S0-BBX-788

SALES &

OPERATIONS PLANNING

Also by Tom Wallace and Bob Stahl

Learning Resource:

The Education Kit for Sales & Operations Planning, by Tom Wallace

Books:

Sales & Operations Planning: The How-To Handbook, 3rd Edition

Sales & Operations Planning: The Executive's Guide

Sales & Operations Planning: The Self-Audit Workbook, 2nd Edition

Building to Customer Demand

Sales Forecasting: A New Approach

Master Scheduling in the 21st Century

Videos:

The Executive S&OP Briefing: A Visual Introduction, by Tom Wallace

Building to Customer Demand

Procurement in the New World of Manufacturing, by Bob Stahl

SALES &

OPERATIONS

PLANNING

The How-To Handbook

Third Edition

How It Works

How to Implement It with Low Risk and Low Cost

How to Make It Better and Better

Thomas F. Wallace and Robert A. Stahl

T. F. Wallace & Company
2008

© 2008, 2004, 2000, 1999 by T. F. Wallace & Company. All rights reserved.

Third Edition

First Printing: March, 2008

Second Printing: April, 2008: Minor text corrections

Third Printing: January, 2009: Minor text corrections

Fourth Printing: July, 2010: Minor text corrections

Fifth Printing: May, 2011

This book or parts thereof may not be reproduced in any form without written permission from the publisher except by a reviewer, who may quote brief passages in conjunction with a review, or except where specifically noted in the text.

International Standard Book Number: 978-0-9674884-5-5

Printed in the United States of America

Books and videos by Tom Wallace and/or Bob Stahl may be ordered online from: www.tfwallace.com

Also available from the APICS bookstore: www.apics.org
                                          800-444-2742

Contact information: Tom Wallace   Bob Stahl
                          tom@tfwallace.com   RStahlSr@aol.com
                          www.tfwallace.com   www.tfwallace.com
                          513-281-0500   508-226-0477

Table of Contents

Part One — Sales & Operations Planning: Its Role, Benefits, and Structure

Part Two — Implementing the Live Pilot

Part Three — Expansion and Full Financial Integration

Part Four — Getting It Right and Making It Better

Appendixes

List of Figures

* Attached to Inside Back Cover

Dedication

This book is dedicated to the men and women who have pioneered Sales & Operations Planning and thus helped it develop into one of today's primary management tools.

This includes teachers, writers, and consultants but — most of all — the people working in companies that have successfully implemented the process. They can be found in many different departments within these companies: Sales, Marketing, Manufacturing, Supply Chain, Finance, New Product Development, and most important, in general management with titles such as CEO, COO, General Manager, Managing Director, President, and so forth.

Our thanks to all of you.

Acknowledgments

Thanks also go to the talented and highly experienced professionals who reviewed the manuscripts of all the editions of this book and gave invaluable feedback.

First Edition:

Ross Bushman
Vice President, Sales and Planning
Cast-Fab Technologies

Mike Campbell
President and CEO
Demand Management, Inc.

Mike Kremzar
Former Vice President, Product Supply
The Procter & Gamble Company

Linda LeBlanc
Vice President, Human Resources
Formica Corporation

Dick Ling
President
Richard C. Ling, Inc.

Walt Pietrak
North American MRP II Coach
The Procter & Gamble Company

Arvil Sexton
Former Vice President
Drexel Heritage Furnishings, Inc.

Bing Sherrill
Vice President, General Manager
Moog, Inc. Systems Group

Chandler Stevens
Production Planning
CTL Aerospace

Second Edition (additions only):

Chris Gray
President
Gray Research

Bill Montgomery
Orange County CA APICS Chapter

Rebecca Morgan
Principal
The Fulcrum Consulting Works

Third Edition (additions only):

Jack Childs
VP Value Engineering
SAP, America

Phil Dolci
Former VP/General Manager
Sanford/Sharpie

Jeff Greer
VP Operations
KVH Industries

Ken Kahn, Ph.D.
Professor, College of Technology
Purdue University

Larry Lapide, Ph.D.
Director, Demand Management
MIT Center for Transportation & Logistics

Bruce Smythe
President
ImagePoint Corporation

Duncan Johnson,
Director Planning, Customer Service
Albemarle Corporation

Jerry Kilty
President
Quality Management Solutions, Inc.

Jay Nearnberg
Senior Director, Demand Planning
Wyeth Consumer Health Care

Thanks, folks, you made the book a lot better.

Many thanks also go to Kathryn Wallace (page layout), Kim Nir (copy edit), and David Mill (cover design). These folks did their usual superb job, for which we're very grateful.

Last but certainly not least, we give a heartfelt "thank you" to Pat Stahl and, again, Kathryn Wallace for putting up with us during the writing of this book.

Preface: A Terminology Issue

Sales & Operations Planning traditionally referred to a decision-making process for balancing demand and supply at the *aggregate* level. This is an executive-centered activity.

However, over the recent past, common usage of this term has broadened to include tools and techniques, which operate at the *detail* level, for individual products and customer orders. These are not executive-centered processes; they carry too much detail and require more time than executives have to devote. This has created confusion, because the term "Sales & Operations Planning" no longer has a clear meaning. One doesn't know if the speaker is talking about aggregate volume planning or detailed mix planning. It's too bad this has happened, but it has.

To help reduce the confusion, we use the term *Executive S&OP* to refer to the executive activity. We use *Sales & Operations Planning* to refer to the larger set of processes, which include the processes for forecasting and planning at the detail level as well as Executive S&OP.

Executive S&OP is not something new. It's what we previously called Sales & Operations Planning. It simply has a new name, to help reduce the confusion.

We'll look at this issue more closely in Chapter 1.

Foreword

Executive S&OP is a superior decision-making process that helps people in companies to provide excellent customer service and to run the business better. It's a great tool when it's done correctly. However, in our travels, we see too many companies:

- trying to use Executive S&OP but struggling, because they really don't understand it; or,

- trying to implement Executive S&OP but having a hard time, because they really don't understand it; or,

- not considering Executive S&OP, because they really don't understand it.

There's a fair amount of misinformation and mythology about Sales & Operations Planning that's getting in the way. For example …

Myth: *Sales & Operations Planning is one of a number of tools used in the area of planning and scheduling. It's on a par with Master Scheduling or Capacity Requirements Planning.*

Fact: It's a lot more than that. Yes, S&OP "grew up" as a part of the closed-loop planning process known as Manufacturing Resource Planning or Enterprise Resource Planning. However, it's evolved into a great deal more. It's become a decision-support tool for top management to use in setting and controlling the future course of the business; it operates in both financial and operational modes; and it provides a "window into the future."

****

Myth: *S&OP is just a once-per-month meeting.*

Fact: Executive S&OP operates on a monthly cycle, which culminates in the Executive Meeting held around the middle of the month. Prior to that, three important phases take place: Demand Planning, Supply Planning, and the Pre-Meeting, where middle management people make decisions and formulate recommendations for the executive session.

All of these activities make it possible for the Executive Meeting to take place in two hours or less, thereby making very effective use of top management's time. Executive S&OP is an ongoing, multistep process that occurs every month.

****

Myth: *S&OP's no big deal —it's mainly looking at numbers on a spreadsheet.*

Fact: The essence of Executive S&OP is decision-making regarding customer service goals, sales volumes, production rates, levels of finished goods or intermediate inventory, customer order backlog, and, last but certainly not least, financial performance. The S&OP spreadsheets and graphs, one for each major product family, bring all of these elements together into one display.

Executive S&OP enables people to view the business holistically — to see the interplay between demand and supply, between customer orders and inventories — and to make solid, informed decisions. Viewing different parts of the business separately can lead people to make suboptimal decisions, as in "The inventories are too high; cut the inventory!" and "Our customer service is lousy; we've got to put more into inventories!" An organic, holistic view of the business makes it far easier to avoid such decisions —and to avoid getting into that kind of trouble in the first place.

****

Myth: S&OP deals with product families, so how can it be helpful? You can't learn anything from looking at aggregate numbers.

Fact: We do it all the time. Take investing, for example. When we want to know how the stock market's doing, we check the Dow Jones Industrial Average, the S&P 500, and the Nasdaq. Those three numbers alone give us a good feel for what the market's doing. If they haven't changed a lot from yesterday, last week, last month, then we're okay and we can think about something else. If there's a lot of movement, however, then we may want to get down into the detail and check individual mutual funds and stocks.

It's similar for a business enterprise. The picture on aggregate product families shows:

- their levels of customer service;

- how their sales are trending;

- if production is meeting the overall plan; and

- whether the finished inventories and customer order backlogs are where we want them to be, and so on.

With this high-level information, executives and managers can make effective decisions regarding the direction of these important elements of the business. We liken this view of the business to flying in a plane at 10,000 feet off the ground. You can see a lot from up there; you can get the big picture.

Of course, the company has to do more than deal with aggregate volumes. It needs to handle the mix: individual products, customer orders, stockkeeping units (SKUs). This is the job of tools such as line-item forecasting, customer order promising, Master Scheduling, and plant and supplier scheduling. Mix is not the big picture; it's the details. Mix is 200 feet off the ground at about 400 knots. You can't see the big picture down there.

****

Myth: We're using Lean Manufacturing. We don't need S&OP.

Fact: Lean Manufacturing and Sales & Operations Planning are two very different things.

Lean is a superb set of processes used to eliminate waste, reduce time, and increase quality. It has been heavily focused on the plant floor, the suppliers, and the immediate customers.

Executive S&OP is a medium-to-long-term planning process that provides visibility into the future, to recognize demand variability early and thus to keep demand and supply in balance.

Toyota, the "poster child" for Lean, doesn't have much of a demand variability problem; it ships cars at a relatively constant rate to a group of happy, contented Toyota dealers. Most companies — Lean or otherwise — don't have that luxury. They ship to WalMart, GE, Boeing and the like, whose demands can be quite variable. Whether your company stabilizes demand with a huge finished goods inventory buffer (like Toyota), or ships to variable demand, you'll still need Sales & Operations Planning.

****

Myth: We can't use S&OP because we don't do any of our own manufacturing. We use contract manufacturers exclusively.

Fact: Do you need to balance demand and supply? Of course you do. In some situations, the presence of contract manufacturers puts an even greater premium on the demand/supply balance because the degree of control is lessened. Does it matter who owns the factory? S&OP doesn't care. We'll see examples of this throughout the book.

****

We wrote this book to dispel the myths and to raise awareness of the facts. Our hope is that it will help more and more companies take advantage of the powerful decision-making capabilities of Executive S&OP, which in turn will help them to run their businesses better.

Tom Wallace	and	Bob Stahl
Cincinnati, OH		Plymouth, MA

What's New in the Third Edition

The second edition of this book added substantial new material to the first edition:

Lean Manufacturing

Global Businesses

Highly Seasonal Products

Finish-to-Order/Build-to-Order/Postponement

Supply Chain Management

In this third edition, we've added new or enhanced material on:

Implementation Methodology

Behavioral Aspects of Implementation

Change Management

New Product Introduction

Highly Variable Supply

Risk Management

Graphical Displays

Software Selection Criteria

Fixing a Broken S&OP Process

Examples from Real World Companies

Much of the material in the first edition remains, and that's gratifying. The body of knowledge making up Sales & Operations Planning (S&OP) remains much the same; it's evolving but not changing dramatically.

Last, and most certainly not least, Bob Stahl has joined Tom Wallace as co-author of this book. Bob and Tom's collaborations have brought forward a number of books and videos, all of which are better than if they had been done solo. So we're applying the same approach to this book: two pairs of eyes and ears, and two brains, are better than one. We hope you agree.

How to Use This Book

This book has four major sections.

Part One introduces and describes Sales & Operations Planning and its top management component, Executive S&OP.

Parts Two and Three focus on implementing Executive S&OP.

Part Four addresses post-implementation issues and discusses the future development of Executive S&OP.

Time is money, and typically we don't have enough of either. Not everybody will need to — much less want to — read this entire book. So here are some thoughts as to who might read which chapters, in order to learn what they need to know and still make efficient use of their time.

Companies Operating Executive S&OP

A number of companies today are using Executive S&OP to help manage their businesses, some very successfully. If you're in that category, you probably know quite a bit about the process already. Therefore, Part One of this book, which describes the process, may not add much value for you. However, Part Two, which gets into the details of how to implement it, might help you make improvements. Our advice for you folks is to read Chapters 17 through 21 and double back into Parts One and Two if you feel the need for clarification.

Many people we talk to in companies using Executive S&OP are curious about how they're doing and how they stack up against other users. If you're in that category, you might first look at the Executive S&OP Effectiveness Checklist in Appendix F. It should give you insight into the good and the not-so-good aspects of your process and help you prioritize the needed changes

Companies Implementing Executive S&OP

People in these companies fall into several categories (described in Chapter 8):

- Members of the Executive Team should read at least Chapters 1 through 9.

- The Executive Champion[1] and the Executive S&OP Process Owner should read the entire book.

- Anyone else who will be "hands-on" with Sales & Operations Planning should read the entire book, including all members of the Design Team (Core Team, Project Team).

- The senior Information Systems executive should read Chapters 1 through 7, 11, and 16.

---

[1] For clarity, we will capitalize the first letter of each word for all project-related positions

- The person charged with the development of the graphical displays and spreadsheets should read Chapters 1 through 12.

Companies Considering Executive S&OP

This book can also be helpful to people in companies that have not yet begun an implementation. Typically they want to know what it is, how it works, why it's important, and how it might help them. They should read Chapters 1 through 5. Then, if that gets their interest, they might want to cover the remaining chapters.

Part One

Sales & Operations Planning:
Its Role, Benefits, and Structure

Prologue to Part One: What's New

TOM WALLACE: First, Bob, I'd like to welcome you to the writing team of this, the third edition of the *How-To Handbook*. It's great to have you on board.

Maybe we could start by you giving the readers a bit more input on what's new: what's in this book that's not in the second edition.

BOB STAHL: Thanks, it's great to be here. Regarding what's new, I'd estimate about half of this book, give or take, is new material: things that we just didn't know four years ago when the Second Edition was written. Happily, the fundamentals haven't changed: balancing demand and supply, aligning units and dollars, and the Five-Step Process are all alive and working well.

Now for some specifics:

- Perhaps the most major change concerns implementation and issues such as change management and the behavioral aspects of successfully implementing Executive S&OP. This is where the rubber meets the road: if you can't get the stuff to work, it doesn't matter how potentially powerful it is.

- As a part of this, we've added a new framework for implementation: a three-phase approach, carrying low risk and low cost.

- There is substantial new material on establishing and controlling what we call "simplifying assumptions" — the enablers of effective decision-making across the medium- and long-term horizons.

- We've added material on risk, focusing on S&OP's role in anticipating and recovering from supply chain disruptions.

- There's quite a bit of new material on graphical displays of the S&OP information — in color fold-outs, so they're easy to understand.

- Plus, as we pointed out earlier, this book contains new material on other topics including:

new product introduction	highly variable supply
software selection criteria	fixing a broken S&OP process

We've added a number of "Reports from the Field" throughout the book. These are, in effect, mini-case studies about the experiences of actual companies in implementing and using Executive S&OP. Where possible, we identify the actual companies except where the news is bad, not good, or where we were unable to get permission from the company to identify it.

TOM: What's that saying you have about being smarter?

BOB: We reserve the right to be smarter today than yesterday, and not to have to apologize for it.

TOM: Well said. Let's get started.

Chapter 1

Introduction to Executive S&OP

Let's eavesdrop on an executive staff meeting at the Acme Widget Company. The participants are not happy campers.

President: *This shortage situation is terrible. When will we ever get our act together? Whenever business gets good, we run out of product and our customer service is lousy.*

VP Operations: *I'll tell you when. When we get some decent forecasts from Sales and Marketing . . .*

VP Sales (interrupting): *Wait a minute. We forecasted this upturn.*

VP Operations: *. . . in time to do something about it. Yeah, we got the revised forecast — four days after the start of the month. By then it was too late.*

VP Sales: *I could have told you months ago. All you had to do was ask.*

VP Finance: *I'd like to be in on those conversations. We've been burned more than once by building inventories for a business upturn that doesn't happen. Then we get stuck with tons of inventory and run out of cash.*

And the beat goes on: back orders, dissatisfied customers, high inventories, late shipments, finger pointing, cash-flow problems, demand and supply out of balance, missing the Business Plan. This is the norm in many companies.

It doesn't have to be that way. Today many companies are using a business process called Executive S&OP to help avoid such problems. To learn what it is and how to make it work, read on.

What Is Sales & Operations Planning?

How would you like to have a process that has helped many companies give better customer service, lower inventories, shorten customer lead times, stabilize production rates, work better with suppliers, give top management a real handle on the business, and build teamwork among Sales, Marketing, Operations, Finance, and Product Development?

Such a process exists. Would you like this tool to not cost much and start to generate results within a few months of getting started? It's all of those things. It's called Executive S&OP, and a growing number of companies are using it to sharply improve their ability to run their businesses. It helps them to get demand and supply in balance, *and to keep them in balance.* Balancing demand and supply is essential to running a business well, and this balancing must occur at both the aggregate, volume level and at the detailed, mix level.

We've identified four fundamentals: demand and supply, volume and mix. Let's look at the first two.

Demand and Supply

What happens when demand and supply aren't in balance? Well, if demand exceeds supply by more than a little bit for more than a little while, bad things happen:

- Customer service suffers. The company can't ship product to its customers when they want it. Customer lead times stretch out as the order backlog builds. Business is lost as customers go elsewhere.

- Costs rise. Unplanned overtime goes up. Material costs and freight costs may increase.

- Quality often "gets lost in the shuffle" as the company strives mightily to get product shipped. Specifications get compromised or waived. Temporary subcontracting yields a less robust product. Material from alternate suppliers often doesn't process well in the plant.

Isn't this great? Owing to demand exceeding supply, performance can deteriorate on three fundamental attributes: delivery, cost, and quality. Business is lost, costs go up, and thus the bottom line takes a hit. Similarly, when supply substantially exceeds demand, bad things happen:

- Inventories increase, carrying costs rise, and cash flow can become a problem.

- Production rates are cut. Volume variances turn unfavorable. Layoffs are a possibility and morale suffers. People in the plant slow down and efficiency numbers start to drop.

- Profit margins get squeezed. Prices are cut. Discounting increases. Deals and promotions become more frequent.

Well, that's not good either. Supply exceeds demand and the company is stuck with lower margins, higher costs, a cash crunch, and the possibility — or reality — of layoffs.

Now, is it always bad if demand and supply aren't in balance? No, sometimes it can be a good thing. It depends on where the imbalance lies. For example, if projected demand ten months in the future exceeds current capacity, and if the company can economically add more capacity sooner than that, that's fine. Demand is growing; business is good. Being able to see the projected imbalances soon enough is what's needed, so that the *potential* imbalance problems can be eliminated before they become *real* problems.

At the risk of stating the obvious, we'd like to point out that demand and supply are not the same thing. Demand is what the customers — external and internal — want; supply represents the resources we have available to meet that demand. We all know that, so why are we taking up your time with it?

We sometimes see companies struggling with demand/supply issues, but not being very effective. They're often unable to answer the fundamental question: Is this a demand problem or is it a supply problem? The result is a lack of focus, which can lead to a less than desirable outcome. Rather, in our thinking, we should *decouple demand from supply*. Study and analyze them separately, so that they can be brought together in the real world.

The next time you're in a discussion about bad customer service, excessive inventories, erratic plant schedules, or the like, ask yourselves: Is this primarily a demand problem or a supply problem? Get agreement among your colleagues on that point, and often you'll be well on the way to a solution.

The name of the game is to get demand and supply *in balance* and to keep them there. It's that simple. Balance demand and supply. Have processes in place to do it. Have early warning capabilities to alert people that they're getting out of sync. Make the necessary corrections early — surgically, with a scalpel — so that they can be small, as opposed to making large, radical corrections later with a meat cleaver.[1]

Volume and Mix

The other two fundamentals are volume and mix. As with demand and supply, we need to treat them separately in our thinking. If volume is handled effectively, it's much less difficult to deal with mix problems as they arise. On the other hand, if volume is not planned well, then mix issues become substantially more difficult to cope with. Many companies get themselves in trouble because they can't distinguish volume-related problems from those of mix. In the box below, we can see the difference between the two: volume is the big picture and mix is the details.

Questions of volume precede those of mix, so smart companies plan their volumes first, and spend enough time and effort to do it well. They find that doing so makes mix problems easier to deal with. But where do most companies spend almost all of their time? On mix. Many look at volumes only once per year, when they do the Business Plan. They probably wouldn't do it even that often, except that the folks in Finance & Accounting make them do it. Once each year, the CFO says, "Well, folks, it's budget time again."

Volume	Mix
"The Big Picture"	"The Details"
• How Much?	• Which Ones?
• Rates	• Sequence
• Product Families	• Individual Products, Customer Orders

Why is that? Why do most companies spend more than 99 percent of their time on mix issues to the exclusion of volume? It's simple: mix — individual products — is what companies ship to their customers. That's where the pressure is. Mix is seen as important and urgent. The effective planning of future volumes may be seen as important, but it carries less urgency.

As a result, many companies set their volumes — sales rates and production rates — no more than once per year, when they do their annual Business Plan. But how often during an average year do volume needs

[1] Sooner or later, demand and supply will be brought into balance. You can do it, or you can let the imbalance fester and another party will get it balanced. Perhaps it will be the customers who defect — when demand is chronically higher than supply — or perhaps it'll be the bank when your inventories are going through the roof due to continued overproduction and overprocurement and your credit line is at its limit.

change? It's almost always more often than once every twelve months. For most companies, it's more than once per quarter.

Most companies don't work hard enough at forecasting and planning their volumes and spend *too much time trying to predict mix*. They overwork the details and don't focus enough on the big picture.

Back to the four fundamentals: demand and supply, volume and mix. Shipping product to customers with world-class reliability and speed requires that all four of these elements be well managed and controlled.

One of Executive S&OP's missions is to balance demand and supply at the volume level. Volume refers to rates — overall rates of sales, rates of production, aggregate inventories, and order backlogs. Companies have found that when they do a good job of planning and replanning volume (rates and levels) as they go through the year, then problems with *mix* (individual products and orders) become less difficult to deal with. Companies have found that when they do this, they can ship better and more quickly, and do it with less inventory.

In the Preface to this book, we addressed the terminology issue. We'd like to expand on that now.

The Terminology Shift

As we indicated, terminology in this field has changed. Originally, the term *Sales & Operations Planning* referred to an executive-centered decision-making process focusing on *volume* issues. This process utilizes techniques for Demand Planning (forecasting) and Supply (capacity) Planning to accomplish its mission.

However, the meaning of Sales & Operations Planning has broadened. Today, many people view Sales & Operations Planning as dealing with mix in addition to volume. Thus it now can include Master Scheduling and other mix-related tools such as customer order promising, supplier scheduling, plant scheduling, distribution replenishment, and more (sometimes done via the use of Advanced Planning Systems). Your authors have watched this development, and we endorse it. However, this morphing of the term *Sales & Operations Planning* has generated confusion.[2] People today frequently don't know if a person is talking about the Executive component of S&OP or the detailed mix pieces. At times we wonder if the person using the term knows what he or she means.

So, since Sales & Operations Planning now means more than the executive process, how is the executive process to be identified?

Well, consistent with the principle of keeping it simple, we call it Executive S&OP. Therefore, Sales & Operations Planning — the larger entity — has a number of component parts. These include Executive S&OP, Demand Planning, Supply (capacity) Planning, along with Master Scheduling and related detail-level tools for the managing of mix, including both conventional plant and supplier scheduling techniques as well as Kanban/demand pull from the world of Lean Manufacturing.

---

[2] Some observers predict that Sales & Operations Planning will become the successor term to Manufacturing Resource Planning and Enterprise Resource Planning.

Here are two key points:

- Executive S&OP does not refer to anything new. It's what we've always called Sales & Operations Planning. The only thing new is the term, and that's to reduce the very real confusion.

- Executive S&OP is the heart of Sales & Operations Planning; when that critically important piece is missing, much of the power of the total process goes away.

For those of you who like formal definitions, we offer the following:

Sales & Operations Planning (S&OP) — A set of business processes that helps companies **keep demand and supply in balance.** It includes Executive S&OP, Sales Forecasting and Demand Planning, Resource Requirements Planning, Master Scheduling, and other detailed scheduling tools for both plants and suppliers, both conventional and demand pull. Originally used to identify only aggregate planning, its meaning has expanded to include those elements that operate at the detailed, mix level.

Executive S&OP — That part of Sales & Operations Planning that balances demand and supply at the **aggregate volume** level, aligns units and dollars, and helps to establish relevant policy and strategy at both the volume and mix levels. It occurs on a **monthly** cycle and displays information in both **units and dollars,** for profit planning, asset management, and so forth. Executive S&OP is **cross-functional,** involving General Management, Sales, Operations, Finance, and Product Development. It occurs at **multiple levels** within the company, up to and including the **executive in charge of the business unit,** (e.g., division president, business unit general manager, or CEO of a smaller corporation). Executive S&OP links the company's **Strategic Plans and Business Plan to its detailed processes** — the order entry, Master Scheduling, plant scheduling, and purchasing tools it uses to run the business on a week-to-week, day-to-day, and hour-to-hour basis. Used properly, Executive S&OP enables the company's managers to view the business **holistically**, provides them with a **window into the future**, and serves as the forum for discussing relevant policy and strategy.

What Are the Benefits?

Benefits resulting from effective Executive S&OP include:

- For Make-to-Stock companies: higher customer service and often lower finished goods inventories — *at the same time.*

- For Make-to-Order companies: higher customer service, and often smaller customer order backlogs and hence shorter lead times — *at the same time.*

- For Finish-to-Order/Postponement companies[3]: higher customer service, quicker response, and often lower component inventories — *at the same time.*

---

[3] This refers to the practice of not finishing the product until receipt of the customer order, and then finishing it very quickly. Think Dell Computer.

- More stable production rates and less overtime, leading to higher productivity.

- Better visibility into future resource problems, both too much work and too little.

- Enhanced teamwork within the executive group.

- Greater accountability regarding actual performance to plan.

- Enhanced teamwork among the middle-management people from Sales, Operations, Finance, and Product Development.

- A better demand/supply balance across the company's supply chain.

- A monthly update to the Business Plan, leading to better forward visibility and fewer surprises late in the fiscal year.

- The establishment of "one set of numbers" with which to run the business.[4] The primary functional areas of the business — Sales/Marketing, Operations, Finance, Product Development, and General Management — all operate with a common game plan.

- The ability to make changes *quickly* off of that common game plan.

- A sharp decrease in the amount of *detailed* forecasting and scheduling required, because the volume plans in S&OP drastically reduce or eliminate the need for detailed mix plans extending out across a long horizon.

- A "window into the future." It's uncanny, but the process — when done well — truly does enable people to better see future problems coming at them: a large increase in workload several months out, an upcoming new product launch that will consume substantial plant capacity, a forecasted downturn in demand later in the year. Executive S&OP enhances proactive decision-making.

- Better control of the business; becoming masters of your own destiny.

Our colleague, Chris Gray, makes a good point about communications as a benefit: "People complain that 'our company doesn't communicate well' and this becomes the diagnosis for all the ills in the company. Of course by saying that, they don't mean that the solution is better voice mail or e-mail or another technology approach. They know that they need better processes to *institutionalize* communications, so that Charlie doesn't have to remember to tell Fred about the slip in the new product roll out and so that Betty doesn't have to remember to communicate with Finance about a potential problem in hitting the sales targets for the year, and so on. For us, S&OP is as much about institutionalizing good communications throughout the organization as it is anything else."

---

4 Many publicly traded companies operate on the principle of: "under-promise and over-deliver." They'll use two sets of numbers: one for Wall Street, containing plans expected to be attained, and one for internal purposes with stretch goals, which many or may not be completely achieved. That's fine. They run with one set of internal numbers — the stretch goals — and that's what we re talking about here.

Executives who've implemented Executive S&OP swear by it. Let's hear from some:

- *Sales & Operations Planning addresses the very same issues that are vital to our customers — what they need and how we're going to get it to them.* — Vice President, Sales

- *Because we're looking ahead every month, we're able to make production rate changes sooner and, at times, spread the impact. This means these changes are easier for us and our workforce to respond to. And they cost less.* — Vice President, Operations

- *In some of our Make-to-Order businesses, as a direct result of S&OP we've reduced lead times to customers by up to 50 percent.* — Vice President/Group General Manager

Perhaps the best testimonial of all came from the head of the North American component of a UK-based multinational. At the conclusion of an S&OP meeting where some very difficult decisions were made effectively, he turned to one of your authors and said:

> *Tom, when I think back to a year ago, before we had Executive S&OP, I wonder how we were able to run the business without it.* — Division Chief Executive

Executive S&OP really is top management's handle on the business.

Why Is Top Management Necessary?

Saying it another way, does the boss really need to be involved, and if so, why? Well, we believe that active, hands-on leadership and participation by the head of the business unit (president, CEO, COO, and so on) is essential for Executive S&OP to work anywhere near its full potential. The two main reasons are stewardship and leadership:

- Many of the decisions made in Executive S&OP affect the Financial Plan for the current year, and top management "owns" that Business Plan. They have a *stewardship* responsibility for it, because they represent the shareholders, partners, family, etc. Thus, only they can make decisions to change it. When the Business Plan is not changed to reflect the new Sales & Operations Plan, there's a disconnect between the financial numbers top management is expecting and the sales forecasts and operations plans being used to operate the business. "Best in class" performance in this area means that the business is managed using only one set of internal numbers.

- Participation by the *head* of the business makes a strong *leadership* statement that Executive S&OP is the process being used to manage these important activities: integrating operational and financial planning, balancing demand and supply, and enhancing customer service. This "encourages" people throughout the organization to do their part. Without such leadership by the senior executive, participation in the Executive S&OP process can be viewed as optional, with the result that through the passage of time, the process erodes and goes away, or deteriorates into a high-level shortage meeting.

Hands-on participation by the executive group shouldn't be a problem, because so relatively little of their time is required. We're talking about one meeting per month, lasting for two hours or less. This event, called the Exec Meeting, can often replace several other meetings and thus result in a net reduction in meeting time. For the president, preparation time is zero. For members of the president's staff, some preparation time may be helpful — mainly in the form of briefings by their people — to enable the necessary sign-offs to take place.

So how can something so productive require so little time? Well, most of the heavy lifting is done in earlier steps: middle-management people update the Sales Forecast and Demand Plan, identify resource issues and raw material problems, and formulate recommendations for the Exec Meeting.

How Does Executive S&OP Connect the Pieces?

In companies without Executive S&OP, there is frequently a disconnect between the Strategic and Business (financial) Plans on the one hand, and the detailed plans and schedules on the other. In other words, the plans developed and authorized by top management are not connected to the plans and schedules that drive day-to-day activities on the plant floor, the receiving dock, and most important, the shipping dock.

The vice president/general manager of a two billion dollar per year consumer goods business had an interesting way of putting it. He said, "Before we had Executive S&OP in the company, I spent a lot of my time turning knobs that weren't connected to anything." What he was saying is that the decisions he made at his level may or may not have gotten transmitted down to impact directly what happened on the receiving dock, and perhaps most important of all, in the customer order department and on the shipping dock. Or, if they did get communicated, they might get garbled on the way down. Or two or more other things might get messed up along the way. There was a disconnect in the process.

He went on to say, "Executive S&OP connects the knobs." It links the top-level strategic and financial plans of the business to the week-to-week, day-to-day, or shift-to-shift activities of receiving and promising customer orders, acquiring material, converting it into finished product, and shipping it to customers.

Report from the Field: The Procter & Gamble Company

Company Description: Procter & Gamble, following its acquisition of Gillette, is now the largest consumer packaged goods company in the world, with annual sales of over $75 billion. It is a very large, very global business — selling into grocery chains, drug chains, mass merchandisers and, since the Gillette acquisition, electrical distributors and electronics shops (with Duracell batteries).

Their Experience: The Executive S&OP process is not new to P&G, having been implemented during the 1990s. Over the years, it has become deeply imbedded in most of the company's business units.

Mike Kremzar, formerly Vice President, Product Supply, Customer Services Worldwide, was the S&OP champion and the force behind its successful implementation. Mike had the following to say: "The general managers of the business units now can operate their profit centers with the knowledge of the impact of their decisions on the total system. The S&OP process provides the data, the forum, and the measurement tools that lets these leaders continue to make good decisions for their brands, but now with full team understanding including cost, inventory, and service impacts."

One of these general managers, fully experienced with the process, stated: "For the first time, Sales & Operations Planning lets me feel like a true general manager. I now know the cost implications of the decisions that we make every month. Our entire business team — Marketing, Sales, Product Supply, Finance, R&D — is working more effectively since we have stopped defending different volume estimates all month. We can pull together with a 'single number' forecast that has everyone's full support."

Benefits, per Mike Kremzar: "Some of our business units have experienced a 20 percent improvement in inventory with a 25 percent improvement in customer service levels while costs have decreased!"

One last point: the P&G/Gillette merger will probably go down in business history as one of the smoothest, best managed mergers ever. Not surprisingly, perhaps, both companies prior to the merger had excellent Executive S&OP processes.

The Moral of the Story: Executive S&OP is truly "Top Management's Handle on the Business."

How Much Does Executive S&OP Cost?

Surprisingly little. It involves relatively few people: dozens, not hundreds, in an average-sized business unit of, say, $100 million to $1 billion in annual sales. Thus, the education and training costs are low. It normally doesn't require a full-time project team or even a full-time project leader. Software plays a relatively minor role in Executive S&OP, so computer costs range from moderate to zero.

This is not to imply that "S&OP is free" or anything like that. Rather, the costs are largely in people's time, not in out-of-pocket dollars. The primary resource consumption is people, not money.

Back to software. Many companies have found that Executive S&OP will require that they do a better job of forecasting and that good forecasting software will help them do that. Some companies already have all they need; Excel™ has surprisingly good support for forecasting. For the S&OP spreadsheet itself, most companies also use a spreadsheet package such as Excel.™ More on software later; for now, just be aware that it doesn't need to cost you very much at all.

The other expenditure that some companies incur is consulting costs. We'll discuss this aspect of implementation in Chapters 7 and 8, but for now let's just point out that these costs are typically less than $100,000 over the life of the eight- to ten month implementation cycle. If you don't need software and are able to use an experienced internal advisor, your out-of-pocket costs will be near zero.

*   *   *   *

FREQUENTLY ASKED QUESTIONS

This process sounds very formal. Is it too rigid?

Executive S&OP is all about managing change. Think about it: if things never changed, or changed only once per year, there would be no need for Sales & Operations Planning. It's there because things change.

Executive S&OP gives you the ability to make changes very quickly because there's an agreed-upon game plan already in place. Without Executive S&OP, there's seldom a total plan; each department has its own. With Executive S&OP, the foundation's in place because the key players have already bought into one single plan. All that needs to be addressed are the changes arising from new conditions.

Yes, there is a structure and a logic to Executive S&OP but it's far from rigid. It's a tool to manage change.

Chapter 2

Where Does Executive S&OP Fit?

In this chapter, we'll focus on how Executive S&OP relates to three well-known initiatives: Enterprise Resource Planning, Supply Chain Management, and last but certainly not least, Lean Manufacturing.

How Does Executive S&OP Interact with Enterprise Resource Planning?

First, a point of clarification: Enterprise Resource Planning (ERP) is not a set of software. That may surprise some of you, since the business press and some business research firms have twisted this around a good bit. ERP is a set of *business functions* for resource planning, focusing largely on mix. A set of software that supports ERP is properly called an Enterprise Software System (ESS).[1]

The predecessor to ERP was Manufacturing Resource Planning (MRP II). The differences between it and ERP are not great. One way to think of ERP is that it's essentially MRP II running on an Enterprise Software System (ESS). In that context, ERP/ESS is more robust and is better able to integrate operations across diverse business units. At the heart of all of this are the *business processes* to balance demand and supply, provide superior customer service, and manage the resources of the business well.

Executive S&OP was originally developed as a part of the resource planning process. It started out as *Production Planning* and then, thanks to pioneering work by Dick Ling and others, developed into Sales & Operations Planning. As we saw earlier, Executive S&OP forms an essential linkage. It ties the Strategic and Business Plans together with the tools for detailed planning, scheduling, and execution.

How Does Executive S&OP Support Supply Chain Management?

Executive S&OP does more than support Supply Chain Management; it's an integral part of it. A given supply chain probably won't work well if its various members don't have good volume plans in the first place and if they're slow to react to the inevitable changes in volume. Sales & Operations Planning can be considered as a *lubricant* between partners in the supply chain, enabling the total chain to function harmoniously and with minimum disruption.

Supply chains extend in two directions: forward to the customers and backward to suppliers, with the company itself at the center of that chain (see Figure 2-1). If that company, the one at the center of the chain, doesn't do a good job of balancing its own demand and supply, then what are the chances that its supply chain partners will receive valid statements of future demand and supply to produce against? Two chances: slim and none.

---

[1] For more on this distinction, please see Thomas H. Davenport, *Mission Critical — Realizing the Promise of Enterprise Systems* (Boston: Harvard Business School Press, 2000) and Thomas F. Wallace and Michael H. Kremzar, *ERP: Making It Happen — The Implementers' Guide to Success with Enterprise Resource Planning* (New York: John Wiley & Sons, Inc. 2001).

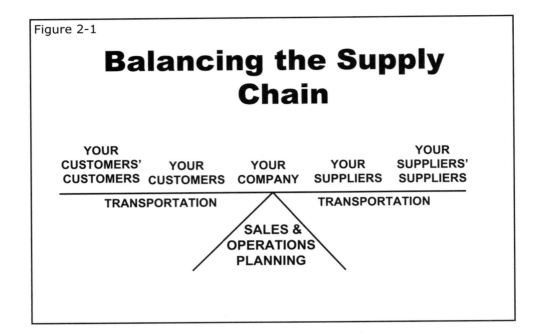

Regarding customer service, in Chapter 1 we saw examples and heard testimonials from executives on Executive S&OP's contribution to improved customer service performance. And for us this is the biggest supply chain benefit of all: *Executive S&OP will help you provide superior customer service.*

Regarding moving backward in the supply chain, toward the suppliers, Executive S&OP's contribution is also significant. The benefits can be much the same for suppliers as for a company's internal production processes. Provided the company shares some of its Executive S&OP results with key suppliers, then these suppliers should experience:

• more stable production rates,

• volume changes made sooner and smaller, and hence more economically — rather than later and larger, and thus more expensively, and

• a greater ability to respond to mix changes, because volume is under control.

Supplier partnering calls for shared information and plans. This is based on the premise that the more advance notice you can give suppliers, the better they will be able to support your needs. Very simply, Executive S&OP can help to provide the future volume plans for suppliers — off the same common plan that top management has authorized for internal production.

How Does Executive S&OP Support Lean Manufacturing?

Executive S&OP supports Lean Manufacturing in much the same way that it supports a conventional manufacturing environment:

- It involves decision-making.

- It operates at an aggregate level and ties the aggregate to the detail.

- It integrates financial plans and operational plans.

- It involves top management in decision-making on these issues.

- It provides a window into the future.

To understand better how Lean Manufacturing and Executive S&OP work together, let's first point out that they're not the same thing at all. Lean is an approach, a methodology, a mind-set focusing intensely on the elimination of waste. It's centered largely, but not exclusively, on physical processes. Its mission is to improve the operating environment.

Executive S&OP, however, is a decision-making process that focused on the future. See Figure 2-2.

Figure 2-2

Lean Manufacturing	**Executive S&OP**
• Tools to reduce waste, cost, and time	• Tools for decision making and coordination
• Strong on execution	• Strong on planning
• Short future horizon	• Long future horizon
• Drives improvements to the operating environment	• Balances demand and supply across the supply chain
• Works best with stable and linear demand	• Can be used in many different environments

---

Many successful users of Lean Manufacturing also use Executive S&OP. However, it's not always clear to people, particularly Lean enthusiasts, why that should be so. In response to many questions received on this topic, a few years ago we wrote a one-pager, patterned after quality guru Phil Crosby's well-known Elevator Speech of several decades ago. It's shown on the next page.

Lean Manufacturing and Executive S&OP: You Need 'Em Both

They work best when they work together. They do different — and very necessary — things, and you need 'em both.

Lean Manufacturing is a powerful approach whose objective is to eliminate waste, reduce costs, cut lead times, and improve quality. It does these things superbly. Sales & Operations Planning is a set of forward planning tools to help people balance future demand and supply, and it does this superbly.

Lean is strong on execution; Executive S&OP is strong on decision-making for the future.

The scheduling tools within Lean look most closely at the plant and its immediate suppliers. S&OP, which includes Sales Forecasting and Capacity Planning — along with its companion tool, Master Scheduling — can extend its future vision out in both directions along the supply chain: to the customers and the suppliers — and in some cases, beyond.

Some of the "leanest" companies in the world use the Sales & Operations Planning and Master Scheduling tools — or variants of them under different names. They do this to balance demand and supply out into the future. Thus the plants and suppliers have good visibility into the future, and are positioned to meet that demand — with material and capacity — effectively and economically.

These companies recognize that "they need 'em both." You probably do too, because they work best when they work together.

So, in terms of Strategic and Financial Planning, aggregate Sales Forecasting, Demand Management, and Master Scheduling, there are far more similarities than differences. In companies using both Executive S&OP and Lean Manufacturing, Executive S&OP operates much as it does in a traditional environment, with perhaps some enhancements to the S&OP spreadsheet format such as Takt Time, Operational Takt Time, and Engineered Cycle Time — values required by Lean.

*   *   *   *

FREQUENTLY ASKED QUESTIONS

Is Executive S&OP primarily a strategic process or is it more tactical?

It's primarily tactical, although it frequently gets involved with strategic issues. Topics such as rates of sales, rates of production, aggregate inventory levels, and the like are certainly tactical, as are their related financial views.

On the other hand, Executive S&OP frequently gets involved with the evaluation of competing alternatives, risk assessment and mitigation, and so forth, which some would consider more strategic than tactical. We refer to Executive S&OP as the *forum* for discussing relevant strategy and policy issues.

One thing's for sure: it's Executive S&OP that *links* the company's strategic plans to its tactical planning and execution. George Gage, formerly head of strategic planning for the EG&G Corporation and an old friend of ours, put it this way: "It's more important to do the *right things* than to do things right." What George was getting at is that not all problems can be solved with tactical solutions. Some require strategic change. We've tried to sum this up in the adjacent diagram.

Chapter 3

The Structure and Logic of Executive S&OP

What follows is an example from a fictitious manufacturer of widgets for home and industry. This company is not yet using Executive S&OP.

Bad Day at Acme Widget

Mike Marshall, a marketing manager at Acme Widget, is doing his quarterly review of the forecasts for his products. He's looking at a summary spreadsheet for the Medium Consumer Widget product family.

	FEB	MAR	APR	MAY	JUN	JUL	AUG	SEP
FORECAST (in 000 units)	100	100	100	120	120	120	120	120
ACTUAL SALES	90	95	85					
DIFFERENCE	-10	-5	- 15					
CUM DIFFERENCE		-5	-15					

Mike is concerned that sales are consistently below forecast. Over the last three months, actual sales have been 10 percent less than forecast. Mike scratches his head, checks a couple of reports he recently received from field sales people, and concludes that this product family is losing business to another family that the company introduced recently. He decides to revise the forecast downward and, with a few quick strokes on his computer keyboard, does so.

	FEB	MAR	APR		MAY	JUN	JUL	AUG	SEP
FORECAST (in 000 units)	100	100	100	OLD FORECAST	120	120	120	120	120
				NEW FORECAST	90	90	80	90	90
ACTUAL SALES	90	95	85						
DIFFERENCE	-10	-5	-15						
CUM DIFFERENCE		-5	-15						

Mike has reduced his forecast by 10,000 per month in May and by 30,000 per month after that, thereby wiping out the forecast increase that he had made for June and beyond. Remembering a conversation he had recently with Carol Clark, the chief financial officer, about high inventories, he decides to notify the plant of the forecast change. He sends Pete Prentis, the plant manager, an e-mail containing the spreadsheet shown above.

Pete reacts to the e-mail message by checking his production plan for Medium Consumer Widgets:

	FEB	MAR	APR	MAY	JUN	JUL	AUG	SEP
PLANNED PRODUCTION (in 000 units)	100	100	100	110	120	120	120	120
ACTUAL PRODUCTION	98	100	101					
DIFFERENCE	-2	—	+1					
CUM DIFFERENCE	-2	-2	-1					

Pete scratches his head and thinks to himself, *Man, this is a double whammy. Not only is he dropping the forecast, he's taking out the increase in June. And we're already ramping up to 120, 000 per month. Nuts!* Pete calls Mike; they talk a bit, and Pete concludes there's no choice but to cut production back. He lays out a new plan, recognizing that there's not much he can do to cut back the May output, since the month is already more than half over:

	FEB	MAR	APR		MAY	JUN	JUL	AUG	SEP
PLANNED PRODUCTION	100	100	100	OLD PLAN	120	120	120	120	120
				NEW PLAN	110	100	100	90	90
ACTUAL PRODUCTION	98	100	101						
DIFFERENCE	-2	—	+1						
CUM DIFFERENCE		-2	-1						

Meanwhile, back in the Finance department, Carol the CFO has just finished a difficult phone call with the company's banker. It centered on such things as excess inventories, poor cash flow, and the need to increase the line of credit. Carol promised the banker that she personally would dig into these problems and get them fixed.

She takes a look at her finished goods inventory report and soon comes across the page for Medium Consumer Widgets:

		FEB	MAR	APR	MAY	JUN	JUL	AUG	SEP
PLANNED INVENTORY		100	100	100	110	120	120	120	120
ACTUAL INVENTORY	103	111	116	132					
DIFFERENCE	+3	+11	+16	+32					

Carol's concerned about the inventory build-up on Medium Consumer Widgets. They now have 132,000 units in stock, which is much higher than the budgeted one-month supply. At a standard cost of $100 each, that's $3,200,000 over plan. She calls Pete at the plant: *Pete, the inventory of Medium Widgets is way up there — 30 percent above authorized. Are you guys working on bringing that down? If so, can I count on the inventory starting to drop?*

Pete replies, *Carol, you don't know the half of it. It's a lot worse than your numbers are showing.* He tells her about Mike's downward forecast revision, and they arrange to meet that afternoon. Later, at their meeting, Pete shows Carol Mike's new forecast and his new production plan.

Mike's Forecast:

	FEB	MAR	APR		MAY	JUN	JUL	AUG	SEP
FORECAST	100	100	100	NEW FORECAST	90	90	90	90	90
ACTUAL SALES	90	95	85						
DIFFERENCE	-10	-5	-15						
CUM DIFFERENCE		-15	-30						

Pete's Production Plan:

	FEB	MAR	APR		MAY	JUN	JUL	AUG	SEP
PLANNED PRODUCTION	100	100	100	NEW PLAN	110	100	100	90	90
ACTUAL PRODUCTION	98	100	101						
DIFFERENCE	-2	—	+1						
CUM DIFFERENCE		-2	-1						

Carol, fearing the worst, picks up a pencil and calculates the projected inventory out into the future. She does this by starting with the 132 finished inventory balance at the end of April, subtracting the forecast for each month, and adding in Pete's planned production. Here's what she comes up with:

	APR	MAY	JUN	JUL	AUG	SEP
INV.	*132*	*152*	*162*	*172*	*172*	*172*

Carol's response: *Good grief! This is awful. The inventory's going over 170, 000 — and staying there! That's almost twice as much as we need. At $100 each, we're going to have $17 million tied up in Medium Widgets. Our budget for all finished goods is $25 million. What's going on here?*

Hey, don't blame me, counters Pete. *I just got the new forecast this morning. Seems to me they should have called those numbers down months ago. I've been saying for a long time that the Marketing Managers don't look at the forecasts often enough.*

Carol: *I'm afraid you'll need to cut production back a lot more than what you've got here. We just can't live with that inventory.*

Pete: *Well, if we gotta then we gotta. But that means a layoff, which not only costs money but will really drag down morale. And when morale goes down, so does productivity.*

Carol: *I'll get this on the agenda for Monday's executive staff meeting and we can present the issue then. In the meantime, I'll touch base with Mike to see if maybe they can do something to jack up sales.*

What's Wrong with This Picture?

A lot. Let's give some constructive criticism to Mike, Pete, and Carol:

• Mike's not reviewing his forecasts frequently enough. A once-per-quarter review simply isn't adequate for most businesses; they're too fast-paced, too dynamic, too subject to change.

• As a result, demand and supply have become way out of balance. Pete, the plant manager, is faced with a severe cutback in output rates and a likely layoff.

- The activities are disconnected. Each person is looking at his or her part of the business, but nowhere is the entire picture being brought together. The CFO, Carol, is in this particular loop primarily because the bank has been hassling her.

- The problem is sufficiently serious that Carol will escalate it to the executive staff meeting. This will most likely consume a fair amount of time, be a difficult discussion, and include some finger-pointing and fault-finding. It will not enhance teamwork among the top management team.

Bottom line: Acme Widgets lacks a process to routinely review the status of demand and supply, and to make timely decisions to keep them in balance. They're lacking Executive S&OP.

A Better Way to Look at It

Let's pretend for a moment that Acme was just beginning to implement Executive S&OP. Sally Smith, the sales administration manager, is heading up the implementation project and she has just put together an S&OP spreadsheet for Medium Consumer Widgets, a Make-to-Stock product family. Here's what it might look like.

	FEB	MAR	APR	MAY	JUN	JUL	AUG	SEP
FORECAST	100	100	100	100	120	120	120	120
ACTUAL SALES	90	95	85					
DIFFERENCE	-10	-5	-15					
CUM DIFFERENCE		-15	-30					
PLANNED PRODUCTION	100	100	100	110	120	120	120	120
ACTUAL PRODUCTION	98	100	101					
DIFFERENCE	-2	—	+1					
CUM DIFFERENCE		-2	-1					
PLANNED INVENTORY (1-MO SUPPLY)	100	100	100	142	142	142	142	142
ACTUAL INV. (JAN=103)	111	116	132					
DIFFERENCE	+11	+16	+32					

Let's examine this display for a moment. Notice how both the demand data and supply data are shown adjacent to each other. They're followed by the inventory projection, which in effect is the critique of the demand/supply relationship.

The result is a holistic view of the status of the Product Family. This kind of display contains information specific to each of the three key functions: Sales Forecasts and actual performance for Sales, the Production Plan and performance to that plan for Operations, and the inventory status and outlook for the people in Finance, among others.

Each function can view not only its own numbers but also those from other areas. That makes it much easier for managers from a variety of functions to view the business as an organic whole, rather than looking only at their part of it. In the example on the previous page, we can see the inventory growth far above plan. We can also track back to the cause: actual sales below forecast. If Sally Smith and her colleagues at Acme Widget had been looking at these numbers every month, they would have been able to take action sooner — and not have had to deal with such a major problem as the one they're now facing.

One of the early users of Executive S&OP was the U.S. Pharmaceutical Division of Abbott Labs. Its president stated, *Marketing can challenge Production proposals, Finance can question advertising concepts, and all disciplines participate in the finalization of the production rate proposed by Materials Management. My goal is to get everyone seeing the business through my glasses.*[1]

Executive S&OP is a monthly process that involves both middle management and the executive group. It's done in aggregate groupings (families, categories), not in detail. For each of a half-dozen to a dozen major product families, the process focuses on a review of:

- **Recent past performance.** It compares actual performance against plan for sales, production, customer service (on-time shipments), inventory or customer order backlog — and highlights the deviations. This visibility into past performance highlights bias[2] and enhances accountability, and those can be major benefits. The future plans represent commitments by Sales and by Operations; the actual numbers show how well they did in hitting those plans. In a number of companies, we've seen this fact alone help reduce the gap between plans and actual performance.

- **The outlook for the future.** New, updated Sales Forecasts and the resulting Operations Plans[3] are developed, modified where necessary, and authorized. (The Operations Plan is the Sales Forecast plus or minus changes in inventories or backlog to meet the customer service targets, seasonal requirements, plant shutdowns, and so forth.)

The Make-to-Stock View

An important aspect of Executive S&OP is the ability to focus on customer service and its interplay with inventories (or customer order backlogs for a purely Make-to-Order business). See Figure 3-1, which is a somewhat simplified example of an S&OP spreadsheet. This spreadsheet shows the three prior months' sales and production performance, the finished goods inventory, and the customer service levels achieved. We can see that sales have exceeded forecast by 44,000 units (over three months), and this has reduced the finished goods inventories to an unacceptably low level. Why unacceptably low? Because customer service is plummeting. It's nowhere near the target of 99 percent.

---

[1] "Game Planning," by David Rucinski. *Production and Inventory Management Journal,* First Quarter 1982, pp. 63–68.

[2] Bias in this context refers to forecasts that are consistently over or under actual sales. Bias is a particularly bad form of forecast error.

[3] Throughout this book, we'll use the term Operations Plan rather than Production Plan because it's more inclusive and more representative of the operational environment here in the twenty-first century.

Figure 3-1   THE ACME WIDGET - SALES & OPERATIONS PLAN FOR OCT. 2008

FAMILY: MEDIUM WIDGETS (MAKE-TO-STOCK)   UNIT OF MEASURE: 1000 UNITS

TARGET LINE FILL: 99%   TARGET FINISHED INVENTORY: 10 DAYS ON HAND

SALES	J	A	S	O	N	D	J	F	M	3rd 3 MOS	4th 3 MOS	12 MO TOTAL	MOS 13-18	FISCAL YEAR LATEST CALL	BUSINESS PLAN
		HISTORY													
FORECAST	200	200	200	210	210	220	220	220	220	690	690	2670	1335	$25,540M	$25,400M
ACT SALES	222	195	227												
DIFF: MO	22	-5	27												
CUM		17	44												
OPERATIONS															
PLAN	200	200	200	210	220	230	230	230	230	690	690	2735			
ACTUAL	200	206	199												
DIFF: MO	0	6	-1												
CUM		6	5												
FINISHED GOODS INV.															
PLAN	100	100	100	61	71	81	91	101	111	111	111				
ACTUAL	78	89	61												
DAYS ON HAND	8	9	6	6	6	7	8	9	10	10	9				
LINE FILL %	97%	98%	89%												

DEMAND ISSUES AMD ASSUMPTIONS
1. FORECAST REFLECTS LAUNCH OF NEW DESIGNER WIDGET LINE IN 3RD QTR.

2. ASIA FORECASTED TO REACH 2005 VOLUME

SUPPLY ISSUES
1. XMAS FULL PLANT SHUTDOWN RESCHEDULED TO STAGGERED PARTIALS THRU FALL AND WINTER

The forward decisions will then focus on:

- the possibility of an increase to the Sales Forecast,

- how quickly production can gear up to get the inventories back to their target level, and

- actions that can be taken in the short run to minimize the negative impacts of the sub-par customer service levels.

One of the important things we've learned from quality initiatives such as Six Sigma or TQM is that *facts are our friends.* Executive S&OP gets all of the relevant facts on one sheet of paper. This helps to avoid suboptimal decisions, where one aspect of the business is improved at a disproportionate cost to another. For example, decisions are sometimes made by looking solely at inventory levels, and the outcome is a mandate to cut production in order to get the inventories down. Several months later the customer service statistics show horrible performance, so the word goes out to crank up production so we can start to ship on time. And on and on.

Executive S&OP avoids this by displaying planned and actual data for sales, production, inventories, and most important, customer service — all on the same page. In our experience, executives find this very helpful, because it helps them make better decisions.

Please notice that this display goes out 18 months into the future. This is to enable both efficient budgeting and effective resource planning, which we'll talk more about in Chapter 14. We'll use an 18-month forward planning horizon in all our examples.

Many S&OP spreadsheets show the number of work days in each month, which can help to explain month-to-month variability. The spreadsheet examples in this book do not do so, for reasons of clarity and ease of understanding.

Graphs versus Spreadsheets

In addition to spreadsheets, most companies will also use graphical displays. Graphical displays have significant advantages over tabular ones: they're simpler; they are easier to understand; and they direct one's attention to the more important elements.

The downside to graphs is that they lack detail that is sometimes necessary. For this reason, most successful users of Executive S&OP will use both graphical displays and tabular, spreadsheet displays. In the Exec Meeting (see Chapter 5), the graphical display for a family would be shown first and discussed. The tabular display would not be shown unless more information were needed to fully understand the situation, make decisions, and so on.

Following the last page in this book, there is an example of a graphical display (labeled CG-1) for the Make-to-Stock product family we've been studying. This is a fold-out sheet and it's in color (as are most of the real-world graphical displays used in Executive S&OP). We suggest you take a moment to fold out the graph and see how it relates to the tabular display on p.26. We've used the following conventions:

1. Color coding: red is demand, blue is supply, green is inventory, and yellow is the inventory target.

2. Vertical bars are actual data; lines are plans or targets.

3. Volume data is scaled on the left-side Y axis; days-on-hand is on the right side. In addition, there are also graphical displays for Make-to-Order and Finish-to-Order families, which we'll cover now.

A disclaimer: these graphs have been modified from their original Excel™ format to enhance readability.

The Make-to-Order View

First, let's contrast Make-to-Stock with Make-to-Order. Make-to-Stock says, "Make the product and then wait for the customer orders to come in." In essence, Make-to-Order says, "Wait for the orders to come in and then start to make the product." Make-to-Order, at least within the context of S&OP, refers to companies that do *very little* work on the product prior to receipt of the customer order.[4]

There are two gray areas here:

- Some companies make products that are specific to only one customer. This sounds like Make-to-Order. However, for contractual or other reasons, they must carry a finished inventory for a given customer. Big-Mart might be saying: "We want you to always have two weeks' supply of our products in your warehouse." For S&OP purposes, this is not a Make-to-Order situation but rather it's Make-to-Stock, because the products flow through a finished goods inventory. The challenge is to balance demand and supply in a way that results in a two-week finished inventory.

- Some companies finish products after receipt of the customer order, using standard components. For S&OP, this also is not Make-to-Order but rather Finish-to-Order, covered later in this chapter.

| Figure 3-2 | | | | | | | THE ACME WIDGET - SALES & OPERATIONS PLAN FOR OCT. 2008 | | | | | | | | |

FAMILY: LARGE WIDGETS (MAKE-TO-ORDER)   UNIT OF MEASURE: EACH

TARGET LINE FILL: 99%   TARGET ORDER BACKLOG: 6 WEEKS

	HISTORY									3rd 3 MOS	4th 3 MOS	12 MO TOTAL	MOS 13-18	FISCAL YEAR LATEST CALL	BUSINESS PLAN
BOOKINGS	J	A	S	O	N	D	J	F	M						
FORECAST	20	20	20	20	20	20	20	20	20	60	60	240	120	$1,800 M	$1,800 M
ACT BOOKINGS	22	20	21	20	10										
DIFF: MO	2	0	1												
CUM		2	3												
PRODUCTION/SHIPMENTS															
PLAN	20	20	20	20	20	20	20	20	20	60	60	240	120		
ACTUAL	20	21	20												
DIFF: MO	0	1	0												
CUM		1	1												
ORDER BACKLOG															
PLAN	30	30	30	30	30	30	30	30	30	30	30				
ACTUAL	28	30	29												
BACKLOG (WKS)	6	6	6	6	6	6	6	6	6	6	6				
ORDER FILL %	99%	100%	100%												

<u>DEMAND ISSUES AMD ASSUMPTIONS</u>   <u>SUPPLY ISSUES</u>
1. FORECAST ASSUMES NO CHANGE IN
   COMPETITOR PRICING OR BACKLOG

---

[4] A subset of Make-to-Order is called *Design-to-Order* or *Engineer-to-Order*. This is for products whose detailed design is not even begun until receipt of the customer order. Products in this category tend to be large, specialized, complex machinery — often one of a kind. For S&OP, this is treated in much the same way as Make-to-Order.

The logic of Sales & Operations Planning for Make-to-Order products is *almost* identical to Make-to-Stock. The big difference, as shown in Figure 3-2, is that the finished goods inventory is no longer in the picture but is replaced by the customer order backlog. (You may want to take a look at the graphical display for this product, CG–2, on the fold-out immediately following the one for Make-to-Stock.)

"Backlog" refers to all customer orders received but not yet shipped, regardless of when they're due to ship. It's actually "negative inventory." Finished goods inventory is what has been produced ahead of receiving customer orders for it. Backlog represents orders received ahead of producing the products.

The size of the customer order backlog can be an important competitive factor. The backlog is a primary determiner of lead time to customers because the bigger the backlog, the longer the lead time. If the backlog gets too big and hence the lead times get too long, then the customers might not want to wait. They may go somewhere else where they can get the product sooner. If the backlog gets too small, Operations and possibly other departments can have problems; there may not be enough work to stay efficient. Executive S&OP helps Make-to-Order manufacturers manage the size of their customer order backlogs; thanks to Executive S&OP's superior visibility, it's easier to keep those backlogs where they should be.

Here's an example. Let's imagine that Acme Widget salespeople see an opportunity in the marketplace: if they could cut their lead times from six weeks to four, they feel they would capture business from the competition. Operations agrees that this is practical and lays out a plan to cut the backlog by two weeks. The resulting plan, which could easily become a formal recommendation to the executive group, might look like Figure 3-2a, on the next page. Operations is committing to a temporary 15 percent ramp-up in production, from 20 units per month to 23. They could possibly ramp up higher and thus reach the four-week backlog target sooner, but as the supply comment points out, this plan is conservative and cost-effective. Starting in March, the plan is to drop back to 21 and then 20. Of course, the hope is that the new four-week customer lead time will bring in more business and thus Acme might not have to drop back at all from 23 per month.

The Finish-to-Order View (Postponement)

Does the word "postponement" ring a bell? How about the phrase "mass customization"? Ever hear about — or perhaps experience — Dell Computer's highly successful "build-to-order" strategy? Well, all of these terms are getting at much the same thing: finishing the product to the customer's specifications *only after receipt* of the customer order.

But there's more: the product needs to be finished and shipped *quickly*, within a short time, so the customers don't wait long at all to get their products. This contrasts with a standard Make-to-Order process, which most often involves order fulfillment times of weeks or months, not days.

Let's stay with the Dell Computer example since most of us are familiar with that company. If you want to buy a computer from Dell, you can't have them ship one to you off the shelf. That's because they don't carry a stock of finished computers.[5]

---
[5] With some exceptions, which are not relevant here.

Figure 3-2a   THE ACME WIDGET - SALES & OPERATIONS PLAN FOR OCT. 2008

FAMILY: LARGE WIDGETS (MAKE-TO-ORDER)   UNIT OF MEASURE: EACH

TARGET LINE FILL: 99%   TARGET ORDER BACKLOG: 4 WEEKS

		HISTORY									3RD 3 MOS	4TH 3 MOS	12 MO TOTAL	MOS 13-18	FISCAL YEAR LATEST CALL	BUSINESS PLAN
BOOKINGS	J	A	S	O	N	D	J	F	M						
FORECAST	20	20	20	20	20	20	20	20	20	60	60	240	120	$1,800 M	$1,800 M
ACT BOOKINGS	22	20	21	20	10										
DIFF: MO	2	0	1												
CUM		2	3												
PRODUCTION/SHIPMENTS															
OLD PLAN	20	20	20	20	20	20	20	20	20	60	60	240	120		
NEW PLAN				20	21	22	23	23	21	60	60	240	120		
ACTUAL	20	21	20												
DIFF: MO	0	1	0												
CUM		1	1												
ORDER BACKLOG															
OLD PLAN	30	30	30	30	30	30	30	30	30	30	30				
NEW PLAN				30	29	27	24	21	20	20	20				
ACTUAL	28	30	29												
BACKLOG (WKS)	6	6	6	6	6	5	5	4	4	4	4				
ORDER FILL %	99%	100%	100%												

DEMAND ISSUES AMD ASSUMPTIONS

1. FORECAST ASSUMES NO CHANGE IN
   COMPETITOR PRICING OR BACKLOG

2. FORECAST DOES NOT REFLECT INCREASED
   SALES DUE TO SHORTER BACKLOG

SUPPLY ISSUES

1. PRODUCTION RAMP-UP TO REACH 4-WK BACKLOG IS
   CONSERVATIVE BUT COST-EFFECTIVE

They do, however, have all the components necessary to make their computers readily available. When the customer order arrives, they create a bill of material that specifies which options the customer has selected: things like processor speed, amount of RAM, size of hard drive, screen size, and so forth. They then *finish* the product using these available components.

Dell calls this approach "build-to-order." Other companies use the term *Finish-to-Order*, and that's what we'll call it in this book. Similar terms include assemble-to-order, package-to-order, late-stage differentiation, blend-to-order (in chemicals), and perhaps the one most frequently used — postponement.

Well, is this Finish-to-Order approach a good thing? In most cases, it definitely is. It can drive customer service up to very high levels and simultaneously reduce the finished goods inventory to near zero. It can be particularly helpful in companies whose products have lots of options and are under pressure to ship quickly. To follow a Make-to-Stock strategy in a case like this is difficult, because of high finished inventories coupled frequently with poor customer service (because the forecasts of the many individual items are almost always wrong).

Some people have difficulty understanding how Executive S&OP can support Finish-to-Order. Unlike Make-to-Stock, there is normally no finished inventory and hence, no finished inventory target of days' supply. Unlike Make-to-Order, the customer order backlog is near zero; the goal is to ship soon after receipt of the order. So what can serve as the target if not finished inventory or order backlog?

The key to Finish-to-Order is to produce quickly using *available* components. Only by having the components readily accessible can production occur quickly. Therefore, the target is the size of the component inventory available to be used in the finishing operations. It's normally expressed in day's supply, and often employs a key component — one might think of it as a surrogate — to represent the total component inventory. Here are some examples:

- A manufacturer of electronic products focuses on "modules." They try to keep several days' supply of each of their various key modules ready for production. Their purchasing and fabrication processes — for power supplies, housings, sensors, packaging, and so on — are tied to this surrogate target in their Master Schedule; if not, they might run out or have too much.

- A chemical company, in its latex division, targets its inventory of primary product prior to final blending. Given the right amount of primary product, it's able to blend to order quickly and on-time — and to complete its "packaging" operation, which is to fill tanker trucks and rail cars.

- A company making tape has its S&OP process focused on the number of "rolls." These are the wide rolls of tape, in about ten different colors, prior to slitting (width) and cutting (length). Upon receipt of the customer order, they quickly slit, cut, package, and ship. Here, the surrogate (rolls) drives the planning for components (packaging, cores, and so forth) via the Master Schedule; some of these items are replenished via a demand-pull, Kanban process and others via supplier scheduling.

Please note: in all of these examples, they are not keying on finished inventory. There is little or none of that, and that's the way they want it. They do need availability of components, and that's where they have Executive S&OP focused.

Figure 3-3 shows an S&OP spreadsheet for a Finish-to-Order product family (the graphical display, CG–3, immediately follows the one for Make-to-Order). It calls for a target module inventory of five days on hand. Now note the section labeled Module Inventory. In September, the module inventory dropped to three days on hand and customer service dropped. Consequently, the Operations Plan for the next several months has been set higher than the forecast to build that inventory up to the five-day target.

Please note: all of the above data relative to sales, operations, and module inventory must be in the same unit of measure. Sometimes the nature of the surrogate is such that it must be expressed in a unit of measure different from that of the sales forecast. In those cases, the sales forecast is usually converted into the surrogate's unit of measure and is shown accordingly.

For example, sales forecast for the tape manufacturer cited above might be expressed in cases, while the surrogate (rolls) is expressed in linear feet. What's needed here is to convert cases to feet and to show that on the S&OP spreadsheet. Some companies will show both in the Sales area (cases and feet of rolls, in our example) but do the arithmetic using the surrogate unit of measure, because that's how the Operations Plan and inventory are shown.

```
Figure 3-3                    THE ACME WIDGET - SALES & OPERATIONS PLAN FOR OCT. 2008

FAMILY:  DESIGNER WIDGETS (FINISH-TO-ORDER)              UNIT OF MEASURE:           EACH

TARGET LINE FILL: 99.9%                                  TARGET FINISHED INVENTORY:   5 DAYS ON HAND
```

	HISTORY									3rd 3 MOS	4th 3 MOS	12 MO TOTAL	MOS 13-18	FISCAL YEAR LATEST CALL	BUSINESS PLAN
SALES	J	A	S	O	N	D	J	F	M						
FORECAST	2000	2000	2000	2100	2200	2200	2200	2200	2200	6900	6900	26900	15,000	$51.080	$50,800
ACT SALES	2220	1950	2270												
DIFF: MO	220	-50	270										MARGIN	33.0%	32.5%
CUM		170	440												
OPERATIONS															
PLAN	2000	2000	2000	2200	2300	2200	2200	2220	2300	6900	6900	27350		$34,250	$34,390
ACTUAL	2000	2060	1990												
DIFF: MO	0	60	-10												
CUM		60	50												
MODULE INV.															
PLAN	500	500	500	410	510	510	510	510	610	610	610			$1958	$2,000
ACTUAL	480	590	310												
DAYS ON HAND	5	6	3	4	5	5	5	5	6	6	6				
LINE FILL %	99.5%	100%	98.7%												

DEMAND ISSUES AMD ASSUMPTIONS
1. HOUSING STARTS FORECASTED FLAT FOR NEXT YEAR

2. WILL START SHIPPING BIG-MART 10/20

3. MARKET SHARE PROJECTED +5% BY SUMMER

SUPPLY ISSUES
1. WILL BEGIN SOURCING MODULES 3A, 4A & 4B FROM ASIA 12/1

The View for Seasonal Products

Acme Widget has a line of products — Christmas Widgets — with a highly seasonal sales curve. Over three-quarters of the total year's sales for Christmas Widgets are shipped during September, October, and November. Here's next year's sales forecast for Christmas Widgets, in thousands.

J	F	M	A	M	J	J	A	S	O	N	D	
0	0	0	0	0	0	0	100	300	400	300	100	= 1,200

Acme doesn't have enough capacity to produce such a large volume in just a few months, believing that having that much capacity would not be cost-effective. Therefore, they must produce early in order to meet their customers' demand. They start this early production, called the "pre-build," in April.

Figure 3-4

THE ACME WIDGET - SALES & OPERATIONS PLAN FOR OCT. 2008

FAMILY: CHRISTMAS WIDGETS (MAKE-TO-STOCK)   UNIT OF MEASURE: 1000 UNITS

TARGET LINE FILL: 97%   TARGET FIN INV (WEEKS):   MAX: 20, END: 0

		HISTORY									3rd 3 MOS	4th 3 MOS	12 MO TOTAL	MOS 13-18	FISCAL YEAR LATEST CALL	BUSINESS PLAN
SALES	M	A	M	J	J	A	S	O	N	D						
FORECAST	0	0	0	0	0	100	300	400	300	100	0	0	1200	700	$10,800M	$10,800M
ACT SALES	0	0	0													
DIFF: MO																
CUM																

OPERATIONS																
PLAN	0	80	100	120	140	160	200	200	200	0	0	300	1200	800		
ACTUAL	0	73	104	123												
DIFF: MO	0	-7	4	3												
CUM			-3	0												

INVENTORY (F.g.)																
PLAN	0	80	180	300	440	500	400	200	100	0	0	300				
ACTUAL	0	73	177	300												

LINE FILL %	–	–	–	–												

DEMAND ISSUES AMD ASSUMPTIONS
1. ANTICIPATING LATER ORDERS THAN LAST YEAR, AND MORE FOLLOW-ON ORDERS IN DECEMBER

SUPPLY ISSUES
1. WILL BE ABLE TO CONTINUE PRODUCTION ONE OR TWO WEEKS INTO DECEMBER

Obviously, this has the effect of building inventory sharply during the period April – August, and thus the concept of a single, fixed-quantity finished inventory target doesn't work here. Over the summer, the inventory will be increasing to a quite high level — by design. At the end of the selling season, Acme would like to have nothing left in inventory in order to avoid the costs of carrying it over until the next season. Thus, a seasonal inventory target that builds up based on a defined maximum and then falls to a defined minimum at the end of the season is far more valid. This is shown in Figure 3-4.

Note the target finished goods inventory in the upper right part of the display: a maximum of 500,000 units with a desired inventory at year end of zero. The plan as laid out accomplished those directives, with the inventory rising to the half million level early in the pre-build and sold out by December.

Let's go back to the graph for a moment. Notice it displays not merely the upcoming season but also the one for the following year. In highly seasonal businesses, this can be quite helpful: to get an advanced look at what's coming at us next year.

New Product Introduction

Many companies believe, validly, that their toughest challenge is the introduction of new products. Some don't feel that way; these are companies where new products are almost always line extensions, perhaps packaging tweaks or minor enhancements to existing products.

For others, launching new products is very difficult and, at the same time, critically important. These companies often refer to new products as the "life blood of our business. If we don't do it and do it well, we will die."

Extreme examples of both difficulty and criticality exist in industries whose products carry a life-and-death aspect: pharmaceuticals, medical equipment, and aircraft come to mind; lead times are measured in years, and millions — often billions — of dollars are involved. Frequently there is a high degree of government oversight.

For virtually all companies, new product introductions and Executive S&OP go together like ham and eggs. Here's why:

- New products are hardly ever launched in a vacuum; they can impact both demand and supply of existing products. Those impacts need to be predicted and monitored, and Executive S&OP is the ideal process for that.

- New product launches require a high degree of cross-functional coordination: Marketing, Sales, Operations, Finance, and of course, the New Product folks themselves. Well, cross-functional collaboration is what Executive S&OP is all about.

- Future demand is highly uncertain, not only for new products but also for existing products whose demand might be cannibalized by the new ones. Forecasts need to be very closely monitored in the run-up to the launch, during the launch, and for a while after it.

- Demand data for new products need to enter into the financial projections.

- Supply Plans also can be uncertain, one reason being the degree of resource consumption — both in materials and capacity. Often the true resource consumption picture — time on the finishing line, for example — is not known until after scale-up. Here, also, the impact on existing products can be substantial.

- Supply data for new products, including the impact of pipeline fill on inventories, need to enter into the financial projections.

- S&OP helps to monitor for and to minimize "surprises," which are most often part and parcel of introducing new products.

- The Executive Team wants to be in the loop but not get into the nitty-gritty. They want to know: Are the milestones being met?; Is the product testing satisfactorily?; Will the product be available in sufficient quantities to support the launch?; Will the marketing and merchandising materials be available in time?; Will the sales force receive training at the right time?; and so forth.

- Plus there will be occasions when top management needs to make decisions. Often these decisions are triggered by milestones being missed (or perhaps bettered), and thus adjustments to the launch timing may need to be made. These can include not only the phase-in of the new product(s) but also the phase-out of existing ones.

So, there seems to be an excellent fit here. But that doesn't mean that Executive S&OP should replace the company's current processes for new product introductions. Rather, it should be the primary mechanism that blends the specific new product plans into the company's overall Sales and Supply Plans.

Recommendations for New Product Launch

We recommend that you include new product launch issues in your Executive S&OP process. Make new products a permanent agenda item in the Demand Planning step, the Supply Planning step, the Pre-Meeting, and the Exec Meeting. Even if you introduce new products only rarely, having the item on the agenda will help to get it into the process when the need arises.

Have New Product Development people present and active in the Demand Planning phase, the Supply Planning phase, the Pre-Meeting, and the Exec Meeting. For companies that introduce new products only rarely, this could be a temporary situation; for others, the New Product people would be permanent participants in these activities.

The new product launch information — demand, supply, inventories, backlogs — must be visible. Here you have two choices, one being to use separate S&OP spreadsheets and graphs for the new products. The other is to display the new product information on the spreadsheet and graph for the family where the new product will reside. This would require separate rows for sales, supply, and inventories or backlogs.

This separate visibility into new product performance should be maintained for more than just a short while, perhaps six months to a year depending on product and industry characteristics.

On whichever type of display you use, document and display the assumptions that underlie the new product's forecast and supply plan as you would for existing products, but with more detail due to the uncertainties involved. Professor Ken Kahn from Purdue University states: "New product forecasting is all about assumptions."[6]

---

[6] For more on this, see Ken's new book, *New Product Forecasting: An Applied Approach,* 2006, Armonk, NY: M.E. Sharpe.

Some companies carry more than one forecast: a high-side and a low-side forecast. This enables them to develop multiple sets of plans for supply and inventory, which aids in risk assessment. More on this in Chapter 21.

Report from the Field: Eli Lilly[7]

Company Description: Eli Lilly is one of the world's leading pharmaceutical manufacturers, with nearly 40,000 employees. Lilly excels at new product introduction in an industry which has perhaps the toughest environment of any for bringing new products to market. The relationship between pharmaceutical companies and, in the United States, the Food and Drug Administration (FDA) is extremely close. The FDA must approve most of the steps in the product development cycle and this all takes time.

Their Experience: In their book, *Sales & Operations Planning — Best Practices*, authors John Dougherty and Chris Gray state: "Eli Lilly launched ten new products from 2001 through 2005, a rate over five times higher than the pharmaceutical industry average. Further, Lilly can bring new products to the market faster, averaging less than eleven years from product concept to market, versus an industry average of over fourteen years."

This performance resulted in substantial shareholder value in the following months and years, as the stock price substantially outperformed most others in the pharmaceutical industry.

John and Chris go on to say: "Lilly has also added new manufacturing sites, and outsourced products for both capacity increases and the offloading of late life cycle products to make room for new products. Many of these sourcing changes and product development projects have highly variable conditions and timing. This has resulted in a great dependence upon principles, organization, and processes to effectively manage it all, with S&OP providing a forum to manage, approve, and communicate change effectively."

Here's another quote, this one from Stephan Bancel, Executive Director of Manufacturing Strategy and Supply Chain at Eli Lilly: "The value of S&OP at Lilly has been the ability to launch all of our products in a very complex environment without adding significant cost, resources, or inventories. We have managed a strong customer service performance metric while controlling our growth in assets." Lilly people pride themselves on their customer service performance, which routinely runs close to 100 percent.

The Moral of the Story: Executive S&OP is providing significant support for new product introduction in an extremely difficult environment. It can probably help in your environment too.

---

[7] This material is taken primarily from *Sales & Operations Planning — Best Practices*, John Dougherty and Christopher Gray, 2006, Victoria, BC: Trafford Publishing.

Operations Plan Choices:
Level, Chase, or Hybrid

Broadly, there are three choices when laying out the Operations Plan:

- Produce (or procure) at a level rate all year called, appropriately, a *level* strategy.

- Set the Operations Plan to match the Sales Forecast, called a *chase* strategy.

- Do a combination of the two, a *hybrid* approach.

In actual practice, most companies use the hybrid approach, as in the case of the Christmas Widgets at Acme. In other words, they will do some chasing of the sales curve while trying to maintain a reasonably level production rate.

Lean Manufacturing calls for a level rate, but only in the short run. In practice, many Lean shops find that the demand picture for their families changes as they move through the year, and hence employ either a chase or a hybrid strategy, adjusting their leveled schedules upwards or downwards to reflect volume changes in increments, such as month to month. For highly seasonal products, trying to produce at a level rate all year could generate a great deal of inventory. This would qualify as waste, and thus it runs directly counter to the principles of Lean Manufacturing. This then, is another example of needing a chase, or at least a hybrid, strategy. Some Lean companies attempt to offset seasonality with counter- seasonal products. Sometimes they're successful, but what if the counter-seasonal products run counter to the business strategy? Or there's not enough volume? Or they require extensive capital investment?

We'll return to the issue of the S&OP spreadsheet in Chapter 12. There we'll get into the nitty-gritty of spreadsheet design, formulas, and enhancements to what we've seen here, including some thoughts on how to display the information via graphs as opposed to the purely numerical tables we've seen thus far.

*   *   *   *

FREQUENTLY ASKED QUESTIONS

Why do the Make-to-Stock and Finish-to-Order spreadsheets show finished goods or component inventory only? What about raw materials and work-in-process (WIP)?

There are other tools available to manage raw material and WIP inventories: Master Scheduling, Kanban, MRP, and Plant and Supplier Scheduling. These processes take their marching orders — directly or indirectly — from S&OP.

Another reason is that often it's impossible to tie the raw-material inventory to specific product families. A given raw material may go into a number of different product families. On the other hand, if you can segregate the data validly, there's nothing wrong with displaying raw material and WIP numbers on the spreadsheet as memo entries, provided it would add value and not just clutter.

Chapter 4

Inputs to Executive S&OP

The two major inputs to Executive S&OP are, quite simply, demand and supply. That figures, because one of Executive S&OP's most important jobs is to help people get demand and supply in balance — and to keep them in balance.

Demand Input: Sales Forecasting

In many companies, the toughest part of implementing Executive S&OP is overcoming an aversion to forecasting. Let's look at five fundamental questions that surround this problem.

Question #1: Why Bother with Forecasting?

It's amazing, but we still hear this question from time to time. Often it comes from the same people who say, "You can't forecast this business."

Our response is: Nuts. Of course the business can be forecasted — perhaps not with great accuracy, but it certainly can be done. As a matter of fact, virtually all businesses do a significant degree of forecasting. (The only ones who may not are those whose order fulfillment time to their customers is *longer* than their total lead time to get material and capacity — and who don't need to do financial planning. Have you seen many of those lately?)

The problem in many companies is that people in Operations do the "forecasting" by default, i.e., they order the long-lead-time materials and release the long-lead-time production items. Not having a forecast, they must guess. Unfortunately, most of those folks aren't close to the customers and markets; they don't know about planned promotions, price changes, sales force incentives, industry trends, and the like; and thus they rely heavily on history rather than on the future outlook in the marketplace. When things go wrong, it reinforces the beliefs of the people who are saying, "You can't forecast this business. See? I told you so."

Thus, **Point 1: Forecasting is being done in virtually every company. The issues are who does it, at what level it's done, and how often**. Now, let's look at the second point: the level where forecasting is done.

Question #2: Where Should You Forecast?

We don't mean where physically to forecast, as in "Should we do the forecasting in Joan's office or Doug's? Joan's got a window, but Doug's coffee is better." No, we're talking about where in the overall product structure to forecast. In other words, at what level should you forecast? Some choices are shown in Figure 4-1, on the next page.

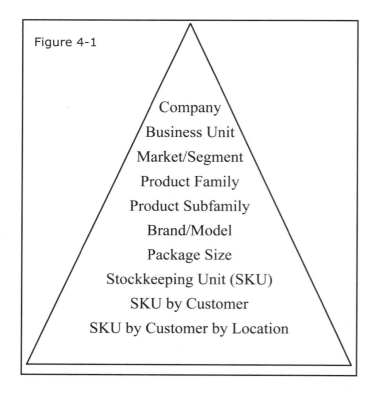

Figure 4-1

Company
Business Unit
Market/Segment
Product Family
Product Subfamily
Brand/Model
Package Size
Stockkeeping Unit (SKU)
SKU by Customer
SKU by Customer by Location

How about forecasting at the top of the pyramid? Obviously forecasting only one line item — the total company — won't do the job; it's just not specific enough to provide good direction to Operations and others.

How about forecasting down at the bottom, stockkeeping unit (SKU) by customer by location? Well, it contains all the detail, and it gives you the capability to aggregate upwards in lots of ways. But don't jump to the conclusion that it's the best. It's most likely to be too much detail; forecasting at this lowest, most detailed level will probably cause more forecast error, not less. One reason is that it fails to take advantage of the law of large numbers (which states that larger numbers are generally easier to forecast). Another reason is that, in many cases, it can be a lot more work.

One company in the spirits business learned that forecasting at the lowest possible level would be counterproductive. There was simply too much unneeded detail. For example, a case of Old Loudmouth Bourbon, 750 ml, going to Pennsylvania is a different SKU from the identical product going to Ohio, because they take different case labels. The company decided it didn't have to forecast SKUs, but rather found it was able to do most of its forecasting at the brand/package size level.

Let's digress for a moment, just in case you're wondering about the supply side of this story. Well, the plants printed their own case labels, with virtually zero lead time. If they were filling an order for Ohio, they'd print Ohio labels. This is a good example of how operational effectiveness — in this case, ultra-short lead times — can make life easier for the forecasters. There's a principle here: "Plan the volume; manage the mix." When you can finish products very quickly, adding the optionality at the end of the production cycle, you can often get out of the business of forecasting mix and focus on volumes.

So you should not necessarily forecast at the most detailed level possible. Higher is often better. On the other hand, it's best to *store* the actual data at the lowest level possible, which in some companies means storing by stockkeeping unit by customer by location. That makes it possible to capture and retain very specific demand for certain customers and to view it when necessary.

For example, in the case cited above, let's say that the state of Ohio had decided to have an aggressive promotion on Old Loudmouth Bourbon, 750 ml, from April through June; they anticipate that sales will be 300 percent of normal during that period. It's important to get that kind of intelligence into your formal forecasting system on a rigorous and managed basis.

So the question arises: should you forecast in aggregate or should you forecast at the detail level? Our answer is: yes. And that leads us to a discussion of what some people call "the forecaster's best friend."

The Planning Time Fence

The Planning Time Fence is that future point inside of which we need high granularity; we need to know the details. It represents the cumulative lead time to acquire material and to build the product, plus a short time allowance for planning and order releasing.

For many companies, the Planning Time Fence (PTF) is four to eight weeks into the future. For companies doing a good job with Lean Manufacturing, the PTF can be a week or less — except for those obtaining widely used components from offshore. In those cases, the PTF could be at eight weeks or more.

This leads us to **Point 2A: Inside the Planning Time Fence, you must forecast at the detailed, mix level.**

You need a high degree of granularity inside the PTF because specific materials and components must be acquired and specific products must be built.

And now for **Point 2B: Outside the Planning Time Fence, you should forecast aggregate volumes, except in rare circumstances.**

The information needed outside the PTF needs to be directional, and the volume view provides that. It's important to know what the overall volumes look like for the next six to twelve months, or perhaps more, for a given resource (line, cell, work center, contract manufacturer, etc.).

What's not necessary is to see which specific SKUs will run on Line 11 during Week 3 of the seventh month into the future. Even if you had that information, would it be of any value? Of course not — because it will change many times over the next seven months as changes occur to forecasts, orders, inventory levels, and so forth. Today's "snapshot" will be obsolete tomorrow.

Now let's consider the disclaimer at the end of Point 2B above: "except in rare circumstances." What's that all about?

Well, let's say we use a raw material that's grown only in a tropical rain forest in a remote corner of Borneo. Let's call it RM 999. The lead time for harvesting, transportation, initial processing, further transportation, final processing, and shipment of RM 999 to our plant is five months. But our Planning Time Fence is set at six weeks. What should we do?

It's simple: forecast and master schedule the individual product(s) using that raw material out for six or more months. But . . . don't move the PTF for all products out to six months; do that for only the one(s) using this raw material. See Figure 4-2 on the following page, and note that the product using RM 999 is projected beyond the Planning Time Fence.

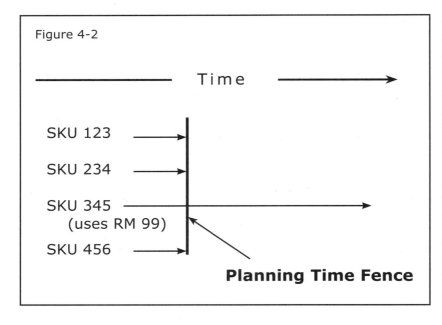

Figure 4-2

Right about now, some of you are no doubt wondering: "But how do we figure out the workload on different resources without the detailed forecast?" Our answer: there is a way. We'll get into that in depth later in this chapter and also in Chapter 14.

A quick word about *time zones*. Many companies using Executive S&OP have a ground rule that says, "The current month is a done deal." They mean that there is not much possibility of changing the production rates *economically* within the current month. Now keep in mind, they're talking about volume. Mix is different; it's easier to change schedules close in as opposed to changing overall run rates.

Will companies using Executive S&OP ever change volumes close in? Yes, if it's practical, if the needs of the business require it, and if the costs and other consequences of not changing exceed those involved in making the change. But normally they'll try to avoid making close-in rate changes.

We've just seen a simple example of a time zone. A slightly more complex example, somewhat similar to that, has been used by Hewlett-Packard:

• Hold the current month.

• Month 2 (in the future) — changes +/– 20 percent are okay.

• Months 3 and 4 — changes +/– 30 percent are okay.

• Months 5 and 6 — changes +/– 40 percent are okay.

• Month 7 and beyond — open.

For companies needing more formal time zone structures like these, it's a good idea to spell them out in the Executive S&OP policy, an example of which is shown in Chapter 16.

Please note: people can decide to override time zone directions. Time zones are there mainly to serve as guides for decision-making and to help avoid jerking the plant around unduly. One of the plant's jobs, we submit, is to become increasingly flexible so that it can respond *economically* to close-in changes. That makes for happy customers and happy colleagues in Sales and Marketing, Finance, and — last but certainly not least — the executive suite.

Question #3: Who Owns the Forecast?

Who's responsible for it? Who actually does the forecasting? In many companies, when we ask these questions, crisp answers rarely come back. We hear things like "it depends which forecast you're talking about" or "well, it's not very clear" or "it doesn't matter, because we use the forecast only for budgeting; we run the business on past history and hunches."

That's too bad, because a good way to increase customer service levels and reduce inventories simultaneously is to do a first-rate job of forecasting. And in order to do a first-rate job, we'd better have clarity on whose job it is.

The issue here is accountability and the underlying principle is this: the people responsible for developing the plan (in this case the forecast, the Demand Plan) should be the same ones who will be held accountable for executing the plan.

So here's **Point 3: Sales and Marketing people "own" the Sales Forecast**. It's their job; they're the experts on the demand side of the business, in both planning and execution. People in other departments may support them, perhaps by operating the statistical forecasting system or otherwise generating basic data. But it's the job of the Sales and Marketing folks to review, update, and modify the Sales Forecast; they own it. They own it, because they *sell* it.[1]

In many companies, Sales and Marketing are separate functions. In these cases, the Sales Department is typically charged with forecasting the near term, because salespeople are in contact with the customers and are in a position to know their plans. These Sales Department forecasts are most often mix forecasts, often at an SKU level.

Marketing, on the other hand, focuses more in the medium to long term; they know the most about plans for future promotions, pricing, new products, and so forth. These forecasts tend to be at a volume level: product families, subfamilies, and the like. These two types of forecasts — volume and mix — need to be reconciled, and we'll get into more detail on that in just a bit.

Question #4: How Accurate Should the Forecast Be?

When people ask us this question, we wince. We try never to use the word forecast and the word accurate in the same sentence. Why? Because it's a turnoff for the folks in Sales and Marketing who will be called upon to do the forecasting.

People who routinely criticize the forecasters for their inaccuracy might ask themselves a few basic questions. First, if the Sales and Marketing people could predict the future with great accuracy, do you really think they'd be working for a living? Would they be knocking themselves out for forty or fifty or more hours per week? Of course not. If they could predict the future with great accuracy, where would

---

[1] Most of us learned this in Management 101: the people who develop the plan should be the same ones who are accountable for its execution.

they be? At the racetrack. And if the track were closed? They'd be home on their PCs, trading in stock options and speculating on pork-belly futures.

Even the best forecasts will almost always be inaccurate to one degree or another. The job of the forecasters is twofold. First, they must get the forecast in the ballpark, good enough to enable Operations people to do a proper job of initial procurement and production, capacity planning, etc. Frequently this does not require forecasts at a detailed level, but works fine with aggregated forecasts — perhaps by Product Family, Subfamily, or Brand.

The second major goal for forecasters is continuous improvement in reducing forecast error. In doing this, they are not trying to reach some nirvana of forecasting accuracy perfection, but to routinely produce forecasts that reflect what we call the "four Rs of forecasting": forecasts that are reasoned, realistic, reviewed frequently, and represent the total demand.

Forecasting is a process. It has inputs and outputs, just like a production operation. See Figure 4-3, which shows the forecasting process in terms of inputs and outputs. Note the output — forecasts that are reasoned, reasonable, reviewed frequently, and reflect the total demand. Nowhere does it say "accurate" because talking about accuracy clouds and emotionally charges the issue. The issue is the process.

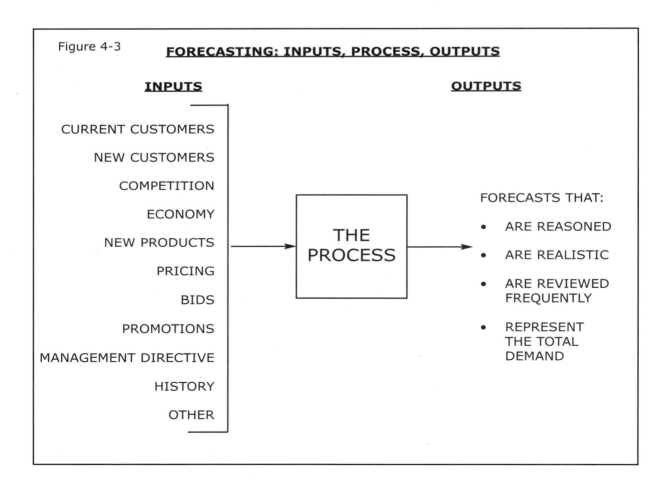

Figure 4-3 — FORECASTING: INPUTS, PROCESS, OUTPUTS

Point 4: Better processes yield better results and forecasting is no exception; better forecasting processes will yield better forecasts. A forecast that's closer to actual demand, one that contains less forecast error, means less inventory in terms of safety stock, reduced expediting, fewer unplanned changes in the plant, and so forth. So although we don't talk about accurate forecasts, we do promote "good" forecasts. Good means that the forecasters are working the process, applying their knowledge of the customers, the marketplace, future sales and marketing plans, and in general doing the best job they can.

Another, probably better, way of saying it comes from Rebecca Morgan of Fulcrum Consulting Works in Cleveland: "*Accuracy* is a term to be avoided. We use the term quality in referring to fitness for use and reduced variability of forecasts over time."

Question #5: How Frequently Should You Forecast?

For a formal review, a good frequency is once per month. Of course, if the demand picture undergoes major changes mid-month, the forecast should be updated at that time. Forecasting less frequently than once per month can lead to the kind of problem that Mike, Pete, and Carol faced in Chapter 3.

Forecasting more frequently than once per month can work well, but before you jump into that, be sure you're doing it for the right reason. We've seen companies changing the forecast very frequently in order to effect changes directly into the near-term production schedule. Almost always this is a result of not having a good scheduling system, so they manipulate the forecast (a statement of demand) to directly affect production, which of course is supply. It is not a good practice, and it almost never yields good results.

Company S produces consumer packaged goods with a highly seasonal sales curve. They used to change the forecast frequently, in the very near term. What do you think the impact was on the plants? It drove them crazy. There were constant changes: stop that, start this, increase that, decrease this.

As we learned more about what they were doing, we saw why: their processes for Master Scheduling and Plant Scheduling processes were right out of the 1950s. The sales and marketing folks felt their only chance of getting the right stuff produced was to constantly change the forecast. It was the informational equivalent of using a saw to drive nails.

The good news is they don't do that anymore. They have a good resource planning system in place and can really manage their Master Schedule and plant schedules. Today they change the forecast far less frequently, run the plant more efficiently, and provide far better customer service than before.

On the other hand, some companies in what's called "fast-moving consumer goods" update their "forecasts" a number of times per week. Typically they're receiving point-of-sale data from their larger customers, and thus can see through the customers' distribution systems right into the retail stores. They can recalculate their customers' expected demands over the next few days, reset their finishing schedules, and produce.[2]

---

[2] A growing number of these kinds of companies have adopted "Postponement," which we talked about in Chapter 3.

This is beyond the scope of most companies' capabilities today. Unless you're really good at it, or have an overriding need, go with a frequency of once per month for your forecast updates. It fits nicely with the Executive S&OP cycle, and you can always go to a greater forecast frequency later if it will help you balance demand and supply at the mix level.

Constrained versus Unconstrained Forecasts

This issue comes up in companies with demand that almost always exceeds supply. Here we're not talking about those occasional periods where demand exceeds supply for a month or two, but rather is cases where supply is chronically less than demand. This could happen when a company decides not to invest in capacity expansion or there is a chronically scarce but essential component or raw material. Thus:

- The unconstrained forecast is what we could sell if we could produce, or obtain, as much as we wanted; future sales would not be constrained by lack of availability.

- The constrained forecast typically represents what we expect to sell, based largely on the amount of product we expect to be available.

So, which forecast should be used on the S&OP spreadsheets and graphs? Many companies in this situation show both the unconstrained and the constrained forecast. However, it must be the *constrained* forecast that enters into the calculations for future inventories and backlogs:

Beginning Inventory – Constrained Forecast + Operations Plan = Ending Inventory

To do otherwise would result in the projected ending inventories going negative and becoming more so throughout the projection. Meaningless.

Plus, there's an even more serious problem if a company were to use the unconstrained forecast in its financial projections. Stated simply, future revenue is not going to come from what we *theoretically* can sell; it will come from what we *actually do sell and ship*. And that means the constrained forecast.

Okay, so is there a role for the unconstrained forecast? Yes, for two reasons:

- Motivation. Some companies will display both forecasts on their spreadsheets and possibly on graphs. They do this so they don't lose sight of how much more they could sell if ample supply were available.

- To serve as an important input for companies with *highly variable supply*. We cover the topic of how to deal with this variable supply issue in Appendix E.

Sell-To versus Sell-Through Forecasts

This issue often comes up in companies that sell to major retailers. Many companies have been "fooled" by looking only at what they ship, versus what their customers are selling. The difference, of course, is the inventory level at the customer. For example, Acme Widget sells its consumer products to Big-Mart, a big-box retailer, which in turn sells the widgets to the end consumer. Thus:

- The sell-*to* forecast is what Acme thinks it will ship to Big-Mart.

- The sell-*through* forecast is what Acme thinks that Big-Mart will sell to consumers (ideally determined with some help from Big-Mart in making this forecast).

Why should Acme care about what Big-Mart sells? Because the sell-through forecast, coupled with Big-Mart's inventory of Acme consumer widgets, will determine what Acme ships to Big-Mart — and that's called the sell-to forecast. The sell-through forecast normally plays a major role in the Demand Planning phase, but it's the sell-to forecast that's the primary forecast input into Supply Planning and later steps.

Supply Input: Resource Planning

The job of the people in Operations — including Production, Supply Chain, Purchasing, Logistics, and so forth — is to evaluate the new Operations Plan for "doability." Can we hit the numbers called for in the plan, or do they represent ten pounds of potatoes in a five-pound bag? Or maybe two pounds in that five-pound bag?[3]

This is a critical step, because what's needed here is either an Operations commitment to hit the numbers in the Operations Plan or, if that's not possible, a revised Operations Plan that can be accomplished. In the latter case, if the doable Operations Plan is not adequate to support the Sales Forecast, then this issue is carried into the Pre-Meeting, described in the next chapter.

In some companies, evaluating a plan is easy; in others, it's more involved — and it's determined by how production resources line up with product families. We need to spend a little time here talking about how production facilities are organized.

Aligned Resources

In some cases, the production departments match up closely with the product families — Product A is made in Department A, Product B in Department B. In this situation, the capacity check can often be performed right on the S&OP spreadsheet itself. Since there's a one-to-one relationship between Product Family and production resource, the Operations Plan for that family represents the entire workload for the resource. The Operations people know what rates they can hit, or can gear up to hit, and it's all visible on one display. We refer to this kind of organization of manufacturing facilities as "aligned," i.e., the resources are closely aligned with the product families.

Nonaligned Resources

In some companies, there is no tight match-up between product families and resources. A schematic of these two different approaches is shown in Figure 4-4 on the next page.

---

[3] Insufficient workload can sometimes be as big a problem — or bigger — than too much work.

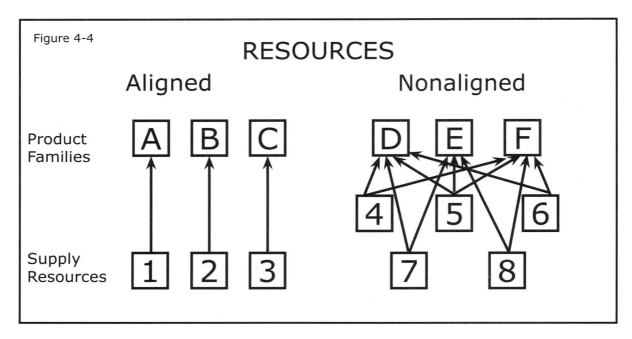

Figure 4-4

The Acme Widget Company had nonaligned resources. Both of their primary product categories — Industrial and Consumer — were made in the same departments in their plant: Fabrication 1, Fabrication 2, Subassembly, and Final Assembly. A further complication was that the low end of the small and medium consumer widget families was outsourced, i.e., purchased as complete products from a contract manufacturer in Asia.

Try as they might, the Acme people couldn't integrate the "operations view" of the business into their product families without making the whole picture terribly complicated and user-unfriendly. They solved the problem by keeping it simple. They set up the product families and subfamilies by major category (Industrial and Consumer) and by product (small, medium, large). They kept the resource picture completely different, as shown below:

Product Families

Large Industrial Widgets	Large Consumer Widgets
Medium Industrial Widgets	Medium Consumer Widgets
Small Industrial Widgets	Small Consumer Widgets

Resources

Fabrication 1	Subassembly
Fabrication 2	Final Assembly
Contract Manufacturer A (Outsourced Products)	

Please note: some plants have both aligned and nonaligned resources. For example, in some chemical plants, the primary operations (for example, the reactor train) are aligned while the packaging operations are not. Thus the capacity for the reactor train can be done as an aligned resource, but packaging cannot. As a nonaligned resource, packaging in this example needs Resource Requirements Planning.

Resource Requirements Planning

The resources are separate elements; they represent the *supply* side of the business. Within the family groupings, Acme people a) do the forecasting of future demand, b) set the Operations Plan to meet the demand and keep inventories or order backlogs at their desired levels, and then c) "translate" the Operations Plan for the individual families into units of workload for each resource, using a process called "Resource Requirements Planning."[4]

This process enables the Operations people to relate the *required* capacity (demand) to their *available* capacity (supply). They're able to evaluate the doability of the plan, changes needed in staffing levels, the need for new equipment, and so on. And please note: it's often necessary to do Resource Requirements Planning on "nontraditional" resources such as order entry and product engineering (in a Make-to-Order or design-to-order environment), distribution center space and staffing levels, transportation resources, and so forth.

After the newly updated Operations Plan is rearranged into aggregate departmental workloads and typically translated from units into hours, it must be displayed so that Operations people can see where their problems are.

How this is done will be covered in Chapter 14, The Supply Planning Process. We're deferring it until then because the mechanics of Resource Requirements Planning, while conceptually simple, require a good bit of time and space to cover adequately. If you absolutely can't wait to learn about this process, you can jump to page 123.

Demand/Supply Strategies

It's necessary to define an operating approach for each Product Family, and we refer to such approaches as *demand/supply strategies*. These strategies spell out whether a given family is Make-to-Stock, Make-to-Order, or Finish-to-Order; what the target customer service levels are; and the desired level of inventory or customer order backlog. These inventory and backlog targets are essential: along with the forecast, they drive the Operations Plan.

In Figure 4-5 on the following page, we can see two examples of demand/supply strategies. In this example, Acme Widget has said that the Medium Consumer Widget family contains primarily Make-to-Stock products, that it wants to provide 99 percent on time and complete customer service for these products, and that doing so will require ten days of finished inventory.

---

[4] Another name for the process is "Rough-Cut Capacity Planning." We've adopted the former because it does seem to be more contemporary in this era of outsourcing, contract manufacturing, and so forth.

Large Industrial Widgets are Make-to-Order. As such, there is no finished goods inventory for them; rather, the variable here is the size of the customer order backlog, which directly determines the customer lead time.

Figure 4-5

EXAMPLES OF DEMAND/SUPPLY STRATEGIES

Product Family: Medium Consumer Widgets
1. Make-to-Stock
2. Target Customer Service Level: 99% Line Item Fill
3. Target Finished Goods Inventory: 10 Days' Supply

Product Family: Large Industrial Widgets
1. Make-to-Order
2. Target Customer Service Level: 98% Order Fill
3. Target Customer Lead Time: 4 Weeks

Let's look at that target customer service level for Medium Widgets. It says 99 percent Line Item Fill. That means that 99 percent of all line items are to be shipped on time and complete. That sounds fine until you consider that Acme Widget averages five line items per customer order, and most orders call for items from different families. The measure that should be used to track customer service should, in almost all cases, not be line fill but rather order fill — the percentage of customer orders shipped on time and complete.

So what is Acme doing messing around with line item fill in their demand/supply strategy? The answer is: they have to. You see, the strategies are specific to a *family*; they drive the forward planning logic of S&OP. But the important customer service measure is *order* fill. Acme recognized that. Early in each Executive S&OP meeting, they address overall customer service performance using order fill statistics. Their *order fill* target is 95 percent. In order to reach that, since they average five items per order, they set their *line fill* target at 99 percent.

Setting the targets for inventory and order backlog is, for most companies, not an exact science. Unless you have very good data readily available, you can't get highly accurate here; don't make a career out of trying to decide what they should be. Regarding the size of the finished goods inventory, our advice is to get started in Executive S&OP by setting the targets at roughly what you have now — unless they're obviously much too high or low. Then, as you move through time and improve your processes, you can adjust them — usually downward.

Part of the issue here involves mix — how many different line items are in a given family. Let's take two product families with identical overall volumes. Everything about these two families is the same except for one thing: Family A has 4 items and Family B has 400. Which family would require the larger safety stock to give the same level of customer service? The answer is B, of course, because the same volume spread over 100 times more items will require much more protection against stockouts.

For Make-to-Order products, the target customer lead time is largely a function of the customer order backlog, which in turn is typically a trade-off between the desire to get the product to the customers quickly and the amount of time needed for pre-production, production, and post-production activities. Here also, our general recommendation is to get started with roughly what you're doing now, and then sharpen it up as you go along.

Let's revisit this issue of Make-to-Order or Make-to-Stock. For purposes of Executive S&OP, many companies who initially think they're Make-to-Order are actually Make-to-Stock. Let's take Company D as an example. They make shopping bags, among other things, for retailers. Many of their bags are customer-specific; they show the customer's name: Nordstrom, Abercrombie and Fitch, Brooks Brothers, and so on.

Sounds like Make-to-Order, right? Well, not quite. Company D has "stocking agreements" with many of its customers that require certain levels of finished goods inventory. For Executive S&OP this is a Make-to-Stock product, not a Make-to-Order one. The question is not primarily whether the product is built for one customer only, but rather whether the product typically goes to a finished goods inventory after it's produced. If it's the latter, it's a Make-to-Stock product for S&OP purposes.

Commercial aircraft manufacturers are largely Make-to-Order. They finish producing the plane for a given airline, take it up for a test hop, slap a green sticker on it, and away it goes. That's Make-to-Order.

To sum up, setting demand/supply strategies means spelling out what you're trying to accomplish with each Product Family in terms of demand and supply. Here are some questions that play into this:

- Is this family Make-to-Stock, Make-to-Order, or Finish-to-Order?

- What is the target customer service level for this family? This refers to on-time and complete shipments to customers.

- If the family is Make-to-Stock, what is the target finished goods inventory level? In other words, how much inventory is needed to enable the target customer service level?

- If the family is Finish-to-Order, what is the target inventory level of modules (or other "surrogates")? Here again, how much inventory is needed to enable the target customer service level?

- If the family is Make-to-Order, what is the target customer order backlog? Remember, in the Make-to-Order world, backlog — negative inventory — is a key factor; it determines how long it will take for customers to get their product from you.

This is important. These demand/supply strategies spell out what we need to do to keep our customers happy and to effectively manage our inventories and order backlogs. They direct us in balancing demand and supply. They're necessary for Executive S&OP because they play a key role in the logic of the spreadsheet. In addition, as we'll see in Chapter 17, they help to keep the need for continuous improvement visible as the company goes through time.

*   *   *   *

FREQUENTLY ASKED QUESTIONS

We have several pieces of equipment that are really bottlenecks. They're individual machines, not entire production departments. Can we do Resource Requirements Planning on them?

Absolutely. These individual units are resources, perhaps small in size but big in impact. For Executive S&OP purposes (overall volume), treat them as you would any other key resource. The issue is not purely one of size, or head count, or throughput; it's whether this resource is a potential shipment stopper.

Chapter 5

The Monthly Executive S&OP Process

The essence of Executive S&OP is decision-making. For each product family, a decision is made on the basis of recent history, current business conditions, and the managers' and executives' judgment and feel for where the business is headed. The decision can be:

- change the Sales Plan,

- change the Operations Plan,

- change the inventory/backlog plan,

- change the strategy and/or policy regarding volume and/or mix, or

- none of the above: the current plans are okay.

These decisions represent the agreed-upon, authorized plans by the president, all involved vice presidents, and other members of the Executive Team. It's important that they be documented and disseminated throughout the organization. They form the overall game plan for Sales, Operations, Finance, and Product Development. These groups break down the aggregate plans from Executive S&OP into the necessary level of detail: individual products, customers, regions, plants, and materials.

Executive S&OP, however, is not a single event that occurs in a one- to two-hour meeting each month. Rather, preliminary work begins right after month end and continues for some days. The steps involve middle management and others throughout the company (see Figure 5-1, on the next page). They include:

- updating the Sales Forecast;

- reviewing the impact of changes on the Operations Plan, and determining whether adequate capacity and material will be available to support them;

- identifying alternatives where problems exist;

- identifying variances to the Business Plan (budget) and potential solutions;

- making decisions where empowered to do so and where consensus exists;

- formulating recommendations for top management on decisions outside their scope of authority, and identifying areas of disagreement where consensus is not possible; and

- communicating this information to top management with sufficient time for them to review it prior to the Exec meeting.

Figure 5-1

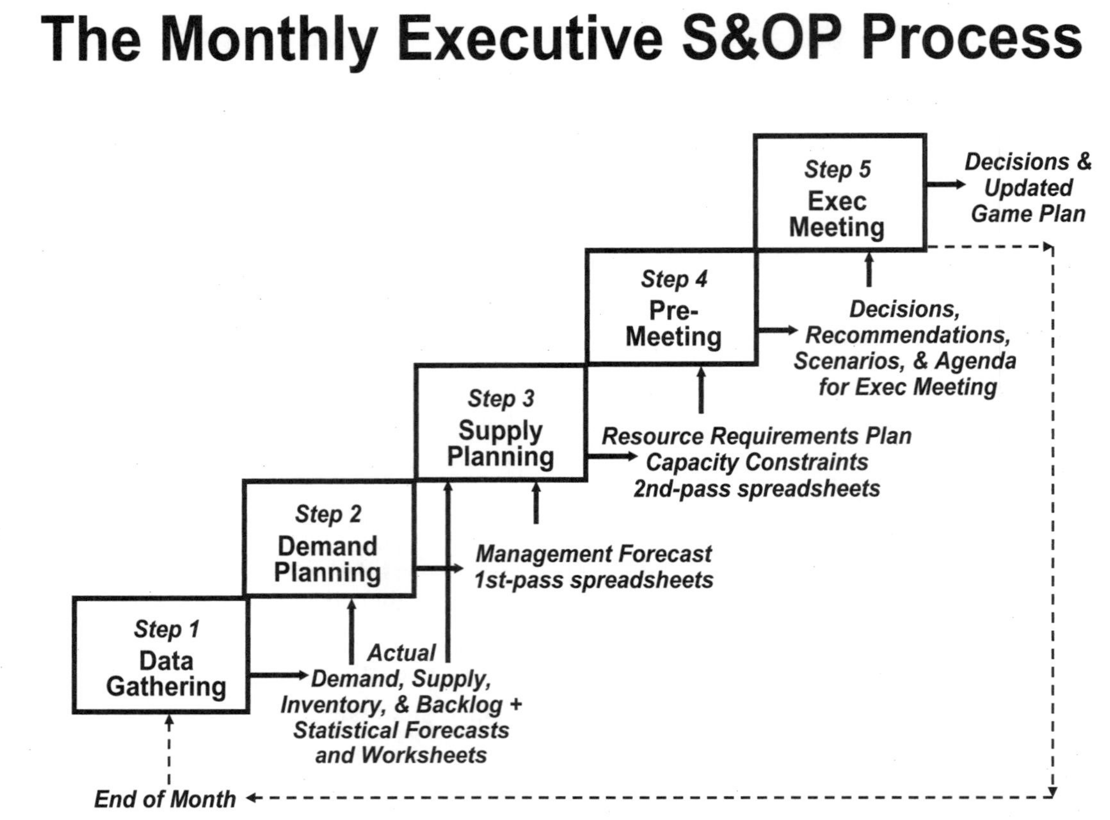

The Monthly Executive S&OP Process

Thanks to the work that has gone before, the Exec Meeting should not take a long time; as we've said, two hours or less is the norm with companies that do this well. The net result of Executive S&OP for the top management group should be *less* time in meetings overall, more productivity in their decision-making processes, and a higher quality of work life. And most of the middle-management people involved in the earlier steps in the process will experience the same benefits.

Another point about timing concerns elapsed time: how long should it take to complete the entire cycle from start (at the beginning of the month) to finish (the Exec Meeting)? The answer is about ten to twelve work days, which puts the Exec Meeting in the third week of the month.

You may be thinking: by then, the month is more than half over. Isn't that a problem? Answer: no it's not. And the reason why it's not a problem gets at what the Executive S&OP process is all about. It's not a detailed scheduling meeting; it's not a shortage meeting; it's not a meeting to decide which customer orders are going to ship next Tuesday. Rather, it's a medium- to long-term planning process, focusing primarily on trends and patterns outside the Planning Time Fence.

A further point: during implementation, companies should not worry about getting the cycle completed in a dozen work days or less. During implementation, the main objective is to get the process working, not to hit some arbitrary timing point. Take your time. Do it right; don't let people burn out by doing all-nighters — and if that means you don't have the Exec Meeting until the fourth week of the month, that's okay. After you get the process working well, then you can focus on pulling in the timing.

Let's take a look at each of the steps shown in Figure 5-1.

Step 1 — Data Gathering

While much of this activity occurs within the Information Systems department, it is a line management responsibility to see that the data has validity. It happens shortly after the end of the month, and consists of three elements:

- Updating the files with data from the month just ended — actual sales, production, inventories, and so on.

- Generating information for Sales and Marketing people to use in developing the new forecast. This could include sales analysis data, statistical forecast reports, worksheets for field salespeople, extrinsic trend data, and so forth.

- Disseminating this information to the appropriate people.

To make Executive S&OP a timely process overall, it's important that this step be completed within a day or two after the end of the month.

Step 2 — The Demand Planning Phase

Step 2
Demand Planning

Step 1
Data Gathering

This is where people in Sales and Marketing review the information they received from Step 1, analyze and discuss it, and generate the new management forecast for the next fifteen or more months into the future. Please keep in mind: this forecast must include both existing products and new products. Let's look at two very different businesses and see how the forecasting process might be carried out.

Demand Planning in Make-to-Order

The Acme Widget Company has two divisions: Industrial and Consumer. The Industrial business is largely a Make-to-Order operation, with relatively few customers taking almost all of the volume. In this business, a very large portion of the forecasting task is customer contact: learning from the key customers their future plans for the use of Acme's products. Statistics on past sales can be helpful, but the key is to capture what the customers think is going to happen.

The biggest help that good information can provide to the forecasters — frequently the field salespeople in this kind of business — is to show, by customer, what products they've taken in the past and to give the Sales folks an easy way to input new forecasts into the system. A good practice here is to direct the salespeople in the field to concentrate on the large customers and/or the high volume products, and not take up their valuable time with less important customers and products.

Even though this is a customer-centric process, once all customer information is updated, it needs to be looked at in total relative to the overall market/industry conditions based on extrinsic information. This "bigger look" is generally a somewhat more centralized activity. More on this in a bit.

Demand Planning in Make-to Stock

Acme's Consumer Division, on the other hand, is almost totally a Make-to-Stock business. Its immediate customers are retailers, who sell the product to the end consumers — folks like us. There are many of these retail customers and, except for several mass merchandisers, no one customer makes up a large percentage of the Consumer Division's sales volume. The foundation for forecasting these products is statistical forecasting; Acme Widget has an effective statistical forecasting package that uses past history as a basis for statistical projections of future forecasts.

We hasten to add that the Consumer Division's approach to forecasting for the mass merchandisers and other large customers should look more like a Make-to-Order process than Make-to-Stock; the field salespeople must be in direct and frequent contact with their large customers regarding future needs.

Arriving at a "Management Forecast"

Let's look at how the Demand Planning phase takes place within the Consumer Division. After the statistical forecast reports are generated, the information is reviewed by managers in the Sales and Marketing areas. Their job is to override the statistical forecasts where appropriate. When would that be appropriate? Any time that past history is not the best predictor of the future. What factors would make history not the best predictor? Well, quite a few:

- field input regarding large customers

- potential new customers

- new products

- promotion plans

- open bids

- price changes

- level of inventory in distribution

- point of sale volume

- competitive activity

- industry and market dynamics

- economic conditions

- intra-company demand (from other business units within the company)

- and, last but not least, a review of the forecast errors from the prior month — focusing on bias and usually by family or subfamily — followed by an analysis of their causes, and a determination of the consequence on the new forecast.

It's the job of people in Sales and Marketing management to use their knowledge of these factors and possibly others to come up with the management forecast.[1] That is their responsibility. And, actually, it's also in their best interest. Most often, the management forecast proves to have a lower error rate. (Okay, it's more "accurate.") Why? Because the statistical forecast is based heavily on past history. As long as the future is going to be much like the past, then everything works. But usually it's not. Changes in the above factors can make the future quite different from the past. It's the job of the people, using their innate intelligence and their knowledge of current conditions and the expected future outlook, to override the statistics and get the best forecast possible.

Some powerful statistical forecasting routines exist that take into account factors such as economic indicators, consumer attitude, and industry trends. If you're using one of these tools, great. However, our point here still applies: human judgment by knowledgeable people is essential.

Documenting Assumptions

Once the numbers that make up the new forecast are put together, the job's not quite done. What's needed is to document the key assumptions that underlie the forecasts. This is important for several reasons. One is that, as the Executive S&OP process goes forward, all of the participants can see the assumptions upon which the forecast is based. This may lead one or more of them to challenge the forecast, which is certainly legitimate. This gives the forecasters the opportunity to defend the specifics of their forecast rather than having to respond to a general comment, such as "it's too high."

The second benefit from documenting assumptions is that, after the period is over, it can be very instructive to review the assumptions and the results and learn, perhaps, why things didn't work out (or perhaps why they did). Learning from one's mistakes — and successes — is one of the best ways to improve.

---

[1] One piece of the overall demand forecast not normally under the purview of Sales is *intra-company demand*. This is often handled by the Supply Chain group, sometimes called Logistics or Materials Management.

New Product Inclusion

Involving New Product Development people is important here, because they typically have the best handle on timing of new product launches. Sales and Marketing should have already made forecasts, not only of the new product but its cannibalization impact on existing products. These forecasts should be reviewed for possible changes. The resulting statements of new product demand must be included here so that the Supply people can make the appropriate plans. This should include new product launches currently underway plus others expected to be launched within the S&OP planning horizon.

Units First, Then Dollars

The forecasts of future demand — for both new products and existing ones — are almost always made in units and then translated into dollars. Forecasts whose base unit of measure is dollars almost invariably lack the kind of focus and utility that Operations needs.

This concept of the base unit of measure not being dollars applies in other parts of the business world, one rather homely example being the annual physical inventory. One can count the items in inventory (in units, of course), dollarize each count, total them up, and derive the value of the inventory. But you can't go the other way: you cannot get a dollar number for the total inventory and derive the units from that.

Having said that, we hasten to add that there must be a dollar view of the updated forecast before it goes further in the Demand Planning process. People from Finance and Accounting should be involved in this update; their participation here is very valuable.

Since the output from this Demand Planning phase is the management-authorized forecast, it's necessary to get the senior Sales and Marketing executive(s) into the loop. In some companies, the forecasters make a brief presentation of the updated forecast to the vice president(s) of Sales and Marketing. Bringing the senior executive into the process at this point does several things:

- It allows him or her to ask questions, challenge the numbers, challenge the assumptions, and, if need be, change some of them.

- It avoids surprises at the Exec Meeting.

- It results in a truly "management-authorized forecast," one that all of the key players have bought into. They've signed off on it. This forecast, then, represents Sales and Marketing's best estimate of future demand.

Managing the Spreadsheets/Graphs

So how does the new forecast enter into the S&OP spreadsheets and graphs?[2] One good way to do it is first to delete all forecasts, plus inventories and backlogs from the month just ended. Then roll the production

---

[2] From here on, we'll use the word "spreadsheet" to mean both the spreadsheet and the graphical display derived from it.

data one month to the left, to reflect the passage of time. Then lay in the newly updated forecasts along with actual sales, production, inventory data, and backlog for the month just ended. The result is what we call the First-Pass Spreadsheets.

You now have the new forecast playing against the current Operations Plan, and the resultant planned inventory or backlog numbers will now be different. Some product families will probably change very little, but others will show major differences from last month. This is due to last month's demand, changes to the forecast, inventory adjustments, and shifts in the backlog. This set of First-Pass Spreadsheets now goes into the Supply Planning step.

Do companies have a formal Demand Planning meeting? Some do and some don't. In general, larger companies tend to hold one or more formal meetings to get the management forecast nailed down, while frequently, smaller companies have a series of smaller, somewhat less formal face-to-face sessions.

People with the following kinds of job titles typically populate the Demand Planning Team:

Demand Manager	Customer Service Manager	Product Manager
Forecast Analyst	Accounting Manager	Sales Manager
New Products Coordinator	Salesperson	Supply Chain Manager
S&OP Process Owner	Sales Administration Manager	

Please note: these are generic job titles. They probably won't match up exactly with yours. Moreover, they are only examples; not all of them should be considered as mandatory. In most companies, there are normally about a half dozen to a dozen people involved in the Demand Planning/forecasting process.

Step 3 — The Supply Planning Phase

The newly updated S&OP spreadsheets are the primary input to the Supply Planning phase, which is Operations' responsibility.[3]

Their first step is to modify the Operations Plans for any families or subfamilies that need it. If little or nothing has changed from last month, then there's probably little reason to change anything this month. On the other hand, changes in the Sales Forecast, inventory levels, or the size of the customer order backlog can readily trigger a change to the Operations Plan.

The new Operations Plan must then be tested for doability. For companies with aligned resources, this can be done using the S&OP spreadsheets themselves. For nonaligned resources, Resource Requirements Planning is needed to focus on the demand/supply picture for specific resources.

Outputs from the Supply Planning step are the Second-Pass Spreadsheets, Resource Requirements Planning reports, and a list of any supply problems that cannot be resolved or that require decisions further up the

---

[3] We're using Operations here in the broad sense: production, supply chain, purchasing, logistics, distribution, and those people responsible for planning and scheduling contract manufacturers and other outsourced providers of products and components.

ladder. In some cases, demand (as expressed by the forecast) simply exceeds supply by too great a margin to reach; the constraints cannot be overcome within the allowable time. Sometimes these constraints are within the company's own production resources; at other times constraints may exist elsewhere in the supply chain, i.e., outside suppliers, contract manufacturers, and the like.

At other times, acquiring the resources necessary to meet the demand may be feasible but will require spending that can be authorized only by top management. These are the kinds of issues that the supply folks carry into the Pre-Meeting.

As with Demand Planning, some companies will conduct a formal meeting for this Supply Planning step, while others find it more effective to simply work the process informally one on one.

This group is made up of people such as:

Accounting Manager	Materials Manager	Purchasing Manager
Distribution Manager	New Products Coordinator	QA/QC Manager
Logistics Manager	Plant Manager	S&OP Process Owner
Master Scheduler	Production Control Manager	Supply Chain Manager

Most of the comments made for the Demand Planning Team apply here also:

• Not all of these job titles need to be represented in the process.

• Formal meetings are held in some companies, not in others.

• Accounting expertise is necessary to evaluate the financial impact of changes to the production plan.

• The impact of new products on plant and supplier capacity must be done here.

• The senior operations executive might serve as a resource to authorize this group's output.

In a multi-plant environment, of course, all of the plants need to be involved in this process to ensure that each plant can meet what's being asked of it. Frequently their participation is via e-mail, conference call, web meetings, and the like.

Step 4 — The Pre-Meeting

Objectives of the Pre-Meeting include:

• making decisions regarding the balancing of demand and supply, within the framework of the existing policies, strategies, and current Business Plan;

• resolving problems and differences so that, where possible, a single set of recommendations can be made to the Exec Meeting;

- identifying those areas where agreement cannot be reached, and determining how the situation will be presented in the Exec Meeting;

- developing, where appropriate, scenarios showing alternate courses of action to solve a given problem;

- setting the agenda for the Exec Meeting.

The Pre-Meeting centers around a family-by-family review of the Second-Pass Spreadsheets, including subfamilies where they exist, and to make adjustments where appropriate. They also check for resource constraints, using either the product family/subfamily spreadsheets for aligned resources or separate capacity displays for matrix resources. Where there are constraints, demand priorities must be established and that, of course, should be done primarily by Sales and Marketing.

In addition, their review should look at actual performance to plan for sales, production, inventories and backlogs, and a once-per-quarter check on the demand/supply strategies for each family to make appropriate changes (see Appendix F, the Executive S&OP Effectiveness Checklist).

```
                                    ┌──────────┐
                                    │  Step 4  │
                                    │   Pre-   │
                                    │ Meeting  │
                           ┌──────────┐────────┘
                           │  Step 3  │
                           │  Supply  │
                           │ Planning │
                  ┌──────────┐────────┘
                  │  Step 2  │
                  │  Demand  │
                  │ Planning │
         ┌──────────┐────────┘
         │  Step 1  │
         │   Data   │
         │Gathering │
         └──────────┘
```

The outputs from the Pre-Meeting include:

- An updated financial view of the business, including matching the latest sales call to the Business Plan for the total company. (This is typically done on a rolled-up, dollarized spreadsheet covering all families.)

- A decision and/or recommendation for each product family, contained on the Third-Pass Spreadsheets, as to the future course of action:

   ✓ stay the course, no change;

   ✓ increase/decrease the Sales Plan; and/or

   ✓ increase/decrease the Operations Plan.

- Any new product launch issues not covered within the product family review.

- A decision and/or recommendation for each resource requiring a major change: add people, add a shift, add equipment, offload work to a sister plant, outsource, or reduce the number of people or shifts.

- Areas where a consensus decision could not be reached, possibly as a result of disagreement or where competing alternatives might be "too close to call." In such cases, it's often very helpful for alternatives to be presented — Scenario A, Scenario B, Scenario C — with dollar data as well as units, to show the financial impact.

- Recommendations for changes to demand/supply strategies where appropriate.

- Agenda for the S&OP meeting, an example of which is shown below.

The Pre-Meeting team includes folks with job titles such as:

Accounting Manager	Forecast Analyst	Plant Manager
Controller	Logistics Manager	Product Manager
Customer Service Manager	Master Scheduler	Purchasing Manager
Demand Manager	Materials Manager	S&OP Process Owner[4]
New Products Coordinator	Supply Chain Manager	

Don't be put off by the apparent size of this group. Yes, there are fourteen job titles identified here, but frequently several functions are performed by the same person.

On the other side of the coin, some job titles may contain more than one person, e.g., three product managers and two plant managers. Therefore, it's possible that you would wind up with a group that's a bit larger than what you're used to. At that point, you can either drop people off the team, or get started with the larger group and see what happens.

We're more comfortable with the second option. We feel it's better to have a group that's slightly larger than ideal than to exclude people who can contribute to the process. One factor in favor of the larger size is that these meetings are not brainstorming sessions. Rather, they're structured meetings with a high degree of focus on the process. Virtually all of the players will have already participated in one or both of the prior steps, so there won't be a large number of surprises or new issues to work through.

To sum up, the Pre-Meeting is in one sense a "get-ready" session for the Executive S&OP meeting. But it's actually a lot more than that: the Pre-Meeting is a *decision-making session*. The mind-set that the participants should have is, "If this were our business, what would we decide to do?"

Virtually all of the decisions to be made in the monthly cycle will be made here or in the two prior steps: Demand Planning and Supply Planning. This is where the true "heavy lifting" is done within the overall Executive S&OP process. Not all of these decisions are easy to come by; frequently differing views are held by strong-willed, articulate people. The corporate culture must foster a willingness to raise conflict and, once raised, to resolve it. More on this later.

Step 5 — The Executive Meeting

This is the culminating event in the monthly Executive S&OP cycle. Its objectives are:

- To review — and accept or modify — the decisions made by the Pre-Meeting Team.

---

[4]   Normally the S&OP Process Owner facilitates this meeting.

- To make decisions about each product family requiring a decision. Typically these are cases where the Pre-Meeting group could not reach consensus or the decision was outside of their scope of authority.

- To authorize changes in production or procurement rates, where significant costs other consequences are involved.

- To relate the dollarized version of the S&OP information to the Business Plan and where they deviate, decide to adjust the Sales & Operations Plan and/or the Business Plan, as appropriate.

- To "break the ties" for areas where the Pre-Meeting Team was unable to reach consensus.

				Step 5 Exec Meeting
			Step 4 Pre-Meeting	
		Step 3 Supply Planning		
	Step 2 Demand Planning			
Step 1 Data Gathering				

- To review customer service performance, new product issues, special projects, and other issues and to make the necessary decisions.

- To review (and change where appropriate) existing policies and strategies with regard to balancing demand and supply.

Outputs from the Exec Meeting include the meeting minutes, which spell out the decisions that were made; modifications to the Business Plan, if any; and the Fourth-Pass Spreadsheets, which reflect changes made at the Exec Meeting.

All these things taken collectively form the company's authorized game plan. As such, there is urgency to get the word out to all involved people, and for this reason we recommend that the meeting minutes and the Fourth-Pass Spreadsheets be made available within two working days of the meeting.

SAMPLE AGENDA

EXEC MEETING

1. Macro Business Review

2. Customer Service Performance

3. New Products

4. Family-by-Family Review and Decisions

5. Production/Procurement Rate Changes

6. Collective Impact on Business Plan

7. Recap of Decisions Made

8. Critique of Meeting

This group should include, at a minimum, the:

President (General Manager, COO)

Vice Presidents of:

Sales

Marketing

Supply Chain

Operations

Product Development

Finance

Logistics

Human Resources

The person who facilitated the Pre-Meeting, usually the S&OP Process Owner.

Most Executive S&OP Teams we've been involved with are not this small. Rather, they include other people who can add value to the process, such as the Demand Manager, Product Manager, Sales Manager, Customer Service Manager, Supply Chain Manager, Plant Manager, Materials Manager, Master Scheduler, Supply Planner, Controller, and New Product Coordinator. The comments that we made for the size of the Pre-Meeting team apply here also.

Here's a tale from Tom: *A company near where I live was implementing Executive S&OP. The two plant managers were on their Pre-Meeting Team but were not included in the Exec Meeting, in order to keep the group small. At the time, the company was facing a number of tricky capacity issues, and they found that their Exec Meetings were difficult and not as productive as they could have been. They just didn't have enough plant-specific knowledge in the room to make decisions crisply.*

I was serving as the company's Executive S&OP expert. My job, therefore, was to address serious issues like this and help to get them resolved. I recommended to the President and the Vice President of Operations that the two plant managers be added to the Exec Meeting team. After a bit of "arm wrestling" on the part of the VP, they did add the two plant managers, and things went a lot better from then on.

Here's a quick point for those of you in smaller companies. You may not need to have both a Pre-Meeting and an Exec Meeting. In some companies or business units, perhaps around $30 million or less per year, the line between operating managers and executives gets blurred. The operating-level managers report directly to the President. I've seen some companies in this category combine the Pre-Meeting and Exec Meeting into one — and it's worked well. What is called for, in that case, is a President with a fair amount of patience, because there's no Pre-Meeting to get all the ducks in a row.

Tips for Effective Exec Meetings

Over time your Exec Meetings should become very effective. Here are some ideas to help achieve that.

- **Send out the agenda in advance.** Getting the agenda out several days before the meeting gives the participants a chance to see what decisions they'll be asked to make.

- **Include the important S&OP graphs and spreadsheets with the agenda.** This will give the participants a chance to review the status of the major product families and resources.

- **Project the graphs and spreadsheets at the meeting.** Don't ask people to look at hard copy, as this dilutes the group's attention. Projection keeps everyone on the same page, and helps people to better understand the pros and cons of the decisions they're making. This used to be a bit of an issue but it's mostly gone away, thanks to the fine presentation and projection tools available today.

- **Use virtual meeting technology to include people at remote sites, traveling, and so forth.** This can greatly ease the difficulties of having the right people in the meeting.

- **Have enough Pre-Meeting people at the Executive S&OP meeting to answer likely questions.** Having to scramble to get information or to reconvene the meeting later represents inefficient use of the Executive Team's time.

- **Have a pre-appointed minute-taker.** This person should be someone other than the facilitators or presenters.

- **Be time-efficient.** If necessary, designate a time-keeper to keep the meeting moving.

- **At the end of each meeting, take five minutes to review the decisions made.** This ensures that all of the decision-makers heard the same thing and understand the decisions coming out of the meeting.

- **At the end of the meeting, take five minutes to critique the process.** Each participant should be asked for comments. This step speaks to continuous improvement and helps to ensure that the meetings get better and better.

- **Distribute the minutes within two work days of the meeting.** This meeting sets the company game plan for the upcoming months, so there should be a sense of urgency to get the word out as to what those plans are.

A word about attendance at this meeting: we've said it's essential that the President participate in this meeting. So what happens if the President can't make it, for the best of reasons: illness, an important meeting at the corporate office, a meeting with a major new sales prospect, and so forth?

Our answer has been, and continues to be, reschedule the meeting. But now, we'll add another possibility: he or she may be able to attend via the internet, and that's fine. And the same goes for other participants in the Exec Meeting; attendance via the internet (not just a telephone conference call) can certainly do the job.

Effective Exec Meetings typically last between one and two hours. If it's taking you more than two hours, there's a good chance that the meeting is not well structured and managed: insufficient focus, too much detail, lack of a good agenda, and so forth. On the other hand, less than an hour can mean that the meeting is rushed. This can result in some missed opportunities, which are often discovered during some of the focused discussion in the Exec Meeting. A good rule of thumb here: plan for about an hour and a half.

The Roles of Finance and New Product Development

Common misperceptions of Executive S&OP include: "It's a supply chain thing." or "It's a demand/supply thing." These are only partially true. Executive S&OP is all of that, of course, but also a lot more. It's much more accurate to say: "It's a company-wide thing."

As we went through the steps in the monthly cycle, you may have noticed that each step included representatives from both the Finance department and the New Product Development group. These folks are essential to make the process work well, and that's depicted in Figure 5-2 on the next page.

There are many companies today operating S&OP processes that do not include these groups. And that's too bad, because they're shortchanging themselves on benefits. If new product launches are an important part of the business, not using Executive S&OP is like trying to play an entire round of golf with only a four wood and a putter.

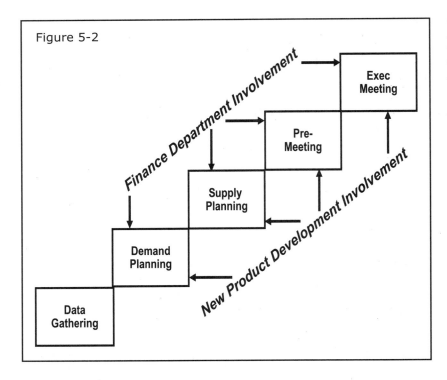

Figure 5-2

Secondly, the overall process loses much of its power without the valid financial view of the future, one example being simulation. Without a dollar view, simulation can happen only in units. Thus the company can answer the question: *can we do it?* But it cannot answer the equally vital question: *do we want to do it?* That's impossible to answer without knowing the financial impact of the alternatives.

We heard Jack Welch, ex-CEO of General Electric, speak forcefully about the great value that first-rate financial people can provide in running a company well. We don't always agree with Jack, but this time we surely did.

* * * *

FREQUENTLY ASKED QUESTIONS

What if there's a major event — affecting demand and supply — that occurs shortly after the Exec Meeting? It doesn't make sense to wait another whole month to address such a big issue.

It certainly doesn't. Many successful users, when confronted with such situations, will use an abbreviated, accelerated Executive S&OP process. They'll go through the early steps — Demand Planning, Supply Planning, Pre-Meeting — very quickly, focusing only on those parts of the business that are affected. If the necessary decisions can be made there, fine — the issue is resolved. If not, within a day or two, they'll conduct another Exec Meeting and make the necessary decisions.

Throughout the abbreviated process they try to keep the steps, the report formats, and the decision-making process the same — because the people are familiar with those processes and know they're solid. (For more on this, see "The 'Mini' S&OP Cycle on pages 181 and 182.)

Part Two

Implementing the Live Pilot

Prologue to Part Two: A Better Way

TOM WALLACE: Bob, this section of the book contains new material on implementation. What was wrong with the implementation section in the second edition? Didn't it work?

BOB STAHL: It worked very well. But over the past five or so years, we've learned some things that can make Executive S&OP easier for the executive group to buy in and also to make the early, critical phases of the implementation more sure-footed.

To put it more simply, we're smarter now than we were then.

TOM: What's the biggest difference between this new approach and the former one?

BOB: We've put even more emphasis on the behavioral aspects of implementation. Today it's clearer than ever that this is a people issue. Substantial amounts of change are required to make this process work . . . and much of that change needs to occur within the ranks of top management.

So here's a group of men and women who have a track record of success; they're holding important positions in the company and are responsible for major parts of the business. Getting them out of their comfort zone and accepting, willingly and enthusiastically, a new way of managing major elements of the business — that's the challenge.

TOM: Any other changes?

BOB: We're recommending an incremental approach to implementation. This means not making an up-front commitment to implement all of Executive S&OP fully. Rather, the first major decision (we call it Go/No-Go Decision #1) is nothing more than a commitment to a Pilot: a live 90-day Pilot Demonstration to experience how this process works in the company. Only then should there be a commitment to full implementation (Go/No-Go Decision #2).

Chapter 6

The Executive S&OP Implementation Path

Would you agree that what you've seen so far is fairly simple? No open heart surgery, no orbital dynamics, no quantum physics. But there's a paradox here: even though this process itself is very straightforward and simple to understand, it is *difficult* to implement. Here's why:

- It's a new process for the company. It is *not* an extension of past experience. It's not doing what you do better; it's doing something very different to *become* better.

- A new process means change: people changing some aspects of how they do their jobs. This results in risk for the organization and discomfort for the people.

- This change cannot be done without the sponsorship and leadership of top management, and these people are usually very busy. When they do get committed, however, they expect progress quickly and consistently. If this rapid, consistent progress doesn't happen, the effort will stall out and almost certainly die.

- In order to address all of this, people need a solid understanding of the process and the benefits it can provide in order to willingly and enthusiastically make the necessary changes.

So it's hard to do this right. The good news is that when you implement it, you don't need to reinvent the wheel. Over the last twenty years or so, through trial and error, we've learned how to do it right — every time. Today, we see the keys to success more clearly than ever:

1. Develop a solid understanding — *before* you get started — of what it is and what it will take to make it work, particularly an understanding of the need for change at all levels.

2. Use a pilot approach to allow for rapid learning in a safe environment.

3. Understand that there will be a learning curve and that you'll be *good* before you're *excellent.*

4. Remember that people are the key to success in this venture. Your success will hinge almost totally on the quality of the change management processes employed.

We will deal with all of these subjects in the chapters that follow. Now please take a moment to look at Figure 6-1 on the next page. It contains a generalized Executive S&OP implementation path. It indicates that the time required for a complete implementation will be about nine months for the average organization. Here also, there's a bit of a paradox. Why does something that involves relatively few people take eight to ten months to implement? It's because of the nature of the Executive S&OP process:

- It's different, almost totally so, from past experience and thus requires time to sink in.

- The pilot approach supports this, and also serves to minimize risk before proceeding with cutover of all the families onto the process.

- Full financial integration can't occur until the operating portion of the process — balancing demand and supply — is working well for all product families.

- Executive S&OP occurs on a monthly cycle, and thus incremental experience and expertise are gained only once each month.

For almost all of the companies that we've assisted in implementing Executive S&OP, benefits come sooner than six months. Some people call these "unintended benefits" because they're by-products of people beginning to communicate and work together better.

Further, once the Live Pilot becomes operational, people begin to see things that they wouldn't have seen without it. It's common to hear comments like, "Golly, if we weren't doing this Pilot, we'd have had a big problem with Medium Widgets. We'd have gotten slammed about four months from now." Getting a better focus on the future means that problems can be avoided by taking early corrective action.

Figure 6-1 shows the three phases of an effective Executive S&OP implementation:

I. Live Pilot, which is primarily a demonstration to Executive Management on how the process works in their company. Please note: the Y axis refers to the amount of business improvement resulting from each phase, and that no improvement is predicted for the live Pilot.

II. Expansion, which cuts over the balance of the product families to Executive S&OP. This is a period of high improvement.

III. Full Financial Integration, including financial simulation and data for the generation of pro forma Profit & Loss Statements and Balance Sheets. Improvement continues, at a slower pace.

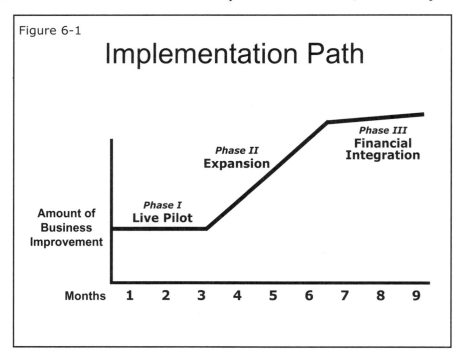

Figure 6-1

Implementation Path

Phase III
**Financial
Integration**

Phase II
Expansion

Phase I
Live Pilot

**Amount of
Business
Improvement**

Months 1 2 3 4 5 6 7 8 9

For each of these segments, a detailed implementation plan is required to enable effective management of the project. Each segment, however, can be looked upon as stand alone. In other words, it's not necessary to have all three segments planned in detail at the beginning. All that's needed is to commit to, and get started with, the first segment — the Live Pilot.

To recap, two important things to keep in mind regarding the implementation of Executive S&OP:

1. Even though the logic of Executive S&OP is simple, implementing it is not. Implementing it requires people to make changes — to do some aspects of their jobs differently — up to and including the senior executive in charge of the business.

2. It will take an investment of time to fully digest and become comfortable with the new methods because this is not an extension of past experience.

In the chapters that follow here in Part Two, we'll discuss each of the elements involved in learning about Executive S&OP, getting started, and implementing the Live Pilot. Let's get started with the Executive Briefing, Education, and the Go/No-Go Decision.

Report from the Field: Oil Patch Industries, Inc.[1]

Company Description: Oil Patch Industries is a multi-billion-dollar, global producer of mechanical drilling devices for the petroleum and natural gas extraction industries. Over the years, the company has grown substantially by acquisition — which has had the effect of bringing in many different information systems.

Their Experience: The company got off to a poor start with Executive S&OP, and it went downhill from there. They skipped the Executive Briefing and thus top management really didn't understand what was involved and how far-reaching it is. This led them to make the further mistake of selecting a relatively weak Executive Champion.

Data issues soon became paramount, with the corporate Information Technology group acting as a huge barrier to progress. The work involved in bringing together all the disparate data elements into a format usable by Executive S&OP was not at the top of their priority list, and they stated that it would be some months before they could get to it. The project dragged on, delayed seriously by the data issues. The weak Champion reflected the conflict-averse corporate culture and was unwilling to "go to the mat" with IT on this issue, and to involve the highest levels in the organization if necessary.

Finally, belatedly, the data was made available and the basic mechanics of Executive S&OP were put in place. But by then, it was too late. The original Champion had moved on. The new Champion was not an S&OP believer and had other priorities. The combination of weak, uninformed leadership

---

[1] The identity of the actual company has been disguised, at the authors' initiative.

and extended delays waiting for the systems work to rise to the top of IT's priority list meant that Executive S&OP was doomed even before the first pilot was implemented.

The result is that today Oil Patch Industries has yet to have an effective process for dealing with their severe business problems, which are solvable via Executive S&OP: huge over-inventories, abysmal service, and cash flow problems. How about profitability — are they hurting there? Not for the time being, because the petroleum industry is in one of its periodic booms. But booms are followed by busts, and one of those awaits Oil Patch Industries sometime in the future. When it arrives, good luck.

The Moral of the Story: Don't underestimate the potential problems with the gathering of the data necessary for Executive S&OP. Getting the data issues off the critical path is essential for success, and this can be particularly challenging in a large organization.

Further, the experience at Oil Patch points up the need for a strong Executive Champion; if the company had had one, that person could have gotten off to a better start and forced the data problems onto the CEO's radar screen by arguing persuasively for their solution.

Chapter 7

Executive Briefing and
Go/No-Go Decision #1

Virtually all business processes center around people, and Executive S&OP is no exception. We, along with many of our colleagues, have been saying for years that people are the A item, as in ABC: the Pareto Principle. The B item is the data, and the computer hardware and software are the C item.

People are by far the most important element in Executive S&OP, and top management is the most important subset of the people category. Thus, a highly important early step is to address their needs via an Executive Briefing, as shown on the implementation path in Figure 7-1.

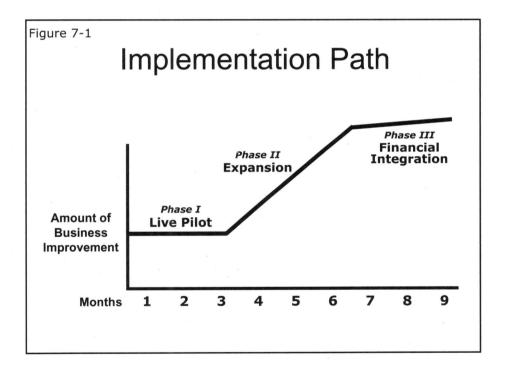

Figure 7-1

Before we get into the Executive Briefing in detail, we need to talk for a bit about a highly important resource.

The Executive S&OP Expert

In the pages that follow, we're going to recommend that you involve an Executive S&OP expert in your implementation efforts — for the initial Executive Briefing, for the education sessions to follow, and for the periodic status and progress checks during the implementation.

An Executive S&OP expert is someone who's been deeply involved in at least one — preferably multiple — successful Executive S&OP implementations. You may have an Executive S&OP expert working in your company, if that person has successful and meaningful Executive S&OP experience at a sister division or another company.

A good example concerns a guy named John. John was the COO at a company implementing Executive S&OP. John served as the Executive Champion (to be discussed in Chapter 8), and the company soon became very successful with the process. John subsequently left that company and became the CEO at a somewhat smaller firm. There, he successfully filled the role of Executive S&OP expert. He could do this because he had "been there." He had experienced how to make it work. Interestingly, John also filled role of the Executive Champion, to be discussed later in this chapter.

More often, however, such a person will not be on board. Thus you'll need to obtain an Executive S&OP expert from among the ranks of consultants active in this field, most of whom are in the supply chain and resource planning fields. They are not rookies; they have many years of experience not only in operating jobs but also as consultants, and they are totally comfortable in communicating with top management. This last point is paramount because communicating with top management is the most important thing they do.

When you're taking to someone regarding an Executive Briefing, education sessions, or other Executive S&OP support, we recommend strongly that you check his or her references. You need positive answers to the following kinds of questions:

- Have you been involved in one or more implementations of Executive S&OP?

- How successful were those implementations?

- What were your roles in those implementations?

- Where were those implementations, and can I talk directly to people at those companies?

- Do you have a process, a methodology for implementing Executive S&OP?

If the answers to all these questions are positive, and if the companies being referenced confirm them, you should be in good shape. If not, look elsewhere.

Still some of you may still be thinking, "What's the big deal? This Executive S&OP stuff is simple." Sure, the basic logic and process is, as we said at the start of Chapter 6. Thus, it's easy to get blindsided by the simplicity of Executive S&OP logic. Don't make the mistake of thinking that because it's not structurally complicated, it'll be easy to make it work. It won't.

Peter Tassi, formerly with the Ford Motor Company's Lean Manufacturing Center, said it superbly: "The soft stuff is the hard stuff." He meant, of course, that the people issues are almost always tougher challenges than hardware, software, machinery, and so forth.

So, implementing Executive S&OP successfully is mostly about dealing with people issues and the most important role of the Executive S&OP expert is to help keep those people issues from becoming people problems and thus derailing the project.

Let's examine those potential people problems, which can be split into two categories: individual and organizational. Individual people problems include:

- Aversion to change

- A schedule that is too busy — or a perception of such

- Reluctance to share information and control

- Apprehension toward the new process

- An unwillingness by the president and staff to devote the time to review and understand the details that underlie Executive S&OP

And, of course, there are others. In the organizational category, here are the three problems we've seen most often:

- Discomfort with accountability: an aversion to hold people accountable for getting things done. Some organizations don't deal with this well and that can be a problem, because Executive S&OP puts a spotlight on accountability.

- A culture of conflict aversion, resulting in reluctance to raise problems and discuss them. The reason for this is often the informal practice of "shoot the messenger" — the person who raises the problem is seen as THE problem. Well, Executive S&OP forces conflict to be raised. It must be addressed in an atmosphere of comfort and positive energy. As former U.S. Senator Everett Dirksen said: "We have to learn how to disagree without becoming disagreeable." And . . . the organizational culture must promote such an atmosphere. Organizations must learn how to deal with conflict and to resolve it.

- Lack of discipline and self-discipline. In some companies, the prevailing mind-set is to do one's own thing. If that means not preparing for a meeting, or even not showing up for them . . . well, the corporate culture says that's okay. With Executive S&OP it's not okay; this is a cross-functional, highly interdependent, team-based process. The members of the various teams must be able to be counted on to do their part.

Most companies can expect to encounter some of these kinds of problems, both individual and organizational. All of the above issues will cause some form of discomfort and stress. To be successful, there must be a willingness to endure this discomfort and thus allow change to take place. Not dealing openly and effectively with these issues will prevent change from happening.

This is where the Executive S&OP expert comes in. Organizations most often need experienced, skilled help and facilitation to work through the process and the issues. The time to start working on problems is when the Design Team (Core Team, to be covered shortly) gets assembled. If you can't make the culture change within the Design Team, it is unlikely that you'll be able to alter it throughout the organization.

Bottom line: most successful implementations have an Executive S&OP expert involved early in the implementation process and throughout it.

Executive Briefing — Making the Business Case

In almost all cases, the best way to get started with Executive S&OP is to conduct an initial briefing — at the executive level. This is a several-hour session facilitated by the Executive S&OP expert.

The purpose of the Executive Briefing is to transfer enough information about the process to enable the senior management group to:

- Understand the capabilities of Executive S&OP. They need to learn what it does, how it works (in very general terms), and what kinds of benefits companies have realized from using it.

- Match Executive S&OP's capabilities to their business problems. This is where the business case is made for Executive S&OP. Show actual performance data and ask what problems the company is experiencing in shipping to its customers on time, running the plants effectively, keeping finished goods inventories low and customer order backlogs in line. Which of these would get better if Executive S&OP were used well?

- Learn how Executive S&OP is different from current practices, even if the current process is already called S&OP.

- Understand how the process is best implemented and what will be required of each member personally.

- Make a decision to implement a live Executive S&OP Pilot within 90 days.[1]

Some companies are reluctant to conduct such an Executive Briefing, because they think they already know all about Executive S&OP. Even if this is the case, and it rarely is, skipping this step is almost always a mistake. The Executive Briefing gains a *collective* and *common* understanding between and among executives. Not to do the Executive Briefing often results in surprises later that delay or derail the implementation.

Go/No-Go Decision #1

At the conclusion of the Executive Briefing, or shortly thereafter, a decision needs to be made: a) get started with Executive S&OP on a limited basis, or b) do not do it. This is practical because the Executive Team is now in a position to make a *semi-informed commitment* about going forward.

---

[1] To be done in parallel with existing practices.

Please note: this is not a decision to implement all of Executive S&OP. Rather, it's a commitment only to go to the next step: the development and execution of a 90-day Live Pilot of Executive S&OP, on one or several groups of products. As such, it carries low risk and low cost — two factors that are almost always appealing to top management.

Let's take a moment and discuss the three types of commitment, two of which we've seen already:

1. Uninformed Commitment: Do an Executive Briefing. Made prior to the Executive Briefing, with little or no knowledge of Executive S&OP. The Briefing moves the group to the next level.

2. Semi-informed Commitment: Do a Live Pilot. Made at, or shortly after, the Executive Briefing, now with some knowledge of Executive S&OP. This is Go/No-Go Decision #1: whether or not to go to the next step. Top management has not yet experienced Executive S&OP and thus should not be asked to risk a complete cutover. They are committing only limited resources to executing a Live Pilot.

3. Fully Informed Commitment: Go to Full Cutover. Made at the end of the Live Pilot. Now the executive group has seen the process in operation in their company, and they're fully equipped to make Go/No-Go Decision #2: whether or not to proceed with full implementation. Top management has now experienced Executive S&OP with their products, in their company, and with their people. This then becomes a low-risk decision.

In our experience, the answer to each sequential go/no-go decision is usually "yes, let's go to the next step."

Stop the Bleeding

But sometimes the decision is "yes, let's go to the next step — but not right now." We've seen this happen in companies experiencing serious problems, so serious that the business may be in jeopardy. In that case, it's often not practical to wait for Executive S&OP to be implemented; they need to fix the problem(s) *now*. Yes, these fixes will be only temporary and will probably not be ideal but they must be done.

There are three sets of activities on the table here:

1. Run the business and stop the bleeding.

2. Implement Executive S&OP.

3. Continue to implement other improvement initiatives already launched.

Our recommendation to a company in this situation is first to discontinue all of the improvement initiatives underway except for those that will contribute directly to stopping the bleeding. All others should be temporarily suspended.

Next, proceed with Executive S&OP only if the resources are available to run the business, stop the bleeding, *and* implement Executive S&OP. If not, defer it until the bleeding has stopped and the patient is stable.

Having said all that, most companies are not in such dire straits and so most of them say yes. We believe the main reason for this is that the inherent logic of Executive S&OP is valid and compelling; for most top management people it exerts a strong pull. It means doing things simpler and better — a powerful combination.

One of your authors recalls the CEO of a consumer packaged goods company, who upon learning about Executive S&OP at the Briefing said, "If we'd had this 25 years ago, I'd be a younger man. I'd have fewer scars — and more hair."

*   *   *   *

FREQUENTLY ASKED QUESTIONS

Some consulting firms advocate a "big bang" cutover — all families being brought on to Executive S&OP at the same time. Why don't you guys recommend that?

Four reasons:

1. It carries a risk of disrupting the operation of the business. The company's ability to ship product might be impaired.

2. It also has the risk of seriously damaging the implementation. People may get overwhelmed with the magnitude of the tasks. If Executive S&OP doesn't work well the first one or two months, the company may give up and drop the process.

3. Executives dislike activities with high risk (as well as high cost). The pilot approach carries very little risk, and not a lot of monetary cost. There is a cost in the people's time though, as we'll see shortly.

4. You need the experiences of one family to do the next families better. If you do them all at once, you will do all of them only as well as the first. (Authors' note: this is a corollary to the principle of being smarter tomorrow than we are today — and not having to apologize for it.)

More on this in Chapter 15.

Chapter 8

Assignment of Responsibilities

Once a company makes the decision to proceed with a Live Pilot, many things need to be addressed.

Figure 8-1 is a more detailed version of the implementation diagram. It shows Month #1 of the Pilot period as being devoted to laying the foundation: selecting people, educating them, setting the project schedule, defining families, and determining data requirements. Month #2 is largely involved with developing the demand and supply planning processes that will be used, and the third month focuses on preparing and executing the Live Pilot.

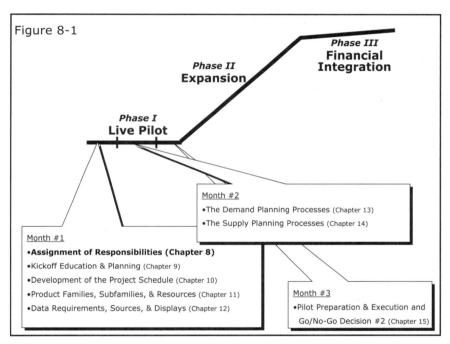

The first item shown in Month 1 is Assignment of Responsibilities. As we said earlier, this can precede the Kickoff Event, or follow it shortly thereafter. The following is what needs to be addressed in terms of roles and responsibilities.

Executive Champion/Sponsor

From the outset, it's important to have one member of the top management team assigned to champion the Executive S&OP implementation. He or she can be a big help in:

- keeping executive attention focused on the initiative,

- removing impediments,

- acquiring needed resources,

- supporting the folks doing the heavy lifting.

He or she should be willing to provide leadership, spend some time, carry the flag for Executive S&OP and, in general, to get personally involved, to "put some skin in the game."

Who should it be? In general, our first choice would be the President — provided he or she had the time and the inclination to do the job. If not the President, it should be one of the VP's who reports directly to the President. Ideally the person selected should be enthusiastic about Executive S&OP and have a solid working relationship with the President. The person should be from one of the line departments: Sales, Marketing, Operations, Finance, Product Development. We've seen Executive Champions from all of those areas.

Despite this job's importance, it's not highly time consuming. It involves:

- mentoring and staying close to the Design Team Leader,

- providing support to the Design Team on tough issues,

- leading discussions with the Executive Staff on the status of the project, on getting commitment to the Executive S&OP Policy (to be covered in Chapter 16), and so forth.

The Design Team (Core Team, Project Team)

This is the group that will do most of the work necessary to make Executive S&OP a reality in the company. The Design Team is typically consists of eight to twelve people, including the Team Leader, covering all of the S&OP-related areas in the company. There may be some overlap: some people may represent more than one area or department.

The role of these people is to represent their home departments in designing how the Executive S&OP process will work in the company. Additionally, they will lead the change processes in their areas of the business. They also become task team leaders for specific tasks that have cross-functional participation and assure that proper resources are assigned to get the work done per the project schedule.

How much time is typically required of Design Team members? An average of about 20 percent, which equals eight hours per week. They'll need to spend more time early in the project and less later.

Design Team Leader

The Design Team Leader chairs the team meetings, maintains the project schedule, and identifies problems to the Champion and the Executive Staff. In small to medium-sized companies ($1 billion per year or less), this normally is not a full-time job. Expect it to take about 50 percent of an individual's time and thus you must do some sort of offloading to relieve this individual of about half of his or her workload for the duration of the project.

So what should this person's qualifications be, and from where in the organization should he or she come? It doesn't have to be a top management person, although we've seen that on occasion. Rather, it should be someone with solid managerial experience within functional departments of the company. Key attributes of the Design Team leader:

- Good people skills

- Proactive and well organized

- Able to lead a meeting effectively

- Knowledge of the business — the customers, the culture, the products, the process, the people, and last but definitely not least, the politics

This last point, knowledge of the business, is the reason that the Design Team Leader should not be someone from the outside. It would take a long time for an outsider to learn these critically important elements of the company and to earn the respect of the people — far longer than it would take an insider to learn the elements of Executive S&OP.

So where should the Design Team Leader come from? Our answer is the same as with the Executive Champion: Operations, Sales, Marketing, Finance, Product Development. Here again take your pick, with one caveat: it's best if the Design Team Leader and the Executive Champion come from different departments. This avoids sending an unintended message that this project resides in one department. One other caveat: neither the Champion nor the Design Team Leader should be from the IT department. This is not because these people aren't capable; it's because it sends a message that this is a "computer project." Nothing could be further from the truth.

A look ahead: frequently the Design Team Leader, following a successful implementation, transitions to become the Executive S&OP Process Owner. This is not a project role, but rather is a permanent position to oversee the operation of Executive S&OP. More on this in Chapter 16.

Spreadsheet Developer

You might find this curious — to include what may seem to be a rather mundane function. Perhaps, but we've learned the hard way not to overlook it. In Chapter 12, we'll get into the spreadsheet topic in depth, but for now let's just say that the odds are very high that your Executive S&OP data will be displayed by spreadsheet software, such as Excel™ or one of its worthy competitors.

What's involved here is both formatting the spreadsheets and extracting the data from the company's data sources, and this can be somewhat complex. It will be a fairly intensive effort during the early part of the Pilot development, and then again on several later occasions as further changes are made. A good rule of thumb here is to expect to modify the format of your spreadsheets and graphs at least three or four times following the Live Pilot and during the Expansion phase.

One of the people assigned to the Design Team from a functional department may be able to handle both the data sourcing and the display. If so, they could fill this role of Spreadsheet Developer. If not, you'll probably need to acquire an IT person to fill that role and to serve on the Design Team. In short — you'll need an "Excel™ Wizard" — don't leave home without one.

Support from the Executive S&OP Expert

Here's some more good news; unlike some other initiatives, with Executive S&OP you won't need to have an army of outsiders — systems integrators, consultants, or whatever — swarming all over your company. On the other hand, as we said earlier, support from an Executive S&OP expert — truly an expert, from either inside or outside of the company — can be a big help in making this process work.

This expert's role is to:

• teach and thus help create a credible vision of the future,

• encourage,

• provide expert advice on the "technical" aspects — families, units of measure, formats, composition of the teams and so on,

• head off problems before they occur,

• help solve problems that have already occurred, and

• communicate directly with the President on problems, impediments, issues, and so forth.

In short, the expert's job is to help keep the project on the rails, to push — hard, if necessary — for visible progress each and every month so that the project doesn't stall out. Remember, we said earlier that this is a people project. The soft stuff is the hard stuff.

Not an enormous amount of the expert's time should be required to do this. Assume for a moment that you do not have an Executive S&OP expert within your organization. For a typical company, then, an average of a day or two every month or two, for about eight to ten months has proven to be adequate — with more days being applied early in the process and fewer later. If the expert is an outsider, make him or her part of the team. Keep your expert in the loop. Don't hesitate to communicate with that person frequently between visits.

Among companies that have used an Executive S&OP expert, the percentage of successful implementations is very high. Among companies that haven't done so, the success rate is much lower.

Report From The Field: The Homac Corporation

Company Description: Homac is a 45-year-old company, privately held, with about 400 employees and headquartered in Ormond Beach, Florida. Their products are electrical power delivery connectors and cable accessories primarily for the utility, construction, industrial and OEM marketplaces.

Their Experience: Homac's Executive S&OP efforts were initiated by Mark McGrane, President. They got off to a good start via an Executive Briefing, but struggled with the selection of the Design Team Leader. There just didn't seem to be a good choice from within the ranks of senior middle management, primarily for reasons of workload — not an uncommon situation in smaller companies.

One of the executives who could have filled the role of Executive Champion was Rick Hall, VP of Operations. Bob Stahl, their Executive S&OP Expert, raised the question: "Could someone from the executive staff be the Design Team Leader?" And further, "Rick's operations seem to be in very good shape; might he be a good choice to head up the Design Team?"

Well, they appointed Mark McGrane, the President, as Executive Champion and Rick Hall as Design Team Leader. It worked superbly. As it turned out, Rick was able to take on some of the Champion's tasks, due to his presence on the executive staff.

Homac has been extremely successful with Executive S&OP, and this is due in no small measure to the superb job by Vice President Rick Hall as Design Team Leader.

The Moral of the Story: Pick the very best people for the key roles of Executive Champion and Design Team Leader. If you don't, you'll probably be sorry; if you do, dividends will almost certainly follow.

---

*   *   *   *

FREQUENTLY ASKED QUESTIONS

What about setting up a full-time and dedicated Executive S&OP project team or task force?

For businesses of average size and complexity, we've not found this to be necessary or helpful. To set up a central team or task force tends to eliminate or diminish the "ownership" factor by those who are running the business. What gets designed can become an imposition from "outsiders," is therefore less effective, and often fails to make any real change.

In large multi-divisional companies, the same principle is true — the more local business ownership, the better. While there may be some benefit to establishing a central project team or task force for setting corporate standards, the real decisions must be made by the people who have to make it work.

Chapter 9

Kickoff Education and Planning

There are two main reasons for taking time to learn about Executive S&OP. One is to enable people to make a solid commitment to implementing it. Second, an education session establishes a common framework, terminology, and vision of the future for the people who will be involved in implementing and operating Executive S&OP.

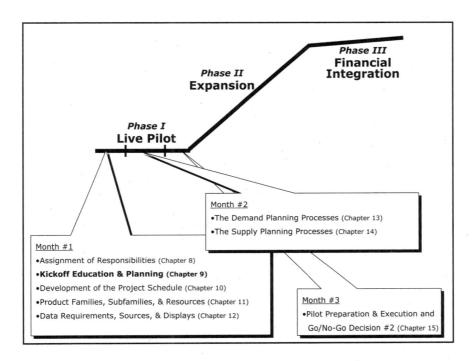

This step, facilitated by the Executive S&OP Expert, should involve all of the people who will be "hands on" with the Executive S&OP process — top management, middle management, and others, such as the forecast analyst, salespeople, planners, and schedulers.

The primary objective of these education sessions is for the people to gain a solid understanding of the Executive S&OP process. They need to see the compelling business reasons for it in order to willingly and enthusiastically make the necessary changes, including some aspects of how they do their jobs.

This is as true with top management as with any other group in the company, because they're so deeply involved with decision making. Making the right decisions today is tougher than ever, one reason being the speed with which things happen nowadays. As we said earlier, better processes yield better results; better decision-making processes yield better decisions. And that's what much of the top management job is all about: making better decisions — on a timelier basis and with higher quality — than the competition's executives are able to do.

Executives and everyone else involved need to understand that Executive S&OP is a superior decision-making process. Therefore, this education step is a very important tool for both top and middle management, and thus those folks need to learn about it.

The Kickoff process is divided into three pieces, with each successive piece involving fewer people and more detail.

First Half-Day

Topic: Basics of Executive S&OP: what it is, where it fits, how it works, how it's different from today's practices, what benefits result, how it's implemented.

Attendees: Everyone who will be "hands-on" with Executive S&OP plus other interested people. This definitely includes top management. But there's a potential problem here, because they've already "heard it" at the Executive Briefing. Why do they need to be here?

Three reasons:

1. They'll "hear more" at the Kickoff session, which contains more material.

2. They'll hear things somewhat differently. Their minds will now be focused on "How will we make the Pilot work?" rather than, in the Executive Briefing, "What is this S&OP stuff?"

3. If top management isn't present, the people in the session will probably be saying: "This Executive S&OP stuff sounds good, but *they'll* never do it." They, of course, refers to top management. Their presence and participation, including that of the President, will make a strong statement that this initiative is for real.

Emphasis: How Executive S&OP can benefit the company and how to implement it successfully.

Second Half-Day

Topic: How to apply Executive S&OP practices to the company.

Attendees: Most of the people who were present in the first session. It's not necessary that the executives be present for this part, although they can stick around if they wish. One exception to this is the Executive Champion. If he or she has already been identified, then by all means that person needs to be present in the afternoon session. If not, then one or several members of the executive group need to be present to provide top management presence and viewpoint.

Emphasis: How Executive S&OP will work in the company.

Third Half-Day

Topic: Development of a detailed 90-day implementation plan.

Attendees: The people who will be hands on with Executive S&OP, less the executive group but including the Executive Champion.

Emphasis: The creation of a detailed implementation plan with tasks, responsibilities, critical paths, timing, and resource requirements, concluding with a Live Pilot within 90 days.

These three sessions should run in sequential fashion, preferably on successive days. Usually the first two half-days occur on the same day, followed by the third half-day the next morning, allowing the afternoon of the second day, if required, to complete the framework for the detailed plan and any other items.

So, whom do you get to present and facilitate these sessions? The Executive S&OP Expert, of course. If that person did a good job at the Executive Briefing, then he or she is the logical person to lead these education sessions.

Coming up next: Development of the Project Schedule.

*　　*　　*　　*

FREQUENTLY ASKED QUESTIONS

What if the President is called away and can't attend the session on the first half-day?

It's simple: reschedule. And this may mean rescheduling the entire event, not just the first half-day, because these three half-days build upon each other.

For the President not to be there sends an extremely bad message to the troops: "The boss doesn't think this stuff is all that important."

The costs and hassle of rescheduling are far outweighed by the costs and hassle of not being successful with Executive S&OP.

Chapter 10

Development of the Project Schedule

Some key points about the project schedule:

- It's essential in order to keep the project on track and ensure that the 90-day Live Pilot does in fact happen within 90 days.

- It needs to cover only the first 90 days or so. Then, following Go/No-Go Decision #2, the schedule should be extended through Phase II, Expansion and Phase III, Full Financial Integration. It's normally prepared on the third half-day of the Kickoff event. Sometimes it takes a few more days to get it totally buttoned up.

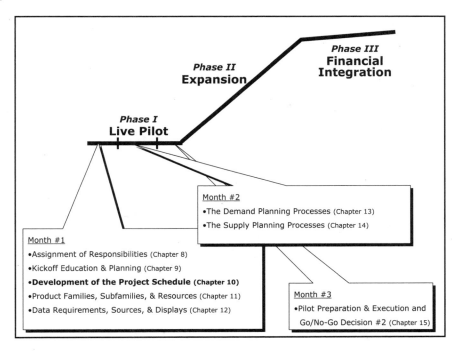

During the three months of the Pilot, much needs to be done, as can readily be seen in the diagram above. This work serves two purposes: a) it enables the Live Pilot to happen and b) it builds the foundation and the core capabilities upon which the full Executive S&OP process will sit.

Most of the work involved in implementing Executive S&OP occurs in this first 90-day period, culminating in the Live Pilot. So let's focus on that Pilot — what is its primary objective?

Well, isn't it to run the business better? Not really — its primary mission is educational. It's to demonstrate to top management that Executive S&OP will work *for our company*. It's to enable them to touch it, taste it, wrap their arms around it — to see for the first time how it will perform within the company and thus allow them to gain more confidence in it.

That's the primary job of the Live Pilot. It enables the top management group to make a *fully informed commitment* to cut over the remaining families onto Executive S&OP, integrate the financials, and so forth (Go/No-Go Decision #2). Remember, this is a low-cost, low-risk approach; take it a step at a time.

Well then, does the Live Pilot ever result in running the business better? Frequently it does. Imagine a top management team in the Live Pilot session: viewing the Executive S&OP information, asking questions, probing. At some point, let's say that one of the executives says: "Look at the situation next April. It seems to me that we're going to have a problem there, because demand is outstripping supply. Am I right about that?"

The Executive S&OP Process Owner, who is no doubt already aware of that problem from the Pre-Meeting says: "Absolutely. It's the additional demand from South America that's going to kick in around March."

Another executive: "Wow. If we hadn't been doing this, we'd have really gotten slammed. Seeing it now gives us time to get some more capacity."

This kind of thing is an early win for Executive S&OP and is not uncommon. You may or may not experience it in your company. But please keep in mind: it's not the primary reason for the Live Pilot. That's education.

The Live Pilot — Month-by-Month

The work involved in bringing up the Pilot fits nicely into this three-month period. Let's look at each month:

Month 1 starts following the Executive Briefing and a decision to proceed with the Live 90-day Pilot. It includes:

- Assignment of Responsibility — identifying and appointing people into key positions of leadership and team membership: Executive Champion, Design Team Leader, Design Team Members, and so forth.

- The Kickoff Education and Planning events, to provide the necessary information to all of the people within the company who will be "hands-on" with Executive S&OP.

- Development of the Project Schedule, out through the completion of the Live Pilot. This, as we said, typically occurs on the third half-day of the Kickoff.

- Families and Subfamilies and the identification thereof. This also includes the identification of the key Resources, the supply counterparts of the marketing-related Product Families. Another part of this step is the selection of the families to be used for the Live Pilot.

- Data Requirements, Sources, and Displays. This involves the design of the basic S&OP spreadsheet, the graphs to be derived from it, and other displays for Demand Planning and Supply Planning. The requirements for the various data elements need to be agreed upon here, and their sources identified.

Probably not all of this work will be completed in the first 30 days and thus will spill over into the next month.

Month 2 is devoted to nailing down the nitty-gritty of the processes to be used in both Demand Planning and Supply Planning, and their related data feeds.

Month 3 is involved with the preparation and execution of the Live Pilot. It brings together all the work that's been done so far to create a presentation package for top management.

The Implementation Schedule Outline

Figure 10-1

SAMPLE LIST OF TASKS

PHASE I-B — PREPARATION FOR THE LIVE PILOT

050 Confirm Responsibilities and Team Memberships

060 Identify Product Families and Subfamilies

070 Determine Product Family Units of Measure

080 Identify Supply Resources to Be Tracked

090 Determine Capacity Units of Measure

100 Determine Planning Horizon

110 Select Pilot Family

120 Set Demand/Supply Strategies for Pilot Family

To help you get started with the development of your schedule, we've developed a verbal version of the implementation diagram you've been seeing for the last few chapters. It's in Appendix A and is a list of tasks to be accomplished, which companies should enter into their project management software and tailor to fit the project schedule. A sample is shown in Figure 10-1.

Use the List of Steps as the starting point for creating your Project Schedule, adding responsibilities, timing, clarifying comments, and even new tasks not shown on the outline but important for your implementation.

For your convenience, we've put the outline up on our Web site to enable an easy download and entry into your project scheduling software. To access it, go to www.tfwallace.com and go to the Free Downloads section.

*   *   *   *   *

FREQUENTLY ASKED QUESTIONS

Is there anything magic about taking 90 days for the Live Pilot? Don't some companies, probably larger ones, need to take longer while other companies may be able to do it in less time?

It's certainly true that in larger organizations, things can take more time. However, the countervailing point is that they typically have more resources to apply. Further, most really large corporations are made up of smaller business units, and Executive S&OP operates at the business unit or divisional level.

We feel that in almost all cases, 90 days is ample time. Beware of "paralysis by analysis," a phenomenon seen all too often in very large organizations. Commit yourselves to 90 days and then hold your feet to the fire. Do it.

Now for the flip side: can a smaller organization do it in less than 90 days? Possibly. It has happened, successfully, in the past. But be careful: some executives, at the Executive Briefing, enthusiastically want to "do it right away" — next week for example. That, of course, does not lead to success.

If you think you might be able to do it in less than 90 days, say 60 or 75, we recommend that you lay out the Project Schedule and see where it winds up. All the while, please keep in mind that people are the A item, and that a willingness to do one's job differently does not come overnight for many people. So assume 90 days unless the evidence is quite strong that you can do it sooner.

Chapter 11

Product Families, Subfamilies, and Resources

We often see companies that have too many product families to allow for an effective Executive S&OP process, and rarely do we see companies with too few. So let's tackle that issue first.

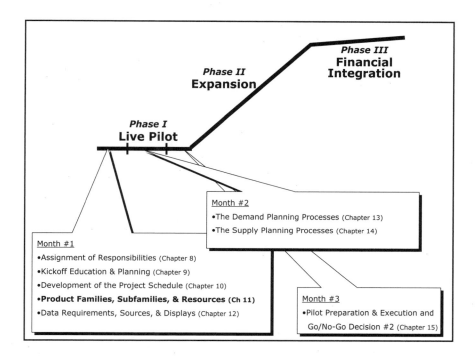

Product Families — How Many?

If you have more than about a dozen product families, you probably have too many. Why? Well, it gets down to the mission of Executive S&OP: it's a decision-making process for top management. Having worked with numerous top management teams over the years, we can assure you of several of their characteristics: they're very busy; thus, they have limited attention spans; and therefore they are not interested in getting into lots of detail unless it's absolutely necessary. Having to review twenty or thirty or more product families once each month does not fit that profile.

If you have too many families, top management will tune out. If top management tunes out, the process will die. One more time: hands-on, active participation by top management is essential for this decision-making process to be effective.

The best number of product families is around six to twelve. When you start to get above that, you're asking for trouble.

Product Families — How to Select Them

Many companies, prior to getting into S&OP, have their product families effectively identified. In their budgeting and business planning processes, the families are spelled out, and they make perfectly good sense. If you're in that category, great. Use what you already have for Executive S&OP. In other companies, they haven't yet spelled out a good product family array and doing that is an important early step. Among the options for structuring your families are:

- product type (scotch, bourbon, gin)

- product characteristics (high performance, deluxe, standard)

- product size (large, medium, small)

- brand (Impala, Malibu, Trailblazer, Tahoe, Corvette, and so on)

- market segment (industrial, consumer)

- distribution channel (mass merchandisers, original equipment manufacturers, aftermarket)

- customer

The fundamental question is, simply, how do you go to the marketplace? Acme Widget's products, for example, fall logically into Industrial and Consumer, and then into subdivisions — small, medium, and large — within those two.

Companies with Make-to-Order products will sometimes set up their families by customer, with perhaps the 20 percent of customers who account for 80 percent of the business spelled out as individual families and the remaining low-volume customers grouped into one family.

Does it ever make sense to have the product families based on how Operations views things? Only if that arrangement also works for Sales. If so, what you probably have are aligned resources. If that arrangement doesn't seem to work well for Sales, then the key questions include:

- Will it be more difficult for Sales to do a good job of forecasting?

- Will it be more difficult for Sales to relate the Executive S&OP process to how they go to market and how they work with customers?

If the answer to either of these is yes, we recommend against doing it that way.

Making Use of Subfamilies

How, some ask, is it possible to define a complex business in just a few families? Our question for you is: what is your purpose? If you're talking about filling customer orders and making shipments, you need to work with individual products and customer orders. However, you can't do Sales & Operations Planning at that level even if you wanted to, because Executive S&OP is a tool for aggregate planning. Its focus is on *volume*, not mix.

Company
Business Unit
Market/Segment
Product Family
Product Subfamily
Brand/Model
Package Size
Stockkeeping Unit (SKU)
SKU by Customer
SKU by Customer by Location

In Chapter 4 we discussed at which level to forecast, and we identified the possibilities shown at the left. Obviously we can't do Executive S&OP at the very top of the pyramid, because there's not enough granularity at that level upon which to base demand/supply decisions.

Toward the bottom of the pyramid, there's too much detail; we're flying fifty feet off the ground at 400 knots. We're surely not going to see the big picture down there. There's an area in this pyramid that sits below the high-level product families used in the Executive S&OP meeting and above individual products, and we refer to these intermediate groupings as "subfamilies."

For example, the Acme Widget Company, as we saw, has two product lines — Industrial and Consumer. Within each category, there are three product families: small, medium, and large. The Consumer product line has a further subdivision: seasonal and everyday. Acme people often need to view these separately; the seasonal line requires extensive production prior to the onset of the peak Christmas selling season, while demand and production for everyday products is, of course, more stable. When planning the pre-build, with its attendant rise in inventory, top management people want to see the plan so they can approve it. They also want to view it during the height of the season. However, during most of the year, it's not of interest to them *unless something is going wrong*.

It's the job of the Pre-Meeting Team to monitor the subfamilies to ensure that they're performing to plan. When they're not, the Pre-Meeting people need to fix them, and sometimes that requires a decision from top management (for reasons of cost, impact on other parts of the business, staffing levels, and so forth). In such cases, the Pre-Meeting Team is empowered to elevate a subfamily, along with their recommendation, to the Exec Meeting for a decision. This has the dual advantages of keeping the top management folks in the loop when needed, but not taking up their time unnecessarily.

Report from the Field: ImagePoint

Company Description: ImagePoint is a privately held company, based in Knoxville TN with plants in South Carolina and Kentucky. They are the leading provider of "turnkey image solutions" — primarily large signs — which they sell into a variety of markets: automobile dealers, gas stations, restaurants, banks, and retail stores. They refer to their products as "custom engineered," which in our jargon means Make-to-Order or Design-to-Order.

Their Experience: The most difficult part of ImagePoint's implementation was to identify their product families. This is unusual, because for most companies the difficulty level for this topic ranges from easy to very easy: companies already have their product families identified in a manner that's perfect for Executive S&OP or maybe they have to modify them just a bit, perhaps adding subfamilies.

Not so with ImagePoint. They were faced with a confusing array of ways to look at demand:

- Markets: auto, food, financial, petroleum, and retail

- Customers: Chase Bank, Chrysler, Exxon, Ford, GM, McDonald's, Nissan, Sears, and Sunoco, to name just a few

- Specific Products: large signs, small signs, letter sets, light bands, columns, wall signs, drive-thru's, directionals, and on and on

- Job Types: pylon packages, channel letter packages, architectural element packages, and so forth

How were they able to pull all of this complexity together into a single, coherent set of product families? Well, it wasn't easy. It took a lot of hard work and focus on the end objective: to develop a set of marketplace-oriented families; doing that would make the forecasting job as "least difficult" — notice we didn't say "easy" — as possible. And they were aware that those product families must be translatable into resource requirements.

The end result was a set of families and subfamilies that accomplished all their objectives. They decided that the basic product families are Job Types as mentioned above: pylons, channel letters, architectural elements, and so on. They're broken down further into subfamilies by customer, and that was the key to the forecasting issue. The Sales people were comfortable with forecasting, for example, pylons for Ford, and drive-thru orders for McDonald's. (We've seen this approach before in companies that are heavily Make-to-Order; customers frequently play a large role in how the product families/subfamilies are defined, and subsequently how the forecasts are generated.)

But, a problem remained: how to get a macro view of all of these forecasts once they've been made, to see if the aggregate makes sense. They solved that one by dollarizing the forecasts, rolling them up into Markets: auto, food, financial, petroleum, and retail.

This enables ImagePoint to evaluate the forecasts against current and future market share position, along with industry outlooks, which are necessary for getting reasoned and reasonable forecasts. The translation from Job Type to resource requirements is straightforward, just as we described in Chapter 4.

ImagePoint has become very successful with Executive S&OP, in large measure because they were able to sort through the complexity inherent in their product line, simplify it, and make it work for them.

The Moral of the Story: Defining product families validly is highly important. Two key points apply here:

- Don't lose sight of the fact that product families must have a marketplace/customer orientation, necessary to make the difficult forecasting job less difficult.

- Changing the way people think about their product groupings requires . . . change. So be prepared for some resistance and be prepared to involve the Executive Champion and others to provide the necessary leadership.

ImagePoint did both of these, and was richly rewarded for it.

Unit of Measure

When setting up your product families, it's necessary to specify the unit of measure to be used for each family. Choices for unit of measure include but are not limited to:

each	cases	thousands	pounds
tons	gallons	liters	kilos

For most companies, selecting the units of measure is a no-brainer. On the other hand, some companies really struggle over this issue. Here also, the point about separating demand and supply applies: pick the units of measure based on how you go to the marketplace. Then, if Operations needs something different, derive that with Resource Requirements Planning.

Selecting the Pilot Family

Once you've got the families and subfamilies initially set up, it's time to select which family to use for the 90-Day Pilot. Key issues:

- **Complexity.** Should we pick the toughest family — the most complicated — or the easiest? Answer: none of the above. Trying to pilot with a highly complex, "gnarly" product family may make the Pilot almost impossible to bring up. Don't forget: there's a learning curve here. You'll be better able to handle that kind of complexity after you've done the process on a family of lesser difficulty.

On the other hand, doing the Pilot on an easy product family may not prove much; it may fall short of the primary goal of enabling top management to truly understand how this Executive S&OP stuff is going to help run the business better.

So the middle of the road prevails. Pick a family that's not highly difficult nor very easy.

- **Size.** How about the size of the family in terms of volume? We'd avoid a small family, because here also it may not provide a good pilot demonstration. Top management may be "underwhelmed" by having to look at such unimportant numbers.

  On the other hand, large is fine as long as it isn't unduly complicated. A large family will have greater impact and be more meaningful to top management during the Live Pilot demonstration.

- **Sales Channels.** A family with products going through multiple sales channels may make for a better pilot than a family with only one channel, provided that it doesn't carry too much complexity.

- **Resources.** It's different on the supply side. Here, we recommend that you try to pick a family with fewer sources of supply rather than many. If Family A gets all its products from Plant 1, and Family B gets its products from seven different plants plus two contract manufacturers, go with Family A.

  Further, try to pick a family that has a high degree of aligned resources. That makes the resource planning job feasible, while a family with virtually all unaligned resources may make it impossible to do much Resource Requirements Planning in the Pilot because the full picture on any given resource won't be available until all of the families it supplies are on Executive S&OP.

  If you have no aligned resources at all, then develop the Resource Requirements Planning process and demonstrate it, at the Live Pilot, for a partially loaded resource. Explain what it will look like when it's finally cut over.

  The point about alignment also applies to material. If all of the material supplied by a given supplier is for one product family, then one can do a good job of providing that supplier with forward capacity requirements.

*　　*　　*　　*　　*

FREQUENTLY ASKED QUESTIONS

How about using dollars as the primary unit of measure?

Only as a last resort. Certainly we need to see dollars because the financial view is essential for running a business well. But it's far easier to go from *units to dollars* than the reverse. Moreover, it's more valid. So the message is: plan in units and translate to dollars.

Two other problems with dollars:

- Sales dollars are subject to price increases. This can cause a lack of clarity when sales are projected far into the future and then translated into units.

- Using dollars results in two units of measure on the spreadsheet: sales dollars and cost dollars. The arithmetic becomes less obvious and potentially confusing.

There are, however, times when it's just not possible to use units. One company we worked with, making process control computers, had product families with processors, monitors, modems, badge readers, power supplies, and on and on. There was simply no common unit of measure that spanned all the diverse products within a given family. Therefore, they used dollars because they had no choice, and worked with units at the subfamily level, examples of which might be Family A Monitors, Family A Power Supplies, and so forth. It worked fairly well.

Chapter 12

Data Requirements, Sources, and Displays

Here's where we get into issues of what data is needed, the sources of that data, and how that data gets synthesized into information. Let's talk first about what's needed.

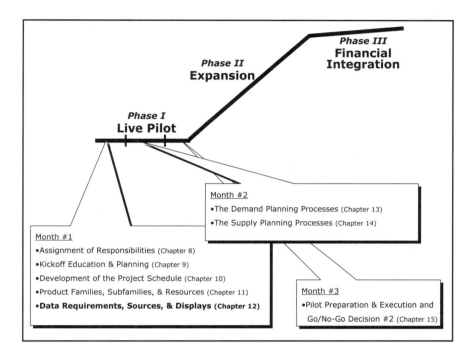

Data Requirements

Executive S&OP requires, broadly, several types of data: Master Data, Actual Data, and Future Data.

Master Data

This includes descriptive information about the product families, subfamilies, and resources. For families and subfamilies, this includes:

- target customer service levels

- target inventory and backlog numbers

- dollar numbers from the financial plan

- data needed to assure the validity of the assumptions underlying the unit-to-dollar conversation (see Appendix B)

On the resource side, one needs:

- output capacities at both standard operating levels and surge levels

- conversion factors to "translate" product family groupings and units of measure into resource-related information (bills of resources)

- data needed to validate the mix assumptions inherent in the Resource Requirements Planning process. (see Appendix B)

Actual (Historical) Data

- actual sales

- actual production

- customer orders booked

- ending finished goods inventories — at the plants, distribution centers, contract manufacturers, and trade partners, if possible

- prior periods' forecasts

- prior periods' production plans

- actual inventory and backlog numbers

- customer service levels from prior periods

Future Data

This refers primarily to the output from the statistical forecasting system, which serves as input to the Demand Planning process within Executive S&OP.[1] There is not, however, a similar situation on the supply side; rather, the Operations Plan is typically developed within the Supply Planning phase, with its primary input being the management-authorized forecast from Demand Planning.

One last point about data requirements — last, but not least. It's important. In addition to the above, you may need other pieces of data for purposes specific to your company or industry. Make sure you bring those into the process along with what we've listed here. And also, of course, ignore those items above that you don't need. For example, if you're a pure Make-to-Order company, you obviously won't need data on the finished goods inventories.

---

[1] Another important element in many companies is data from *outside* the company dealing with market share, economic outlook for one's industry, and others.

Data Definitions and Sources

There's more involved here than just listing the data elements required. It's important — perhaps essential — to take the time to develop a document that spells out what each data element means and from where it comes.

The issue of data sources can sometimes be less than straightforward. In some companies, we see data entering the Executive S&OP process from:

- the Enterprise Software System (ESS/ERP)

- the Customer Relationship Management System (CRM)

- the Statistical Forecasting System

- the Advanced Planning System (for production)

- the legacy system(s)

- and perhaps others

One last point on data. Most companies will develop a document often called a "data element dictionary." This contains information about each piece of data, such as the data term (for example, *sales*), everyday definition (*an item we ship to a customer*), and contents (*SKU number, a quantity, date, ship-to location, invoice number, and so forth*) along with relevant technical information.

Automate Feeds into the S&OP Spreadsheets

Automating the loading of data into the spreadsheets can, in some companies, be quick and easy. In others, not so. In either case, we recommend that this task be completed during the 90-day Live Pilot — even though the volume of data needed for the Pilot could be manually entered.

Why do we feel so strongly about getting this task done early? It's because once the Live Pilot is completed and top management makes an affirmative Go/No-Go Decision #2 (proceed with cutover), then the volume of data required to be loaded each month may quickly outstrip the ability to do it manually. Further, manual data entry is error-prone, and it's inefficient because the folks doing the work usually don't have "data entry" in their job descriptions. They already have full-time jobs.

Our advice is to start looking at this issue as soon as Go/No-Go Decision #1 is made (do the Live Pilot) or even earlier. Do you have a problem here? If so, how soon can it be taken care of?

Some of you are probably thinking, "What's the big deal? This is not a terribly difficult or time consuming task. How do some companies get behind the eight ball on it?" The answer is: *priority*.

Many IT departments have large backlogs of work (owing, no doubt, to a demand/supply imbalance: an excess of demand for their services over the supply of resources they have available). The next job that comes into the department typically goes to the back of the queue, slowly works its way up the priority ladder, and — after a number of months — gets addressed and completed.

Our recommendation is, at the very onset of the project, to establish Executive S&OP as a high-priority activity. Since this data automation step is on the critical path for implementing Executive S&OP, then it also has high priority. Get a commitment from the IT folks to complete this step early in the project. If necessary, the Champion can be called upon to help set the priorities. This task should be completed during the 90-Day Live Pilot — and since it's almost never an enormous amount of work, we can think of no good reason why it shouldn't.

Remember the story of Oil Patch Industries in Chapter 6? Don't make the same mistake that they did.

Spreadsheets and Graphs

In Chapter 3, we looked at a number of S&OP spreadsheets and their related graphs. Now it's time to get into the details and understand how they work. We'll get started with the sample spreadsheet in Figure 12-1 on the following page.

Make-to-Stock and Finish-to-Order Format

In Figure 12-1, for a Make-to-Stock product family called Medium Widgets, the demand/supply strategy specifies a target line item fill rate (shipments on time and complete) of 99 percent. The target finished inventory necessary to support this shipping performance has been set at 10 days' supply (work days, not calendar days). See the area in Figure 12-1 identified by *A.*

Let's examine the 10-day inventory target. Why does this company feel it needs 10 days of finished goods inventory? The answer is that its experience over the recent past has shown that 10 days is a minimum level necessary to provide 99 percent customer service.

Should this 10-day supply target be considered a constant, fixed far out into the future? Not at all. The principle of continuous improvement should drive this company to improve its sales, production, and logistics processes so that 99 percent customer service becomes attainable with only, say, 9 days of supply. And then 8 days. And then 7. But for now, the realities of life are that it takes about a half month's worth of inventory to provide the 99 percent service level.

In *B,* actual sales are compared to forecast. For the past three months, sales are running ahead of forecast by 44,000 units. Actual production performance to the plan is evaluated in *C.* It's close to being perfect.

Area *D* shows inventory performance to plan, and the actual customer service performance. We can see a serious problem developing here: as the forecast was oversold, the actual inventory went below plan. The result is that customer service has dropped to 89 percent for September, quite a bit below its 99 percent target.

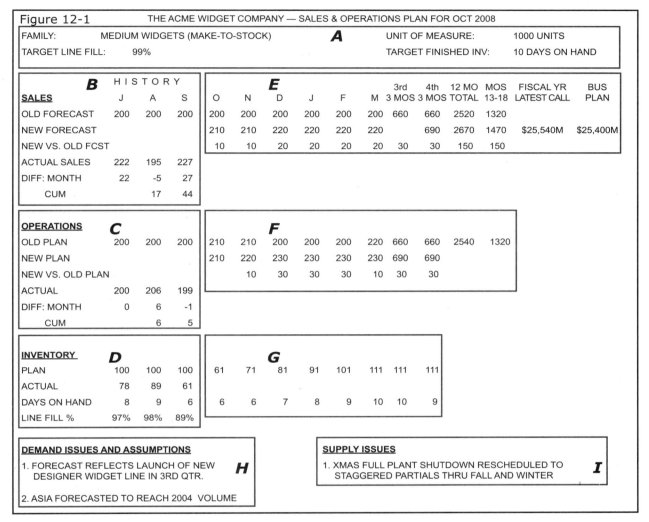

Figure 12-1 — THE ACME WIDGET COMPANY — SALES & OPERATIONS PLAN FOR OCT 2008

A

FAMILY:	MEDIUM WIDGETS (MAKE-TO-STOCK)	UNIT OF MEASURE:	1000 UNITS
TARGET LINE FILL:	99%	TARGET FINISHED INV:	10 DAYS ON HAND

B — HISTORY **E**

SALES	J	A	S	O	N	D	J	F	M	3rd 3 MOS	4th 3 MOS	12 MO TOTAL	MOS 13-18	FISCAL YR LATEST CALL	BUS PLAN
OLD FORECAST	200	200	200	200	200	200	200	200	200	660	660	2520	1320		
NEW FORECAST				210	210	220	220	220	220		690	2670	1470	$25,540M	$25,400M
NEW VS. OLD FCST				10	10	20	20	20	20	30	30	150	150		
ACTUAL SALES	222	195	227												
DIFF: MONTH	22	-5	27												
CUM		17	44												

OPERATIONS C / **F**

OPERATIONS	J	A	S	O	N	D	J	F	M	3rd 3 MOS	4th 3 MOS	12 MO TOTAL	MOS 13-18
OLD PLAN	200	200	200	210	210	200	200	200	220	660	660	2540	1320
NEW PLAN				210	220	230	230	230	230	690	690		
NEW VS. OLD PLAN					10	30	30	30	10	30	30		
ACTUAL	200	206	199										
DIFF: MONTH	0	6	-1										
CUM		6	5										

INVENTORY D / **G**

INVENTORY	J	A	S	O	N	D	J	F	M	3rd	4th	12 MO
PLAN	100	100	100	61	71	81	91	101	111	111	111	
ACTUAL	78	89	61									
DAYS ON HAND	8	9	6	6	6	7	8	9	10	10	9	
LINE FILL %	97%	98%	89%									

DEMAND ISSUES AND ASSUMPTIONS **H**
1. FORECAST REFLECTS LAUNCH OF NEW DESIGNER WIDGET LINE IN 3RD QTR.
2. ASIA FORECASTED TO REACH 2004 VOLUME

SUPPLY ISSUES **I**
1. XMAS FULL PLANT SHUTDOWN RESCHEDULED TO STAGGERED PARTIALS THRU FALL AND WINTER

The new Sales Forecast is shown in **E.** Towards the right of the page you'll find a total for the next rolling twelve months, as well as totals in units and dollars for the fiscal year, ending in December in this example.

As a result, the fiscal totals are made up of both sales history (Jan.–Sept.) and Sales Forecast (Oct.–Dec.). Farther to the right is the forecasted dollar amount in the Business Plan. This latter number allows for an easy comparison between the Business Plan and the S&OP forecast for the fiscal year's volume. On the basis of this, the top management team will probably elect to change the Business Plan accordingly.

Also in **E.** please note that the old forecast is shown in addition to the new forecast. Some companies, certainly not all, like to do this so they can see the magnitude of the changes. The same approach is being taken in the Production section, comparing the old plan with the new.

The assumptions that underlie the forecast are listed in area **H,** in the lower left-hand corner. The future Operations Plan, based on the new forecast and other considerations, is shown in **F,** and the relevant supply (production/procurement) issues are listed in **I.**

Area **G** contains the future inventory projection for finished goods, both in units and days-on-hand. The unit calculation is:

Last month's ending inventory (*for example,* end of September: 60)

minus

This month's new forecast (October: 210)

plus

This month's new Operations Plan (October: 210)

equals

This month's ending inventory (October: 60)

The projected days-on-hand calculation is:

Next month's new forecast (*e.g.*, November: 210)

divided by

Number of work days in month[2]

equals

Daily sales rate (210/20 = 10.5)

divided into

This month's inventory plan (October: 60)

equals

This month's days' supply (October: 5.7, rounded to 6)

In summary, Figure 12-1 is an example of a proven, effective format for Sales & Operations Planning. The intent is to have all of the relevant information for a given product family on one display. That enables each family's situation to be viewed completely and organically, both its recent past performance and its future outlook. For decision-making purposes, this has proven to be far superior to individual displays of information that focus only on sales, or on inventory levels, or on production.

The format for Finish-to-Order looks like the one for Make-to-Stock, except that it deals with "module inventory" or some other kind of surrogate inventory as opposed to finished goods.

A caution: as you get started, try not to let the spreadsheet get too "busy." It's easy to keep adding this piece of data and then that piece, until the display gets very crowded and hard to read. Keep it simple, at least in the beginning. There'll be plenty of time to add things later.

Another caution: for the spreadsheets, use only one unit of measure for demand, supply, inventory, and backlog. To do otherwise means that the arithmetic won't work.

---

[2] We're using a straight 20 days per month in this spreadsheet. Many companies use the number of actual work days in each month.

Make-to-Order Format

A spreadsheet for a purely Make-to-Order family isn't treated much differently from Make-to-Stock, as shown in Figure 12-2. As we saw in Chapter 3, the main difference is that the spreadsheet for Make-to-Order doesn't contain data for finished goods inventory. That's because there is none. (If there were, then the family wouldn't be purely Make-to-Order.) Rather, the inventory numbers are replaced by a display of the customer order backlog — both past and projected.

The other difference is that, in projecting the backlog into the future, the calculations are reversed from Make-to-Stock. In Make-to-Order, demand is added to the projected backlog and production is subtracted from it. (In Make-to-Stock, demand is subtracted from the projected inventory, and production is added to it.)

Here's how the projected backlog calculation works:

Last month's ending backlog (*e.g.*, end of September: 30)

plus

This month's new bookings forecast (October: 20)

minus

This month's new Operations Plan (October: 20)

equals

This month's ending backlog (October: 30)

We used a simplified calculation for the number of weeks of backlog, as follows:

New (production/shipment) plan (*e.g.,* November: 21)

divided by 4 (weeks in a month) equals

Weekly plan (5)

divided into

Ending backlog (October: 30)

equals

Backlog in weeks (October: 6)

Here again, with both Make-to-Order and Make-to-Stock, our advice is to keep the spreadsheet as uncluttered as possible.

One last point regarding the Make-to-Order spreadsheet: in Figure 12-2, we're showing a time fence at the end of the third month into the future. It's labeled "10% time fence," which means that production rate changes within the first 90-day zone should be held to 10 percent or less. As with all time fences, it

Figure 12-2

THE ACME WIDGET COMPANY — SALES & OPERATIONS PLAN FOR OCT 2008

FAMILY: LARGE WIDGETS (MAKE-TO-ORDER) UNIT OF MEASURE: EACH

TARGET LINE FILL: 99% TARGET ORDER BACKLOG: 4 WEEKS

	HISTORY									3rd 3 MOS	4th 3 MOS	12 MO TOTAL	MOS 13-18	FISCAL YR LATEST CALL	BUS PLAN
BOOKINGS	J	A	S	O	N	D	J	F	M						
OLD FORECAST	20	20	20	20	20	20	20	20	20	60	60	240	120	$1,800M	$1,800M
NEW FORECAST				20	20	20	22	24	24	72	72	274	142	$2,055M	$1,800M
NEW VS. OLD FCST				0	0	0	2	4	4	12	12	34	22	$255M	
BOOKINGS	22	20	21	20	5	5									
DIFF: MONTH	2	0	1												
CUM		2	3												
PRODUCTION/SHIPMENTS															
OLD PLAN	20	20	20	20	20	20	20	20	20	60	60	240	120		
NEW PLAN				20	21	22	24	24	24	72	77	284	142		
NEW VS. OLD PLAN				0	1	2	4	4	4	12	17				
ACTUAL	20	21	20												
DIFF: MONTH	0	1	0												
CUM		1	1												
ORDER BACKLOG															
OLD PLAN	30	30	30	30	30	30	30	30	30	30	30				
NEW PLAN				30	29	27	25	25	25	25	20				
ACTUAL	28	30	29	30											
BACKLOG — # WEEKS				6	6	5	5	5	5	5	4				
ORDER FILL %	99%	100%	100%												

10% TIME FENCE

DEMAND ISSUES AND ASSUMPTIONS

1. FORECAST REFLECTS INCREASED SALES BE-
CAUSE OF PROBLEMS AT COMPETITOR
PLUS SHORTER LEAD TIMES

SUPPLY ISSUES

1. UNABLE TO REACH 4 WEEKS BACKLOG UNTIL AUGUST BECAUSE OF:
   A) FORECAST INCREASE, AND
   B) NEW EQUIPMENT NEEDED TO GO BEYOND 24 UNITS PER MONTH
      NOT AVAILABLE UNTIL JULY

should be considered as a guideline only and not a hard and fast rule. Typically it will mean that overriding the time fence carries significant costs or other penalties, so a decision to change it should be made thoughtfully and by the right people.

The Spreadsheet Checklist

As you design your spreadsheets, you might want to keep the following checklist handy. It contains the ten items we feel are essential for an effective spreadsheet:

1. Order Fulfillment Strategy (Make-to-Stock, Finish-to-Order, Make-to-Order, etc.)

2. Unit of Measure

3. Customer Service target

4. Inventory or backlog target

5. Sales actuals and forecast

6. Operations actuals and plan

7. Inventory or backlog actuals and plan

8. Customer Service actuals

9. Financial comparison to Business Plan

10. Demand and Supply issues and assumptions

Insuring that you include all of these on your spreadsheet will get you off to a good start. Then add other items that will be helpful in dealing with your own specific situation.

* * * * *

FREQUENTLY ASKED QUESTIONS

Why does the spreadsheet need to project so far out into the future? What benefit is a forecast for fifteen months or eighteen months out?

One reason is Financial Planning, and there are three pieces to it:

- You need at least twelve months of forward "planning horizon" to compare the S&OP plan with the Business Plan for the current fiscal year. Early in the fiscal year, we'll need forecasts that "reach" to the year's end in order to do that.

- Capital planning should extend outside of the current fiscal year. Not all capital planning involves Sales & Operations Planning, but much of it does.

- Further, you're going to begin work on next year's budget about three to six months prior to the start of the next fiscal year. At that point, you'll need the three to six months of forecast for the current year, plus twelve months for next year. Having this forward forecasting and planning information in the ongoing business planning process makes the entire budgeting cycle much less time-consuming and, dare we say, less painful. One CEO we worked with said that one of their major goals for S&OP was to free people from having to spend large amounts of time in budgeting, so they could focus on the important stuff: serving the customers, developing new products, and running the plants more flexibly and effectively. That works for us.

Another reason for a long planning horizon, of course, is for Operations people to get some feel for what their capacity needs will be down the road. If each month they're looking at a potential bottleneck out in the future, they will be able to start to think about it, kick around some ideas, and check out some possibilities in advance of having to make decisions. A pilot friend of ours once said that Executive S&OP helps to "get your head out of the cockpit" so you can look out longer range.

One last point: we've heard people claim that they're doing Executive S&OP and then say that they have a three- or six-month forward horizon. To us, this is not Sales & Operations Planning. It's not even close.

*　　*　　*　　*　　*

Isn't it confusing to display so much information on one page?

It can be, if the display is not well designed. It's a balancing act between showing the necessary information and not showing unnecessary elements. However, thanks to graphical displays, the spreadsheets themselves are used primarily as back-up and can contain a greater level of detail than ten or twenty years ago, before graphs were widely used.

*　　*　　*　　*　　*

Is it really necessary to use the spreadsheets and graphs in the Exec Meeting? And, if so, is it necessary to view all of them in that meeting, or could we just look at the families where something has changed and a decision is needed?

We recommend viewing all the families in the beginning. They're the heart of the entire process: they're the documents where all of the major demand and supply issues come together and can be viewed holistically.

For the first year or so, we recommend that you look at all of the families. Then, after you're really proficient at the process and you'd like to speed things up, you might try it on an exception basis. But keep an open mind — you may decide it's better to cover them all.

On a number of occasions, we've seen an Executive S&OP group be presented with a family spreadsheet or graph where no changes were recommended, but good things happened. Viewing the information sparks a comment and another comment and then another. This results in a discussion regarding a previously unidentified opportunity, which becomes a follow-up item for further analysis and action.

Our friend Dean Smetana from the Sanford/Sharpie division of Newell-Rubbermaid says: "Executive S&OP is not just about solving problems; it also helps to *spot opportunities*."

Chapter 13

The Demand Planning Process

In more than a few companies, this Demand Planning[1] step can be the most challenging. Frequently, different groups within the commercial side of the business can view the world quite differently when it comes to future demand. We see this frequently within consumer products companies. For example, one company we're familiar with has this situation:

- The Sales Department has a very customer-centric view, focusing on individual mass merchandisers, retail buying groups (for example, Ace Hardware), and so forth. Some call this the "sales channel" view. It tends to be largely close-in — within or near the Planning Time Fence — and thus can be highly granular: SKU by customer by location, for example.

- The Marketing people are focused on product lines, the "brand view." They typically are looking further into the future and are concerned with future promotions, pricing changes, market share issues, and the like.

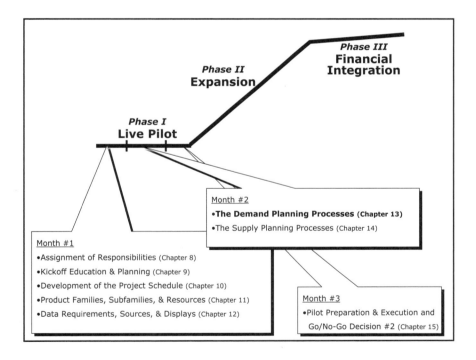

Here's the potentially hard part: these different views must be reconciled into one, single, agreed-upon Sales Forecast, reviewed and authorized by the senior Sales and Marketing executive(s). Now in a smaller company, which has the functions of Sales, Marketing, Merchandising, and so forth combined into one department under one executive, this need not be a major challenge.

---

[1]   Most of the topics in this chapter were introduced in Part One. Here we'll get into more detail on them.

In larger organizations that have this general kind of organization, it can be the toughest part of the entire implementation. Treat this issue as a potential show stopper and give it plenty of respect, time, and brainpower.

Let's think back to the ABCs of implementation: can there be a problem with the C item, computer hardware/software? There may be, but normally not so. How about the B item, the data? Yes, there can also be a problem here, in some cases a challenging one. And the A item, the people? As with so many other aspects of implementation, this is almost always the most difficult part. When we speak of organizational behavior change, this is the kind of thing we mean: changing the way people do their jobs and manage the business; developing new ways of doing things and of working together.

Report from the Field: Whirlpool Corporation

Company Description: Whirlpool is in the appliance business: ranges, refrigerators, dishwashers, washers and dryers, and more. And Whirlpool is actually a lot more than the name Whirlpool; through a series of acquisitions over an extended time, the company's brands now include Maytag, Amana, Kenmore, Kitchen Aid, Jenn-Air, and more. The North American Region (NAR) is Whirlpool's largest business unit, with annual sales in excess of $10 billion.

Their Experience: NAR is implementing Executive S&OP as this book is going to press, so it remains to be seen how well the full process will work there. However, as a part of the implementation, NAR has made great progress in the area of Forecasting and Demand Planning — a very difficult part of their operation.

Why is it difficult? It's because of the many different views of the product line held by people on the Sales and Marketing side of the business:

- Brand Management views the business in terms of individual brands: Whirlpool, Maytag, Amana, and so on.

- Merchandising Management sees the business as consisting primarily of products: washers, dryers, ranges, refrigerators, dishwashers.

- Sales Management thinks in terms of sales channels: Lowe's, Home Depot, WalMart, hardware chains, and so forth.

The challenge lies in bringing together all of these disparate views, and the knowledge behind them, into one coherent statement of expected future demand, one that would service the needs of all parts of the business.

NAR's solution was to create "Product Operations Teams" consisting of people from the above disciplines along with people from the supply side and finance. These Product Operations Teams are organized by product: laundry, cooking, cleaning, and refrigeration, reflecting the basic structure of Executive S&OP. It's focused on product, because products are what are ordered, made, and shipped. These teams are cross-functional teams with representation from Marketing, Merchandising, Sales Channels, and Demand Forecasting (along with others from the Supply and Finance parts of the business). The various demand side representatives do the following:

- Demand Forecasting people generate a new statistical forecast.

- Marketing and Merchandising are charged with creating enhancements to the forecast with regard to launches, pricing, promotions, transitions, and consumer offers.

- Sales and Trade Partner Collaboration people work together to understand the expectations of the Trade Partners and to create a channel forecast. Through this collaboration process, insight is gained to help develop a plan to meet their needs.

- Demand Forecasting people lead the consolidation of the enrichments gathered from Marketing, Merchandising, Sales, and the Trade Partner Collaboration group.

- The resulting Information goes through a "Reasoned and Reasonable" check by the Manager(s) of Demand Forecasting. At the completion of this step, what started out as the statistical forecast now is a valid, blended statement of expected future demand — a result of the best efforts of all of the constituents on the demand side of the house.

Following review by senior Sales and Marketing people, Finance, and the leader of the Product Operations Team, the forecast is now the "management authorized forecast." This is now "re-sliced and diced" into formats that are most meaningful to the various groups: brands, channels, product families.

The NAR people are proud of what they've done here, and enthusiastic about the approach. They expect even better results as Executive S&OP kicks in and takes advantage of this superior forecasting process.

The Moral of the Story: There are two here. First, it's possible — with dedication and hard work — to resolve particularly complex and gnarly issues. Second, an Executive S&OP implementation can facilitate that, because people have the vision of where this will lead and that it will make things better. Thus they're willing to change the way they've been doing their jobs.

Demand Planning for Make-to-Stock and Finish-to-Order

There are five activities here, as shown in Figure 13-1. Let's look at all five:

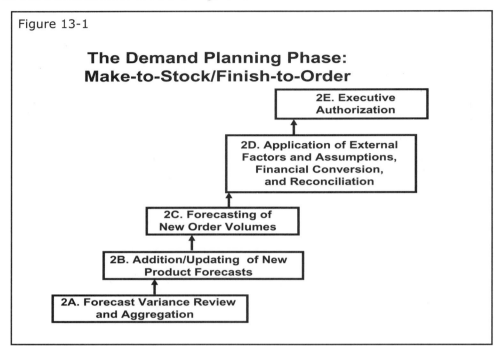

Figure 13-1

The Demand Planning Phase: Make-to-Stock/Finish-to-Order

- 2E. Executive Authorization
- 2D. Application of External Factors and Assumptions, Financial Conversion, and Reconciliation
- 2C. Forecasting of New Order Volumes
- 2B. Addition/Updating of New Product Forecasts
- 2A. Forecast Variance Review and Aggregation

Forecast Variance Review and Aggregation (2A)

This involves reviewing and analyzing the causes of significant forecast variance, and then finalizing the statistical forecast, if there is one.[2] This is typically done by people with the job title of Forecast Analyst or something similar. The computer generation of the statistical forecast occurs during Step 1 of the Executive S&OP cycle, Data Gathering.

In this first activity in the Demand Planning phase, the aggregate statistical forecasts are reviewed and finalized by the Forecast Analysts. One very important thing that the Forecast Analysts should be looking for is bias. As we said earlier, a biased forecast is one that is consistently above or below actual sales, and one type of bias contains an element of timing. This is where the forecast, for example six months in the future, is always quite high relative to the actual sales when they occur six months later. Frequently, the forecast is lowered as the month in question gets closer, with the result that bias becomes smaller to non-existent. However, that biased forecast six or so months out into the future can lead people to over-buy and over-resource — not a good thing.

A tool to help identify and correct this "time-phased bias" is called the *Waterfall Chart*, and is described in Appendix G.

---

[2]   In companies in the Finish-to-Order or Make-to-Order category, statistical forecasting and other statistical methods often play a lesser role.

Also in this step, detailed forecasts (mix) are aggregated into volume forecasts for subfamilies and families inside the Planning Time Fence, and reconciled with the aggregate forecast.

Addition/Updating of New Product Forecasts (2B)

The forecasting of new products is an essential early step in the Demand Planning phase. We treat it separately here, because forecasting for new products is typically quite different than for existing products for the following reasons:

- Different people are involved, specifically key players from the New Products section of the company.

- Different forecasting techniques are used.

- The forecasts often have a different look. As we indicated back in Chapter 3, they're often range forecasts: perhaps a high, a low, and a likely middle.

- New product introductions frequently result in cannibalization; they "steal" volume from existing products. Thus the approximate volume of the new products' forecasts should be known early, as that can be a direct input into the forecasts of related existing products.

Thus the new product forecasts should be worked early in the monthly cycle, perhaps beginning even before the end of the month. This can be practical; new product forecasts are not usually addressed by the statistical forecasting system because sales history has little relevance. Thus there's no need to wait until the end of the month.

Some companies will include Supply people in this step. One reason for this is to enable the development of supply plans for the new products somewhat independently of the Supply Planning phase, so that they can be effectively blended in during that phase.

Another reason is that, for new products, the line between the Demand Plans and the Supply Plans often blurs. Some people approach the new product introduction challenge with a goal of having enough product available to meet the high-side forecast and then adjusting quickly as events unfold. Their mind-set often is: "We know what we can make better than we know what we're going to sell." Thus the emphasis is heavily on the supply side during the early, uncertain periods in the life of the new product, with intense demand monitoring and very close communications between demand and supply people.

Forecasting of New Order Volumes (2C)

This step is used more extensively in Make-to-Order companies, involving primarily field salespeople projecting future business from their customers. However, it has some relevance in the Make-to-Stock/Finish-to-Order world, primarily with major accounts such as mass merchandisers. What's involved here is to obtain the projections from the field and blend them with the existing forecasts.

Application of External Factors and Assumptions, Financial Conversion, and Reconciliation (2D)

First, a disclaimer: these activities are presented here sequentially, one after another. However, companies often find that there is a "looping" kind of process that takes place; there can be more than one financial conversion pass, or several levels of reconciliation. Please keep that in mind as we proceed.

This step breaks out into several pieces, as its name implies:

- We saw a list of **external factors** in Figure 4-3 on page 44. These include new product launch plans, current and new customers, competitive factors, the economic outlook, pricing changes, promotions, outstanding quotes and bids, and others. Judgment plays a big role here as does knowledge of the business and its environment.

- As the various external factors are being evaluated and applied, it's vital to document the **assumptions** being made. Some assumptions may relate to the market or even the expected behavior of specific customers or competitors within that market. Other assumptions may be more macro, relating to the economy, business conditions, consumer confidence levels, and the like. As we said in our book on sales forecasting,[3] there are two primary reasons to do a first-rate job of documenting assumptions:

  Bulletproofing and Buy-In: A number of people, up to and including at least the VP of Sales & Marketing, will be reviewing the new forecast prior to its authorization. Having the assumptions visible to everyone involved in that process enables these folks to question these assumptions, modify them, override them, or — at a minimum — accept them. These assumptions, and thus the forecasts based on them, acquire a wide buy-in as they go through this process. No longer is it just the product manager whose butt is on the line for this forecast. A number of key players are now involved.

  Explanation and Learning: Frequently people scratch their heads and say: "How did we miss the forecast by that much? What were we thinking?" This occurs after the period is over and actual sales are known. Well, being able to see the assumptions upon which the forecast was made can help a lot to answer those kinds of questions. On forecasts that were off by a lot, documented assumptions can help show how the forecast went wrong. We can learn from it and perhaps avoid the same mistake in the future.

  Documenting assumptions is an essential part of a first-rate forecasting process.

- At some point, the unit forecasts must be converted into financial terms and, as we said, this might occur more than once. The **financial conversion** points out the need for Finance Department participation in the Demand Planning phase; their hands-on involvement will lend validity to the financial numbers that result from this process.

As we said earlier, our recommended approach is to forecast at a volume level, not mix, beyond the Planning Time Fence. This is made practical by the use of *simplifying assumptions* regarding the mix of

---

[3] *Sales Forecasting: A New Approach,* 2002, T. F. Wallace & Company.

individual products within a family, based on actual sales history. For example, a simplifying assumption might be that the sales mix for Product Family A is:

50% in SKU A-1 (average selling price of $100) = $50
40% in SKU A-2 (average selling price of $150) = $60
10% in SKU A-3 (average selling price of $180) = $18
$128

These factors yield a weighted average selling price for one Family A product of $128. Therefore, if the forecast for Family A six months from now is for 10,000 units, that converts to forecasted sales revenue of $1,280,000. It's that simple.

But . . . what if the sales mix changes? Couldn't one get badly fooled by using simplifying assumptions that are out of date? Absolutely. And that raises the need for routinely validating these numbers and changing them as the mix changes. Our recommended method for doing this is described in Appendix B.

One last point on the financial conversion: either here or in the next step (reconciliation), this financial version of the forecast should be compared to the Business Plan and the difference between the two clearly documented. On occasion in some companies, the people involved in this phase will loop back to revise a piece of the unit forecast, re-translate into financial terms, and again compare it to the Business Plan. In any event, if the gap is significant, this issue should be made visible throughout the remainder of the five-step Executive S&OP cycle.

One or several **reconciliations** must occur as part of this overall process. First, the various views within the Sales and Marketing groups must be reconciled into one set of numbers. Again, we'll say that this can be one of the more difficult parts of the entire process during implementation. However, there's good news here in the form of a learning curve:

- The various groups within Sales and Marketing will begin to understand what's required of the forecasts to make the overall Executive S&OP process function well.

- Further, they'll learn to work with each other in this forecasting area.

These two factors together usually lead to a more harmonious, more efficient, and less contentious process.

The other reconciliation deals with volume and mix. Inside the Planning Time Fence, there are typically two forecasts at this point:

- the mix forecast, in SKUs or similar, which extends out only to the Planning Time Fence or shortly beyond.[4] This degree of granularity is of course necessary inside the PTF to permit people on the supply side to know which products to make, which materials to procure, and so forth. Often this is primarily a Sales Department responsibility.

---

[4] This is not the case, of course, for Finish-to-Order. There are few, if any, SKU forecasts in these environments.

- the volume forecast, in families, extending out through the entire planning horizon, with primary responsibility falling to Marketing. These two forecasts must be roughly the same; within some reasonable tolerance, the sum of the mix forecast must approximate the volume forecast. The difference between the two must be evaluated and acted upon.

Another step may also need to occur here. If a company's forecasting process uses subfamilies or sub-subfamilies, these must be rolled up to a family level, and tested for validity, reasonableness, and so forth.

Executive Authorization (2E)

This of course is done by the senior Sales and Marketing Executive(s). This essential step validates and authorizes the forecast; it gives an executive "stamp of approval" to the newly prepared forecast before it goes forward to the Supply Planning process. Further, this authorization avoids "surprises" at the Exec Meeting. Some companies call this the "demand consensus meeting."

We recommend that you keep this session short and to the point. The new forecast information should be presented to the Vice President(s) to see:

- the new forecasts in units and dollars,

- a comparison to last month's forecasts,

- the key assumptions that underlie the new forecasts, and

- the comparison of the new forecasts to the business plan.

As we pointed out back in Chapter 5, this does not have to be a face-to-face meeting. When the executives are traveling, it can work nicely to conduct this session remotely, using perhaps a tool such as Web Meeting or similar.

Demand Planning for Make-to-Order

For companies building and finishing products to customer order, the Demand Planning process is a bit different from Make-to-Stock. One difference, as we saw earlier, is that there's no finished goods inventory in a true Make-to-Order situation. Rather, Executive S&OP focuses on the projected backlog of customer orders, to ensure that lead times are competitive and that products can be shipped on time.

Companies building to customer order typically see three distinct time zones for the backlog: the Sold Zone, containing only sold orders; the Partial Zone, containing some sold orders and some forecast; and the Unsold Zone, containing only forecast. In Figure 13-2 on the following page, we can see this graphically.

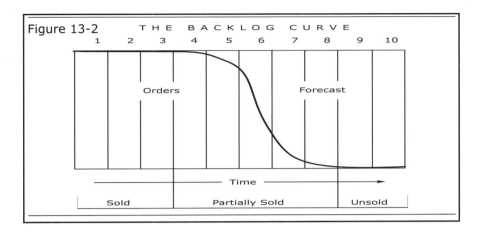

The Demand Planning task in a Make-to-Order environment, therefore, focuses on:

- In the Sold Zone, confirming or adjusting the customer orders.

- In the Partial Zone, confirming/adjusting the customer orders and forecasting the volume of orders expected to be received. Inputs to this zone are quote activity, active projects, and so forth.

- In the Unsold Zone, forecasting the volume of orders expected to be received.

The flow of activities in Demand Planning for Make-to-Order is similar to Make-to-Stock/Finish-to-Order. Differences include the lack of an SKU-level statistical forecasting process, and the fact that this forecasting is largely Sales Department driven; the role of Marketing people is normally not central in this environment. As we pointed out earlier, the forecasting of new order volumes (Step 2C in Figure 13-1) plays a substantially larger role.

The process is heavily involved with customer contact, in an attempt to gain insight into their future buying plans, new product initiatives, and so forth.

*   *   *   *   *

FREQUENTLY ASKED QUESTIONS

Do Sales and Marketing people have to become data management experts to do this job well?

Not at all. There are two parts to Demand Planning: data management and judgment/ownership.

The second part — judgment and ownership — cannot be delegated to anyone else. That is a primary part of the Sales and Marketing job. The data management part can be delegated to anyone in the organization who has the skills and can do the job well. It could be IT, Supply Chain, Finance, and so on. It does, however, have to be done in a way that satisfies the needs of Sales and Marketing.

Chapter 14

The Supply Planning Process

Please note what's happening here: first we concentrate on demand, as seen in Chapter 13. Once the new demand picture is created, we can focus closely on the supply piece.

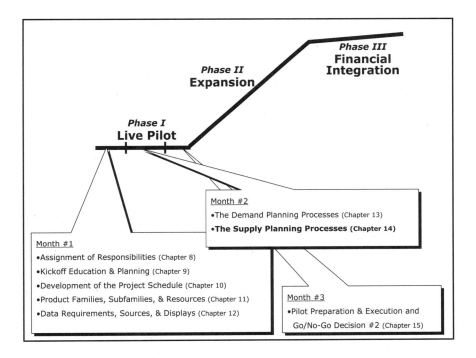

The Supply Planning[1] process, Step 3 in the 5-step monthly cycle, consists of five substeps, as shown in Figure 14-1 on the next page. We'll review them one at a time.

Review Supply Performance to Plan (3A)

This step compares actual performance against the Operations Plan for the month just ended. This is done for both internal supply and outsourced products, and focuses on gaps — both over plan as well as under — between actual and plan.

All significant gaps are analyzed. Based on the cause, a variety of actions could result:

- Fix the problem. Determine the root cause and eliminate it.

- Work around the problem. If the root cause can't be eliminated, develop another way to get the job done, perhaps via reassignment of work to other resources.

---

[1] Many of the topics in this chapter were introduced in Part One. Here we'll get into more detail on them.

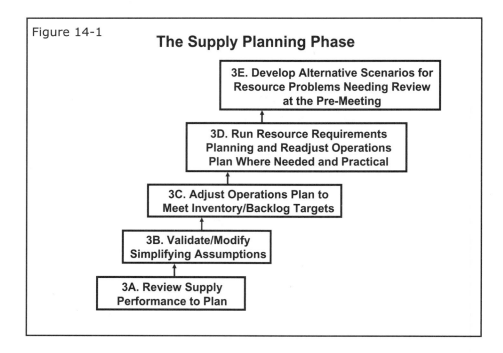

Figure 14-1

The Supply Planning Phase

Reassess the future capacity. Perhaps the desired output won't be attainable for some time to come, and this issue must be communicated widely and factored into future plans.

This part of the Supply Planning step can be done in parallel with the Demand Planning step.

Validate/Modify Simplifying Assumptions (3B)

Several key sets of assumptions are involved here, one being the sales mix of individual products within a family. If that mix changes, and the various items in the family put different amounts of workload on a resource, then the values in the Bill of Resources (to be explained shortly) must be adjusted accordingly. Similarly, if the routing of one or more products has changed, that would probably require an adjustment to the Bill of Resources.

Another example: a resource has a change in its processing speed. Let's say that historically it's taken 1.2 hours in the Filling department to run 1,000 of Product Family A, but that during recent months, Filling has been running those products faster. It takes on average only 1.1 hours to make 1,000. This would call for a change in that factor in the Bill of Resources.

This step can also start before Demand Planning is finished, and we recommend that it be done every month. Figure 14-2 shows an example of how a control chart can be used to validate the simplifying assumption that it takes 1.2 hours of run time in the Filling operation to make 1,000 units of Product Family A.

This chart is a traditional TQM Control Chart. It shows the actuals for the last 15 months, with the mean being calculated and shown. Also shown is a trend line over those 15 months. The upper and lower control

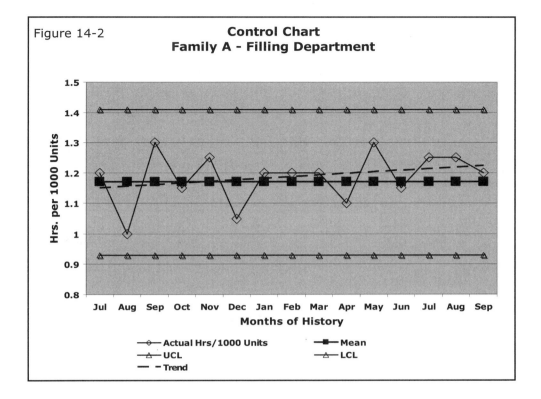

Figure 14-2

Control Chart
Family A - Filling Department

limits (UCL and LCL) are based on three times the mean absolute deviation (MAD), which represent a 99.2 percent statistical probability that all plots in the future will be within those limits.

With this data updated each month, a judgment needs to made that the current assumption about run rate (1.2 hours per 1,000 units in this case) remains valid or needs to be changed. The trend line over these 15 months (seen on the Control Chart) indicates that the amount of time on the average (mean) to produce 1,000 units is increasing. This may or may not cause a change at this time, mainly because the last actual is right on target at 1.2.

It's not enough to verify the assumption (1.2 hours per 1,000), which is almost always an average, a mean. We must also check on the variability of that assumption, and typically that calls for updating the MAD. We'll return to this subject in Section 3D, below.

Adjust Operations Plan to Meet
Inventory/Backlog Targets (3C)

First, a word about another preliminary step, this one with the S&OP spreadsheets. The Operations Plans from the prior month's spreadsheets are "rolled" one month to reflect the passage of time. The new end-of-month inventory numbers are entered, along with actual sales and actual production data for the month just ended. Then, when available, the new forecasts are entered into the spreadsheets.

With this, the Supply people are able to observe where the old Operations Plan (from the prior month) is causing the inventory and/or backlog projections to be higher or lower than target. They adjust the Operations Plan accordingly, thereby creating the new Operations Plan. As they do this, they are aware that they could be causing an overload — or underload — problem in one or another resource. They don't need to solve the problem then, but just know that it'll need to be addressed in the next step.

Run Resource Requirements Planning and Readjust Operations Plan Where Needed and Practical (3D)

This process makes use of the newly validated/updated simplifying assumptions from step 3A. They enable the Operations Plan for the individual families to be "translated" into units of workload for each resource. This process allows the Operations people to relate the required capacity (demand) to their available capacity (supply). They're able to evaluate the "doability" of the plan, changes needed in staffing levels, the need for new equipment, and so on.

The Mechanics of Resource Requirements Planning

The mechanics of Resource Requirements Planning are straightforward. It requires what are called Bills of Resources,[2] a kind of matrix that links product families to key resources.

Let's take a look at Figure 14-3, which shows a simplified display from a company making pharmaceuticals. This matrix tells us, among other things, that making 1,000 units of Product Family A will require, on average, 2.7 hours of time in the Mixing department, 1.2 in Filling, and so forth. The same kind of data is available for the other families, B through F.

Figure 14-3

BILL OF RESOURCES — FAMILY LEVEL (PER 000 UNITS)

KEY RESOURCES	FAMILIES					
DESCRIPTION	A	B	C	D	E	F
MIX (HRS)	2.7	5.0	13.1	—	1.8	14.0
FILL (HRS)	1.2	3.1	2.6	—	11.8	6.0
TEST (HRS)	1.6	2.4	1.1	0.7	—	7.0
LABELER #6 (HRS)	3.3	3.3	—	2.0	—	—
WAREHOUSE SPACE (CUBE)	6.7	3.3	—	2.6	—	19.0
SUPPLIER A (GALLONS)	8.7	6.7	7.1	—	4.2	—

---

[2] Also called Load Profiles.

Those numbers — 2.7 hours in Mixing, 1.2 in Filling and so on — are not only averages, as we said. They are also *assumptions* — the simplifying assumptions we've been talking about. They assume that the demand mix of individual products within Product Family A will stay the same, and that the process steps and speeds will not change.

Bills of Resources can be developed in several ways:

- by analyzing routings and calculating averages for all products within a family. (A weighted average, based on planned volumes, may be required if there are significant variances in the time requirements of different products within the family.);

- by pulling historical data from job cost records;

- by using estimates from knowledgeable people in Production, Engineering, and Purchasing; or

- by using some combination of the above, including judgments about the future.

Adding the Operations Plan into the picture enables the calculation of the Resource Requirements Plan for one month, shown in Figure 14-4.

Figure 14-4									
RESOURCE REQUIREMENTS PLAN (ONE MONTH)									
KEY RESOURCES	**FAMILY PRODUCTION PLAN QUANTITY**						**CAPACITY**		
DESCRIPTION	A	B	C	D	E	F	REQ'D	DEMO	MAX DEMO
	15,000	6,000	21,000	10,000	34,000	6,000			
MIX (HRS)	41	30	275	—	61	84	491	584	621
FILL (HRS)	18	19	55	—	401	36	529	450	482
TEST (HRS)	24	14	23	7	—	42	110	119	146
LABELER #6 (HRS)	50	20	—	20	—	—	90	77	136
WHSE SPACE (CUBE)	101	20	—	26	—	114	261	370	410
SUPPLIER (GALLONS)	131	40	149	—	143	—	463	500	640

Here we can see the result of multiplying the hours in the Bill of Resources by the amount of the Operations Plan. For example, multiplying Product Family A's 2.7 hours of work required in Mixing by the Operations Plan for Family A — 15,000 units — results in 40.5 hours, rounded to 41. Some interesting information is shown in the three right columns:

- The column headed "Capacity Req'd" (Required Capacity) is the sum of all the numbers to its left, representing the *demand* for capacity. To hit the Operations Plan will require that much output.

- The next column, "Capacity Demo" (Demonstrated Capacity) shows the *supply* of capacity, i.e., how much capacity we have available. Please note the word "demonstrated." This refers to average actual output, often expressed in standard hours: what we have proven we can produce, as opposed to a calculated, theoretical output that we may or may not be able to hit.

- The right-most column, "Capacity Max Demo" (Maximum Demonstrated Capacity) refers to an upper limit of output that might be reached with heavy overtime or other means. Many companies will use this as a statement of capacity that can be attained for a relatively short time, not a level they'd like to operate at over the long run.

In Figure 14-4, we can see some problems, an obvious one being Filling. Required Capacity for the month is 529 hours, far in excess of the Demonstrated Capacity or even the Maximum. This says that the Operations Plan as it now stands is not producible. Something has to change, either via increasing the supply of capacity or decreasing the demand for it.

Using the Resource Requirements Planning (RRP) Information

The information in Figure 14-4 shows the picture on *all* of the resources for only *one month*. In actual practice, it's usually the reverse: a Resource Requirements display will show only *one resource*, but for a *number of month*s into the future. See Figure CG-5 in the section of colored graphical displays at the back of the book, which shows a Resource Requirements Plan for Acme Widget's subassembly operation. We suggest you open up that display so that you can follow along with the text.

The required capacity (red bars and green bars) can be related to the demonstrated capacity (blue band) and to the maximum demonstrated capacity (yellow band). The spreadsheet details that back this up can show more information such as actual numeric data, cumulative comparisons, year-end totals, and so on.

Using this information, the Supply Planning people can evaluate the overall load for doability. This resource seems to be capable of doing the overall volume of work if it runs at its normal capacity, with no overtime for many months. A moderate trend upward starts to appear about ten months into the future, which probably does not require action now but may be something to watch over the coming months.

The first step in developing Bills of Resources is to determine which resources to include. A few paragraphs ago, we used the phrase "key resources." That implies that not all resources are visible to Resource Requirements Planning, just the key ones. These are often large resources, which could be entire departments, such as Filling.

Reasons to include a resource in the Resource Requirements Planning process include:

- It's a bottleneck.

- It's not possible to offload work from this resource to another.

- It has a long lead time to change capacity (highly trained Production people).

- It's heavily involved with new products (perhaps Engineering people).

- It's costly to underutilize, such as equipment designed to run 24–7 and/or it's expensive to shut down and restart. Furnaces are a good example.

The resources being addressed can, of course, be production resources but also could be others. Material, warehouse space, refrigerated storage, shipping department personnel, cash, rail cars, trucks, and so on can be appropriate subjects for Resource Requirements Planning when they are constraints to producing and shipping product. In some of these cases, e.g., material, the driver is the Operations Plan. However, the driver for warehouse space would be the Inventory Plan and perhaps the Demand Plan would drive the calculations for shipping workload. In Finish-to-Order, the driver for the Finishing Department would also be the Forecast/Sales Plan.

Not all resources to be tracked need to be from within the company. Contract manufacturers and other key suppliers come to mind. For this kind of planning process, as we said in the Foreword, it's not really important who owns the factory.

Beware of including too many resources in this process. Dozens and dozens are probably too many. One good rule of thumb is to track a number of resources no more than double the number of product families, i.e., ten families, no more than twenty resources.

As with forecasting, many companies are able to do an effective job of Resource Requirements Planning at the family or subfamily level. This occurs when the families or subfamilies are fairly homogeneous, i.e., when the individual items within them create a fairly similar load on the resources. Other companies find that, closer in, they need to generate the capacity requirements from the Master Schedule (using a process called Rough-Cut Capacity Planning). This is because the individual products place widely differing loads on the resources. Hence, individual item detail is necessary in these cases.

In our experience, most companies don't need that kind of precision for projections many months into the future. Some companies feel they need such precision, but if you think your company may be in that category, make sure that you're not confusing precision with validity. Four-decimal-place "accuracy" isn't necessary; what's needed are valid numbers, directionally correct, upon which to base decisions.

Testing the Plan for Assumption Variability

The Resource Requirements Plan shown in Figure CG-5 is based on assumptions of resource consumption in Subassembly by medium widgets and large widgets. These assumptions will almost always be averages. As we all learned in statistics, the mean — one measure of central tendency — goes hand-in-hand with a measure of variability, typically measured by the standard deviation (sigma) or mean absolute deviation. Throughout this book, we've used MAD for our measure of variability, because it's easier to calculate and understand.

So, besides the assumptions of resource consumption, we need to know the variability. Let's say in this case (looking back at the Control Chart earlier in this chapter, Figure 14-2) the upper and lower control limit are set at 3 MAD to represent a 99.2 percent probability of maximum future variability. What that says is that in any short period of time, it could take a run rate of the upper or lower control limit (roughly 1.6 and 0.8, respectively).

With this, one can raise the question: what if we run better than the average? Our output would be up. How different is the effect of that situation? Well, with standard spreadsheet software, it's a simple matter to enter new values into the RRP process and — bingo! — a new RRP plan will appear showing the new picture, given the higher assumed output rate.

And, of course, it's possible to test more than one assumption at a time — and to test them together. In the example shown in CG-5, Subassembly is serving two families of product: Medium Widgets and Large Widgets.

- Let's assume it takes roughly twice as long to run a Large Widget than a Medium.

- You could test with one at the upper limit and the other at the lower limit, or any combination of the two, to see the collective consequence on the RRP.

You would then check for good or bad news in the RRP chart that gets updated based on your choices of variability.

In some Resource Requirements Planning environments, there can be more than one or two assumptions that need to be made. Keeping in mind that simplicity is good and complexity is usually not, try to limit the number of assumptions. The difficulty in testing the plan for assumption variability increases in geometric proportion to the number of assumptions being made.

However, as they say, "if you gotta, you gotta." If you have many assumptions that need to be made, you'll need many control charts to routinely validate those assumptions. Don't make it any more complex than necessary and do make it as easy to do as possible, because it needs to be done once each month.

Develop Alternative Scenarios for Resource Problems Needing Review at the Pre-Meeting (3E)

When a resource is shown to be overloaded, what options are available to rectify that condition? Well, there are many: use overtime, add people, add a shift, offload work to an alternate resource, subcontract, cut lot sizes, and many more. The issue is that the overload must be rectified; if not, then an imbalance exists between the demand for capacity and its supply — and such a plan is not producible.

If the supply of capacity cannot be increased, then the demand for it must be reduced and that typically happens via a reduction in the Operations Plan. Normally this is not a good thing because it means you will not be meeting all customers' demands.

During the prior step, Resource Requirements Planning, problems are identified. In some cases, supply people can solve a given problem on their own; in other cases, not so. This is because they are empowered to make certain kinds of decisions but not others. Here are some examples, but they are not meant to be black and white, as these kinds of things can vary widely from company to company.

- Minor decisions. Examples: add overtime, hire additional people, reduce the staff on the third shift by 10 percent. These are normally within the decision-making authority of the supply people.

- Moderate decisions. Example: add an entire shift. In most companies, this would need to be elevated to the Pre-Meeting to allow for a cross-functional view, discussion, and decision. This could then be presented in the Exec Meeting as a completed decision, as in: "We're going to add a second shift in Fabrication in Plant 4."

- Major decisions. Example: add 90,000 square feet to Plant 2, along with the necessary new production equipment. This would require significant discussion at the Pre-Meeting and one or perhaps more presentations at the Exec Meeting, prior to a decision being made by the Executive Group.

In the case of moderate or major decisions, it's often important that alternatives be explored. For example, the action to "add a shift in Fabrication in Plant 4" is one way to increase capacity. Are there other possibilities? Probably. Perhaps Plant 3 could pick up that additional work. This would result in eliminating the cost of supervision for the new shift, plus the hiring and training costs involved with the new production associates.

On the other hand, Plant 3 is in California and much of the increased volume would need to be shipped east of the Mississippi, with an attendant rise in freight costs. A third option might be to send the additional volume to a contract manufacturer, and that has its own array of costs and benefits. And a fourth alternative, unlikely in most cases, might be to not increase capacity but rather allocate the current level of output to selected customers.

These scenarios need to be presented at the subsequent step(s): the Pre-Meeting and perhaps the Exec Meeting. Obviously they need to be presented in a manner that is clear, concise, and facilitates decision making and — most important — they must carry financial information with them. This points up the need to have Finance people active in the Supply Planning step, Demand Planning, as well as the Pre-Meeting and Exec Meeting.

*　　*　　*　　*　　*

FREQUENTLY ASKED QUESTIONS

If a company has aligned resources, do they need to do Resource Requirements Planning? After all, can't they just compare the Operations Plan on the S&OP spreadsheets to the capacity for the resource and see if there's an overload?

This can happen under only one set of conditions: if all of the products within all of the product families on that resource consume the same amount of resources, and if that is not expected to change. That takes the issue of mix changes off the table.

For example, if the line runs at the same speed when producing all eight SKUs within Product Family M and all 16 SKUs in Family P, then Resource Requirements Planning might be a lot simpler than we've presented here. And, of course, the resource capability check must be made regardless of how the resource requirements were derived.

In our experience, these kinds of cases are quite rare. They do reflect the principle of simplicity/complexity: the simpler the environment, then the simpler the tools needed to plan and control that environment.

Chapter 15

Pilot Preparation and Execution

As we enter Month 3, it's time to get the show on the road: the Live Pilot. In Chapter 7, we saw four reasons to do a Pilot instead of a "big bang" cutover. Now let's ask ourselves: what is the primary objective of the Live Pilot?

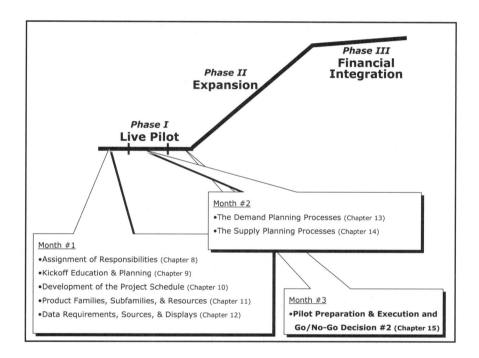

The number one objective of the Live Pilot is *not to run the business better*. As we said earlier, the main objective of the pilot is education: *learning, familiarization, and understanding — primarily for top management*. This must occur before Executive S&OP can be made to work and thereby enable the people to run the business better.

The education we've covered so far has been largely conceptual; the Live Pilot starts the "on-the-job" training. The folks in the Demand Planning and Supply Planning phases learn by doing. Ditto for the Pre-Meeting team.

By the time the Exec Meeting rolls around, most of the people involved with Executive S&OP have had both conceptual education and on-the-job training — except for the top management team. They're the only people who haven't yet experienced how this stuff works in their company.

Therefore, as we said, the Pilot Exec Meeting is more about learning than about making decisions. In this session, the Executive Champion, the S&OP Process Owner, and others[1] should explain – in some detail – how the steps of the process have been done:

- Data Gathering,

- Demand Planning,

- Supply Planning, including Resource Requirements Planning, and the

- Pre-Meeting, including any discoveries — "aha's" — made in that meeting.

This reinforces one of the important aspects of the business case for S&OP: a window into the future.

Part of this meeting should be devoted to identifying changes in roles necessary for the process to work really well. Lastly, the top management folks should be encouraged not only to ask questions but also to provide feedback for design improvements to the displays and the process.

Next, is one product family enough or would you want more than one to get started? Maybe you don't. However, think back to the Acme Widget Company. They have two business units: Industrial and Consumer. The two units have different products; they sell into very different markets; they have separate marketing and sales staffs; and their forecasting processes are quite different. Piloting only one family, say Medium Consumer Widgets, would mean that the folks in Industrial would not have much involvement with Executive S&OP for the entire month. In this case, we'd suggest to Acme that they pick two families: one from Consumer and one from Industrial.

Once you've selected the pilot family or families and accomplished the tasks in the earlier steps, it's time to just do it. What's needed here is to generally follow the steps in the monthly Executive S&OP process, which is diagrammed on the next page.

1. **Data Gathering.** First, run the reports and worksheets that you use to update the Sales Forecasts, and get them to Sales/Marketing so they can get started on the Demand Planning phase. In addition, get the numbers for actual sales, production, and either inventory or customer order backlog.

    Enter the data into the spreadsheet. Later, this data-entry function must be automated because of the volume. However, for now, most companies will enter the data manually if there will be any delay at all waiting for the feeds to be automated.

    At the same time, the target data must be entered for the demand/supply strategies: target customer service levels, target inventories for both Make-to-Stock and Finish-to-Order products, and target customer order backlogs for Make-to-Order.

---

[1] We feel it's a good idea that the entire Design Team attend this session, with each person presenting his or her part of the process. This demonstrates to executive management the widespread buy-in and commitment; in other words, the Design Team members "have their fingerprints on it."

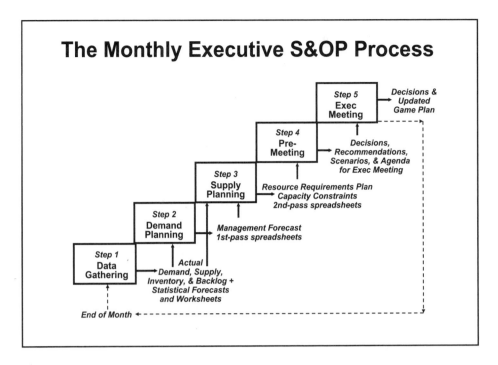

2. **Demand Planning Process.** While this is going on, the Demand Planning phase can kick in. Sales and Marketing people generate forecasts and Demand Plans for the Pilot family. They are entered into the S&OP spreadsheet, which then goes to Operations.

3. **Supply Planning Process.** Here Operations lays in the Operations Plan for the Pilot family. This is set to meet the Sales Forecast and to get the inventories and/or backlogs to their target level. Also, Operations needs to verify that the Operations Plan is "doable" or, if not, how much of it can be achieved, and determine the options to provide the rest of the needed product. Typically this is done using Resource Requirements Planning.

4. **Pre-Meeting.** This is where the Pre-Meeting team prepares the material to be presented at the Exec Meeting, keeping in mind that the primary objective is educational, not operational. It's quite likely that this Pre-Meeting could take most or all of a full day,[2] covering the following topics:

   • Development of an initial set of performance goals and metrics to be presented at each Exec Meeting: customer service, inventory turns, financial performance, and so forth. Keep in mind that this initial list will no doubt change as the total process is implemented and matures.

   • Preparation of the explanation — for top management — of the Data Gathering process.

   • Preparation of the explanation — for top management — of the Demand Planning process, including the roles of the statistical forecast, judgment forecast, and the translation of units to dollars.

---

2 Normally the Pre-Meeting should take no more than a half day. However, it may take longer in the early months.

- Preparation of the explanation — for top management — of the Supply Planning process, including the mechanics of Resource Requirements Planning and its reliance on simplifying assumptions.

- Preparation of the explanation — for top management — of the need for Control Charts for each of the simplifying assumptions, including an example of the mechanics, to be shown to them this one time and probably never again.

- Preparation of the explanation — for top management — of the Pre-Meeting: how the information is reviewed, how decisions are made, how recommendations are formulated.

- Preparation of the explanation of the Exec Meeting: topics, flow, roles and responsibilities, permanent agenda items.

- Making appropriate decisions about the Pilot family: increase/decrease sales, production, inventories, backlog.

- Development of recommendations to top management, typically involving problems with the Pilot family outside the Pre-Meeting team's sphere of authority.

- Establishment of the agenda for the Exec Meeting.

5. **Exec Meeting.** Figure on this meeting taking longer than the typical one to two hours it takes after the process is up and running. We recommend you allocate a half day for this, with the possibility that you may finish after three hours or so. Given that the main objective here is education, top management must have enough time to digest the material being presented, ask questions, raise concerns, and in general get familiar with it.

Here's a meeting outline you may want to follow, which is quite different from the sample agenda presented back in Chapter 5. The reason for this, of course, is that the Pilot is primarily about teaching and learning; the ongoing operation of Executive S&OP is about running the business.

1. Review of Executive S&OP process and logic.

2. History of the Executive S&OP initiative at the company.

3. Initial performance goals and metrics.

4. Explanation of the Data Gathering process.

5. Explanation of the Demand Planning process, including the statistical forecast, management forecast, and the translation of units to dollars.

6. Explanation of the Supply Planning process, including the mechanics of Resource Requirements Planning and its reliance on simplifying assumptions.

7. Explanation of the need for Control Charts for each of the simplifying assumptions, showing an example of the mechanics.

8. Explanation of the Pre-Meeting: how the information is reviewed, how decisions are made, how recommendations are formulated.

9. Review of the proposed standard agenda for future Exec Meetings.

10. Review of decisions made by the Pre-Meeting Team.

11. Decisions needed to be made by the Top Management Team.

12. Go/No-Go Decision #2: whether or not to proceed with Executive S&OP by bringing the rest of the families onto the process and to integrate the financials. (In our experience, this decision is almost always in the affirmative: yes, let's go.)

13. A decision needs to be made as to when and how to discontinue the existing processes, if any, for balancing demand and supply. (The Live Pilot runs in parallel with the old processes, which will no longer be needed.)

14. Establishment of the dates for the next 12 Exec Meetings, being careful to avoid "have-to" events such as corporate meetings, trade shows, and the like.

That's it. You've just completed your first Executive S&OP cycle and, if you did your homework and followed the path outlined in this book, the odds are good that it was reasonably effective. It started your company down the learning curve, and you positioned yourselves for a better, easier cycle next month — when you'll be adding more families.

A caveat: don't try to get the material for the first Executive S&OP meeting to a point of perfection. Rather, in preliminary conversations with the Executive Team, the Executive Champion should set the level of expectations along these lines:

• *Our first Exec Meeting is intended to be primarily a learning experience. It'll be more focused on understanding how the process will work than on making major decisions. We may or may not get some operational benefit from it.*

• *It won't be perfect and may not even be highly polished. Be patient. It will get better in a hurry. We guarantee it.*

• *We may not have all the data we need — but we have enough to get started.*

• *We're working to get all the data, but it'll take a bit longer and we don't want to delay the implementation by waiting for it all to be available.*

The Executive Champion is the best person to present this message. These are some of the most important things he or she can do:

- Set the level of expectations,

- Keep Executive S&OP on the front burner with high visibility, and

- Run interference for the Design Team and others regarding such things as resource allocation, priorities, and so forth.

Our experience with top management groups is that they tend to be quite understanding of start-up problems and will be supportive. However, they won't be happy about seeing the same problems month after month. Making consistent progress over time is far more important than the level of polish of the first Exec Meeting. It should be good, but doesn't have to be great.

Report from the Field: Worldwide Support Group[3]

Company Description: Worldwide Support Group (WSC) is a multi-billion dollar "department" of the Worldwide Equipment Corporation, a very large manufacturer of industrial equipment. The Support Group is responsible for the construction of new plants, process changes/improvements to existing plants, and some preventive maintenance. It employs thousands of people, both employees and outside contractors.

Their Experience: WSC's demands come from the many and diverse product divisions within Worldwide, and are quite variable. To meet these demands, their primary supply resources are people: mechanical engineers, electrical engineers, experienced project management people, and so forth. Increasing these resources carries relatively long lead times. This is a classic demand–supply issue, with the only difference being that the outputs are not physical products.

The leader of this business unit had prior S&OP experience while heading up a product division. Thus, he was able to see clearly that Executive S&OP could help solve the demand/supply problems in WSC every bit as effectively as in businesses with physical products.

For demand planning, WSC uses ten "project families" (similar to product families): large projects, medium projects, small projects, process improvements, process maintenance, and so forth. The unit of measure for most of these is number of projects.

They relate projected future demand against nine primary sets of resources, almost all human resources, in the categories defined above (unit of measure: full time equivalents). In doing so, they make many simplifying assumptions about resource consumption based on data mining and analysis, for example, what's involved in a typical large project: how many mechanical engineers, how many electricals, and so on.

---

[3] The identity of the actual company has been disguised, at the company's request.

WSC used the Live Pilot approach to implementation: they employ the standard Five-Step process for their monthly Executive S&OP cycle, which carries both a unit and a dollar view, and makes extensive use of Resource Requirements Planning in the Supply Planning phase. Once per quarter, their future outlook is presented to corporate executive management for review and spending authorizations as required.

The Moral of the Story: Executive S&OP can work well in areas where the demands are not sales in the traditional sense and where the resources are almost totally "soft," — skill sets as opposed to production machinery and the like.

*   *   *   *

FREQUENTLY ASKED QUESTIONS

Our Top Management Team is made up of some really strong-willed people; they can be contentious, and sometimes in meetings it's difficult for them to stay on track. I'm concerned about the Live Pilot Exec Meeting. I can see them digging into the presentation data early on and never being able to get them back on track. Suggestions?

Yes, we have one which has worked nicely in the past:

- Decouple the demonstration part of the Live Pilot from the decision-making part. Cover agenda items 1 through 8 (above) but no more. Do not use live data, thereby getting most of the potentially emotional elements out of the picture.

- Then, a week or so later, do the decision-making elements: items 9 through 14, using live data of course.

Breaking the Live Pilot into these two steps can make it easier to bring a "frisky" top management group solidly into the process. And, in between the two sessions, perhaps the Champion could visit with the more vocal executives, set their level of expectations, and ask for their cooperation.

****

Does everyone have to sit through the entire meeting (Pre-Meeting or Exec Meeting), or can people come and go as needed?

We feel this question is more relevant for the Pre-Meeting, which can be lengthy. We've seen it work well for the folks from, say, Plant A to be in the first part of the meeting, followed by the Plant B people and so on. But please note: if Plant A and B make some of the same products and have similar resources, this approach might not work. When workload needs to be reassigned, you really need both groups in the room at the same time.

Product managers might need to stay only as long as their products are being discussed — provided also that there's not significant interrelationship or capacity conflicts between their products and those of some other product manager. The same goes for New Product Development. The Finance representative would probably be there for the entire session, as would the demand manager, supply chain manager, Executive S&OP process owner, and others.

We don't think this question is germane for the Executive Meeting. That session lasts no more than two hours, and it's this meeting that gives overall direction to the business. Two hours or less seems to us to be a very good investment of people's time. Even in those parts of the meeting when they're not directly involved, they'll still be getting good input on the overall status of the business.

Part Three

Expansion and Full Financial Integration

Prologue to Part Three:
Low Risk and Low Cost

TOM WALLACE: Any thoughts you'd like to share before we jump into Part Three?

BOB STAHL: Just one: to re-emphasize the low cost/low risk nature of this implementation process.

The first decision — Go/No-Go Decision #1: Live Pilot in 90 days — is a partially informed commitment; it can't be any more than that because top management hasn't seen Executive S&OP in action in their company. That gets accomplished with very little risk and low cost.

After the Live Pilot has taken place, the next decision — Go/No-Go Decision #2: Full Implementation — is made by people who are *fully informed*. There's little risk of Executive S&OP not meeting the company's needs.

Further, our approach is to add the remaining families a few at a time over several months — as opposed to a "big bang" kind of a thing where all the families would be dumped onto the process at one time. That's too risky.

On the other hand, don't drag your feet bringing all the families onto the process. Two or three months is a good pace; perhaps four months if you have a larger number of families, say ten or a dozen.

Low risk and low cost. That's the key.

Chapter 16

Add All Families onto Executive S&OP

Once you've successfully done one or two families in the Live Pilot, it's time to start adding the other families to the process. Also, you'll be adding functions that haven't been included in the Live Pilot; these include Supply Planning, initial Financial Planning, and more mature and complete processes for new product introductions.

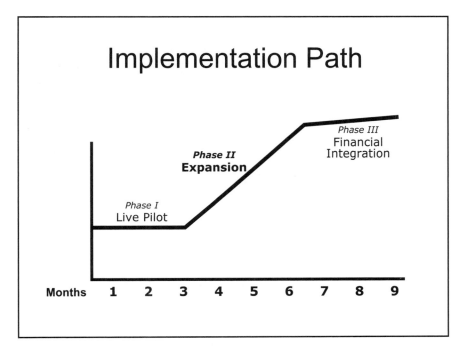

This time period, months four through months six or seven, is the heart of the Executive S&OP implementation process. It's when most of the pieces of Sales & Operations Planning come together.

Company S had eleven product families. They piloted with one family, added three in the second month, three in the third month, and four in the fourth. Along the way, as they were adding these families, they were able to:

• Dramatically improve the process.

• Improve their spreadsheet and graph formats.

• Add Supply Planning. (Company S's resources were heavily nonaligned. They had to get most of the product families on the Executive S&OP process before they could get a complete picture on the collective workload at a given resource.)

- Add initial Financial Planning.

- Add more complete planning for new products.

- Automate the data feeds into their spreadsheets.

Before you start this phase, decide which families you're going to cut over onto Executive S&OP in which months. Then add that detailed cut-over sequence into your overall project schedule.

Add Complete Supply Planning

If you're an aligned company, one where the resources match up very closely with the product families, then you're adding the Supply Planning process as you bring up the various product families. As we saw in Chapter 14, you can display the capacity picture right on the S&OP spreadsheets, provided that all members of the family run at the same approximate rate.

If, however, you're like many companies and you have a matrix relationship between families and resources, then there's a bit of a tricky timing element here. As we just saw with company S, S&OP can't help you evaluate the workload on a given resource until you have S&OP planning on most or all of the product families serviced by that resource.

However, during the next month, Company S added three product families that took all of the output from two of their major production departments. At that point, they were able to start up the Supply Planning part of the process because they had a full picture of the future production requirements for those departments. And, of course, as other families were added, they got an increasingly complete picture of the overall supply side of their business and were able to do a first-rate job of identifying capacity bottlenecks early enough to take corrective action.

So if you're a company with nonaligned resources, set your cut-over schedule for product families with an eye towards the supply side. Bring the families onto S&OP in a sequence that enables Resource Requirements Planning to work sooner rather than later.

Add Initial[1] Financial Planning

The first steps here involve merely dollarizing some of the unit data on the spreadsheet — typically the rolling 15–18 month forecast and the sales projection for the current fiscal year. It's also very helpful to show the Business Plan's dollar number for that family. In that way, the S&OP number (latest call for the fiscal year, i.e., fiscal year-to-date actuals plus forecast for the balance of the year) can be readily compared with the Business Plan number for that family. Some companies show a percentage — S&OP's fiscal year projection versus the Business Plan — and that can be very helpful in quickly identifying where the big problems are. An example of a dollarized S&OP spreadsheet is shown in Figure 16-1.

---

[1] The use of the word "Initial" in the heading for this section implies there's more to be done. That's correct, and it's covered in Chapter 18.

Actually, it's possible to get a start at this during the Live Pilot. However, since it's usually quite a push to get that first Pilot family's unit numbers put together, most companies wait until the following month to get started on the dollars.

The dollarized forecast is normally expressed in average selling price. As we said, the average selling price should be periodically verified to ensure that issues such as new products, changes in the level of promotions, price and discount changes, and so forth are reflected. This is typically done via Control Charts, as discussed in Appendix B.

Figure 16-1				DOLLARIZED - SALES & OPERATIONS PLAN OCT. 2008												

FAMILY: SMALL CONSUMER WIDGETS (MAKE-TO-STOCK) UNIT OF MEASURE: $000

TARGET CUSTOMER SERVICE: 98% TARGET FINISHED INVENTORY: 10 DAYS ON HAND

AVERAGE SELLING PRICE: $10.00 UNIT COST OF GOODS SOLD: $5.00

		HISTORY										3rd 3 MOS	4th 3 MOS	12 MO TOTAL	MOS 13-18	FISCAL YR LATEST CALL	BUS PLAN
SALES (SALES $)	A-M-J	J	A	S	O	N	D	J	F	M						
NEW FORECAST	$5400	$2000	$2000	$2000	$2100	$2100	$2200	$2200	$2200	$2200	$6900	$6900	$26,800	$14,400	$25,590	$23,000
ACTUAL SALES	6150	2200	1950	2270											+11.3%	
DIFF: MONTH		220	-50	270									Y-T-D MARGIN %:		32.7%	33.0%
CUM	750	970	920	1190									Y-T-D MARGIN $:		$8,368	$7,590

OPERATIONS (COST)														
NEW PLAN	$2850	$1000	$1000	$1000	$1050	$1050	$1100	$1100	$1115	$1115	$3450	$3450	$13650	$7200
ACTUAL	2610	1000	1030	990										
DIFF: MO		0	30	-10										
CUM	-240	-240	-210	-220										

FINISHED GOODS INVENTORY (COST)											
PLAN	$450	$500	$500	$500	$300	$350	$400	$450	$500	$550	$575	$575
ACTUAL		350	405	260								
DAYS ON HAND		8	9	6	6	6	7	8	9	10	10	9
CUSTOMER SERVICE		94%	96%	89%								

DEMAND ISSUES AMD ASSUMPTIONS

1. POSSIBLE ACQUISITION OF BIG-MART BUSINESS NOT INCLUDED IN THIS FORECAST

SUPPLY ISSUES

1. NEW EQUIPMENT AT MIDDLETOWN PLANT TO BE INSTALLED THIS MONTH

Dollarized production and inventory data is expressed in cost dollars and it's usually not a big challenge to assemble that information. Adding actual gross margin data for the year-to-date can be helpful and should be easy to get, but projections of margins into the future are subject to the average selling price issue cited above.

Add New Product Planning

During this phase, it's time to get new product introductions completely onto the S&OP radar screen. As we said earlier, new product launch issues need to be visible in all of the S&OP steps: Demand Planning phase, Supply Planning phase, Pre-Meeting, and Exec Meeting.

What's being worked here is the impact of new product introductions on the demand picture, the supply picture, and what problems are being created as a result of the new demand and supply issues. Where practical, the impact of new product launches should be displayed on the S&OP spreadsheets both in the quantitative section of the display and in the comments sections.

Tie the Detail to the Summary

Executive S&OP deals with volume, right? But we don't ship volume out the back door; we ship mix — individual products and orders.

So picture this: Company Z seems to have a great Executive S&OP process. But their Master Scheduling operates independently and never looks at what S&OP is saying. It's disconnected. Therefore, Company Z doesn't really have a great Executive S&OP process after all. People may be doing a lot of good work on the process, but it's not directly affecting the real world.

What's needed is to add up the detail in the Master Schedules, out through the Planning Time Fence. Aggregate it into product families, summarize it by months, and compare it with the Operations Plan within Executive S&OP. The sum of the Master Schedules for all the products within a given family should equal the Operations Plan plus or minus a few percent.

We recommend that the Master Scheduler prepare a concise report, for review at each Pre-Meeting, showing the comparison between the S&OP numbers and the summed Master Schedules. While this may have already been done for the Pilot family, it can now be displayed for all product families. This linkage helps to ensure that the decisions made in Sales & Operations Planning are being transmitted downward into the detailed schedules that affect what happens in the customer order department and on the receiving dock, the plant floor, and the shipping dock.

A similar approach can be applied to the demand side. If you have forecasts for individual products, reconcile them with the aggregate Sales Forecasts in Executive S&OP, thereby insuring that the volume plans and the mix plans are in sync. This was done in the Live Pilot and here we're saying that this practice needs to be continued and expanded.

As we said back in Chapter 4, we believe the best way to develop aggregate sales and operations plans is *not* to develop all the detail and then add it up. Rather, the detailed plans need go out only to around the Planning Time Fence, that point where the specifics of individual products must be known. For most companies, this is a matter of several days or weeks, possibly several months. What we're recommending here is that, within that Planning Time Fence, the detail data match the aggregate. Outside of that time fence, as we've said more than once, there's little or no need for large amounts of detail.

Appoint the Executive S&OP Process Owner

In Chapter 8, we mentioned that the Design Team Leader, following a successful implementation, frequently transitions to become the Executive S&OP Process Owner. This is not a project role, but rather is a permanent position to oversee the ongoing operation of Executive S&OP.

This doesn't always happen. So, during this expansion phase, you should do one of two things: a) confirm that the Project Leader has been appointed to the role of Process Owner or b) select a Process Owner and start to get him or her deeply involved in the Executive S&OP process. Of course, the Process Owner should have all of the same qualifications and characteristics discussed in Chapter 8 with regard to the Design Team Leader.

The duties of the Executive S&OP Process Owner include:

- Supervise the administration of all five steps of the Executive S&OP process.

- Assure timely and quality participation in each of the five steps.

- Facilitate the Pre-Meeting (step #4) to assure that points of conflict are surfaced and resolved, or referred to the agenda for the Exec Meeting (step #5).

- Facilitate the Exec Meeting.

- Administer a periodic process audit/assessment to assure continuous improvement (see Chapter 17 for details).

- Ensure that Exec Meetings have been scheduled for the next six to twelve months.

Develop the Executive S&OP Policy

A lot of people feel the same way about rules and regulations as we do: we're not wild about 'em. Having said that, we hasten to add that a formal Executive S&OP Policy is necessary for the successful implementation and operation of the process. It doesn't have to be anything fancy, and with luck, it will fit on one or several pieces of paper.

Phase II is a good time to go work on this and to complete it. Some companies will get a start on the Policy in Phase I, but it shouldn't be buttoned up because we're simply not smart enough — we haven't even had the Live Pilot yet.

This document should spell out the following:

- The objectives of the company's Executive S&OP process

- The steps in the process

- The participants in each step of the process

- Actions to be taken at each step and what each step owes to the subsequent step

We recommend that this document be signed by the President and others as appropriate.

On the next page is an example of an Executive S&OP Policy patterned after one developed by a company we're familiar with. Please note: This company held formal meetings in its Demand Planning and Supply Planning phases. They were dispersed geographically and thus had to have prearranged meeting times so that all participants could be there, either in person or by conference call. As we said earlier, some companies don't find it necessary to have formal meetings in these early steps; rather, they work the process in individual face-to-face or telephone sessions.

Coming up next: How to keep the process from slipping and to make it better and better.

ACME WIDGET COMPANY — EXECUTIVE S&OP POLICY

Sales & Operations Planning establishes the overall level of sales and manufacturing output, expressed in families, to form the company game plan. Its primary purpose is to establish rates of activity that will achieve the company's objectives, including: meeting customer service and revenue goals, raising or lowering inventories and customer order backlogs, maintaining a stable work force, and enhancing the effectiveness of new product introductions.

1. The Exec Meeting is held monthly in conjunction with the scheduled Officers' meeting. Attendees:

President/CEO	VP Marketing	VP Product Development
VP Finance/CFO	VP Operations	VP Sales
At least two members of the Pre-Meeting Team		

Actions include: resolution of open issues from the Pre-Meeting, authorization or modification of Pre-Meeting plans, changes to the Business Plan, new product issues, and others as appropriate.

2. The Pre-Meeting is held monthly on the third Friday following the fiscal month's close. Attendees:

Controller	Logistics Manager	Product Development Managers
Customer Service Manager	Master Schedulers	Product Managers
Demand Manager/Analyst	Plant Managers	Sales Administration Manager

Actions include: development of plans to ensure a balance of demand and supply, formulation of decisions, recommendations, and agenda for the Exec Meeting, review of long-term capacity constraints, and obsolescence issues. Considerations will include: customer service levels, market strategies, inventory goals, current forecasts and backlogs, new product strategies, financial plans, current status, and capacities.

3. The Supply Planning meeting is held on the third Wednesday following the close of the fiscal month. Attendees:

Capacity Planner	Demand Manager	Plant Managers
Controller	Master Scheduler	Purchasing Manager

Actions include: review of capacity information resulting from the new forecast, review of material availability and lead time problems, manpower planning issues, cost absorption issues arising from production rate changes, and problems with new product introductions and obsolescence.

Any critical resource — manpower, equipment, supplier — whose required capacity varies from its demonstrated capacity by more than +/– 5 percent must be reviewed for action and possible discussion at the Pre-Meeting.

4. The Demand Planning Meeting is held on the second Friday following the close of the fiscal month. Attendees:

Controller	Distribution Planners	Product Managers
Customer Service Manager	Logistics Manager	Sales Administration Manager
Demand Manager/Analyst		

Actions include: approval of a forward 24-month unit and dollar forecast, review of product family trends, new product introduction issues, and special product and customer demands.

Mid-cycle adjustments to the demand and supply plans can be made as required, by following the above steps on a tightly compressed schedule.

Authorized: _____ _____ _____ _____ _____

President   Vice President   Vice President   Vice President   Vice President

Revision #: _____ Effective _____

Chapter 17

Continuous Improvement

There are two main pieces to this important topic: internal and external. "Internal" means within the Executive S&OP process itself, and "external" refers to processes outside of Executive S&OP — other processes that affect customer service, inventories, customer lead times, and so forth.

Internal Improvement — Critique of the Exec Meeting

Two tools exist to help companies make continuous improvements in their Executive S&OP processes, one of which we've already seen. It's the last item on the agenda of the Executive S&OP meeting: critique of the meeting[1]. If you do this periodically, we can almost guarantee that you'll be delighted with how much better the meetings become. It doesn't need to take a lot of time, normally five or ten minutes.

One good way to conduct this critique is to go around the room and ask each person to give his or her reaction to the meeting and point out areas for improvement. We've observed some companies do the critique very effectively by each person assigning a numerical grade to the meeting on a scale of 1 to 10 and stating the reason for that grade. Some companies make it a practice to let the President go last and make the concluding remarks.

Some companies put even more structure to it. They have a short list of elements that are scored collectively by the group. The Executive S&OP Process Owner then keeps track of each element's progress over time. Also, specific issues arising from this process should find their way into the action register for the respective meeting.

Internal Improvement — The Executive S&OP Checklist

The checklist is the second element in continuously improving the Executive S&OP process and is shown in full in Appendix F. As you can see, it contains 33 items that can be rated on a scale of 1 to 4. Also included are instructions for scoring the responses and evaluating how well the Executive S&OP process is being used.

We recommend that you begin using the checklist during the first or second month following the Pilot. It's unlikely that you'll score very high on the first evaluation, but that's okay. Working the checklist at this early stage will point out the areas where you're doing well, and that's good feedback. It will also point out what remains to be done, which at this early stage will be quite a bit.

---

[1] This can also be a valuable process for the Pre-Meeting and others.

Your primary focus should be on completing the items on the project schedule, so the checklist results should be viewed as supporting information to the schedule. In some cases, however, we've seen people modify the project schedule based on results of the checklist. As you go forward into months five and beyond, the project schedule will play a somewhat lesser role and the checklist should become more dominant in directing what needs to be done.[2] The action items that result should find their way into the meeting's action register. In some cases, responses to questions can charter the establishment of an ad hoc project team to address and resolve issues.

External Improvement

Executive S&OP's contribution to continuous improvement in other parts of the company's operations is addressed in item 14 on the checklist, which reads:

> Demand/supply strategies for each product family are formally reviewed quarterly in the Pre-Meeting and Exec Meeting, with a view towards increasing customer service targets, reducing inventory targets, and reducing customer order backlog targets.

Let's say that, for one of your Make-to-Stock families, your target customer service level is 98 percent and your target finished goods level is fifteen days' supply. Let's say further that you've been hitting those targets for some months now. So what should be done?

What should *not* be done is to do nothing. The spirit of continuous improvement should lead the company to target either an increase in the customer service target, a reduction in the inventory/backlog target, or possibly both. So how should that be done?

Well, it's usually not enough to simply change the numbers on the page. What needs to be done is to get into the underlying processes and to start asking some questions:

- Why do we need 15 days of inventory to give 98 percent customer service?

- What process changes could we make to cut the inventory down to 12 days and not hurt customer service?

- What if we reduced the changeover time on the equipment that makes the product for this family? That means we could make shorter production runs, our inventory would go down, and customer service wouldn't drop and might even increase.

- Could we do anything to reduce the forecast error on the items in this family? If so, we'd need less safety stock and could give the same or better customer service.

---

[2] For more on this topic, see *Sales & Operations Planning: The Self-Audit Workbook*. It contains checklists and guidelines for the evaluation process. It includes not only the Executive S&OP checklist, but also ones for *Sales Forecasting* and *Master Scheduling*. The Workbook is available from www.tfwallace.com.

- How about cutting manufacturing and purchasing lead times? If we could do that, we'd become more flexible and that means giving higher customer service with equal or lower inventories.[3]

Another opportunity here concerns time zones and fences. Let's say that Company Y has the following time fence set at the end of month three: inside of here, no production rate changes beyond + or − 10 percent. When was that last changed? If it's been that way ever since they started on Sales & Operations Planning, it seems to us that they're falling down on the continuous improvement side of the process. We recommend that Operations work hard at becoming more flexible so that Company Y can give better customer service, reduce inventories, and improve its financial picture. When they become more flexible, that should be reflected in their time zones.

What we're getting at is that there's a lot more to continuous improvement than changing the numbers on a piece of paper. Rather, the key is to improve underlying processes. The important contribution of Executive S&OP here is that it raises the visibility of process improvements to the top management team and expresses them in terms that are easy for them to understand: customer service, customer lead times, inventory investment, and so forth.

Please refer to Appendix F, which contains the checklist for Executive S&OP, taken from *Sales & Operations Planning: The Self-Audit Workbook*. It details the principles, the checklist items, and scoring instructions.

---

[3] Discussions such as these have led companies to investigate, and subsequently implement, Postponement — with enormous benefits.

Chapter 18

Full Financial Integration

Once all the product families are on Executive S&OP, it's time to tie the financials together fully. However, it's important not to attempt this until the process has become stable and has the full confidence of the executive team.

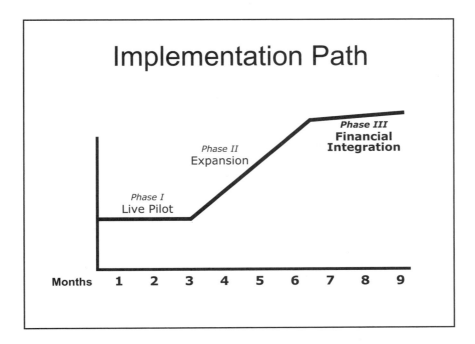

This is because the financial people in most companies have had an effective way to project the financial future of the business. In many cases, they've developed their own forecasts, made their own assumptions, and projected the future in a way that was not always directly connected to changes in demand and supply. Making this change — from independently developed projections to using the demand and supply data from Executive S&OP — can be a major shift in many organizations, one of those difficult behavior change issues that we discussed earlier. However, it's necessary; it's what enables the entire company to operate internally with one set of numbers.

We've already dealt with getting future financial data from the Executive S&OP process — things such as gross revenue, cost of goods sold, finished goods inventory levels, and so on. In this chapter we'll discuss the integration of that data with financial data from other parts of the business. When this is done effectively, several things happen:

- The pro forma[1] Profit & Loss Statement (P&L) and the pro forma Balance Sheet are directly connected to the appropriate data from Executive S&OP.

---

[1]   This refers to projections of future performance in financial terms.

- The budgets can become flexible and change with the dynamics of the business.

- The annual Business Planning process becomes easier and more effective.

Let's take a look at each of these.

Pro Forma P&L and Balance Sheet

The Profit & Loss Statement (P&L) and the Balance Sheet are the primary documents used to report the *current* financial status of a business. When integrated with Executive S&OP, they can become more aligned with the dynamics of a changing business and can show the *future* planned financial status of the business. This pro forma financial information can then be used as part of a powerful simulation process for future planning.

For the pro forma P&L, the primary input from Executive S&OP is the forecast and the related cost of goods sold. Projected overhead absorption, over or under, can be derived using the Operations Plan as the basis for this.

On the pro forma Balance Sheet, the primary input from Executive S&OP is the projection of Finished Goods Inventory. Other Balance Sheet elements getting some S&OP-related help can include Accounts Receivable, Raw Material Inventory, and Work-in-Process Inventory.

Several last points:

- In a traditional budgeting environment, the budgets are developed once per year and often are "frozen" for the year, even if things change. They're often used as a benchmark to measure individual financial performance. Energy must then be spent to explain variances that are the result of agreed-upon business changes.

  In a mature Executive S&OP environment, when a decision is made to accept a change on either the demand or the supply side of the business, the budgets can then be adjusted to reflect that change. As such, financial performance measurements are compared to a budget that reflects accepted changes.

- With Executive S&OP, the yearly process of establishing the annual Business Plan is not nearly as arduous. All of the dynamic demand and supply data is already established by the monthly Executive S&OP process for a rolling horizon of 18 or more months. Much of the data that's needed is already there. Thus, developing the annual plan is not the same old "grind out the numbers" process. It becomes much less of a major energy drain.

Figure CG-6a, in the back of the book, shows the sales projection for the current fiscal year, which includes nine months of actuals and the remaining three months of sales forecast. We can see that Acme is projecting sales of almost $2.7 billion, almost a quarter billion above the original plan.

In CG-6b, we can see the overlay of the fiscal 2008 projection from Executive S&OP, calling for sales of about $2.8 billion.

Managing with S&OP-Generated Financial Information

An important step in the overall financial integration is to aggregate all the dollarized product family information into one view of the entire business, a sort of "master spreadsheet." Obviously, this can't be done completely until all of the families are on S&OP. And even then you might not have it all because of other revenue streams that are outside the array of product families. One approach in such cases that's proven helpful is to create a "Miscellaneous Family," to serve as a collector for atypical streams of income. Other companies just disregard this kind of thing and compare the total sales projection (out of S&OP) with a Business Plan number adjusted to exclude the miscellaneous incomes.

The total company dollar aggregation — the master spreadsheet — serves another purpose over and beyond sales and margin projections. For companies with Make-to-Stock families, it projects the planned levels of finished goods inventory for the total business. This can be valuable in companies whose business is highly seasonal. Frequently such companies engage in preseason production with a corresponding build-up in finished inventories. The inventory dollars can get quite large and can represent a significant cash commitment that should be planned for well in advance. With S&OP operating in dollar mode, this kind of information is always available on the master spreadsheet, updated each month to reflect changing conditions.

Once the master spreadsheet is available, it can be used in a somewhat similar fashion as the product family spreadsheets, particularly as regards performance to plan. Actual financial results can be compared with the plan for those periods. Projected sales and margin dollars can be compared with the Business Plan and appropriate corrective action decided upon.

And this leads us to one of the key issues regarding Executive S&OP and running the business. Sometimes S&OP's latest fiscal year call — actual YTD plus forecast, in dollars — does not match the Business Plan within a few percent. In that case, what should be done? Well, you could do nothing and change neither plan. Or you might change the Sales & Operations Plan, change the Business Plan, or change them both. Let's look at each option, starting with the first one mentioned.

Change neither. We recommend against this. Leaving these two very important plans with a gap between them results in running the business with two sets of numbers. The Sales & Operations Plan is directing our ongoing activities — what we buy, what we make, what we sell. It's saying one thing, while the Business Plan — representing our commitment to the corporate office, the board of directors, and so forth — is perhaps saying something else.

This can create confusion, lack of control, a diminishing of the perceived importance of both plans, and a greater risk of not hitting the Business Plan. Not good.

Change the Sales & Operations Plan. This is appropriate, provided that more is changed than just the numbers. Let's assume that the latest S&OP call for the total company is projecting a five percent shortfall in revenue compared with the Business Plan.[2] Changing that number is easy. The hard part is to determine where the additional revenue is going to come from. Which families can be stimulated to generate increased sales? Are the resources available to support that, or if not, when will they be?

This not only calls for evaluating product families and resources. It means developing specific plans to increase sales, e.g., promotions, pricing, sales force incentives, perhaps accelerating new product launches. It means changing the Sales & Operations Plans for all families affected, then tracking performance against the new plans as the months unfold, and continuing to take corrective action as indicated.

Cost reduction can also play a role here, but that is normally outside the scope of Executive S&OP.

Change the Business Plan. In the abstract, this should be easy to accept. After all, the Business Plan was put together some months before the beginning of the fiscal year. It's old. Doesn't it stand to reason that when a company is some months into the fiscal year, it will have a better handle on how things are likely to go? We think so. Well, then, why do so many companies resist changing the older plan to match the newer plan? Because as we said above, the Business Plan is a commitment to people up the line.

Do those folks up the line care deeply about whether Product Family A is 4 percent below plan and Product Family B is 5 percent above? Normally no. They're interested in the bottom line, i.e., in whether the business is going to generate the revenues called out in the Business Plan. The "mix" of revenue from family to family is normally the concern of the people running a specific business, but not the board of directors or the corporate office.

So we recommend that, as a general rule, the Business Plan numbers for *individual families* should be changed to reflect how the Business Plan numbers will be achieved. When the sum of the individual families doesn't equal the bottom line for the total business, it's time to develop plans to cover the shortfall — and then express those plans into both the Business Plan and the Sales and Operations Plans. And, at the end of the day, if it's not possible to hit the Business Plan, if all else has truly failed, then the bottom line of the Business Plan should be changed also.

All of the above results in running the business with one and only one set of internal numbers. People who do it that way will tell you that it's a very good way to manage. John Jordan, CFO at Graco Children's Products division of Newell-Rubbermaid, says: "Sarbanes Oxley has taken away our ability to manage the results, so predicting the impact of sales and supply performance on a quarterly basis is critical in maintaining integrity with the Street. Executive S&OP is a big help in this."

From elsewhere on the organization chart comes a similar endorsement. Here's Melissa Takas, financial analyst at V&M Star, a manufacturer of pipe for the oil and gas industries: "We are now dealing with numbers that have real credibility."

---

[2] Back in Chapter 1, we pointed out that some publicly traded companies use two sets of numbers: one for Wall Street, containing plans expected to be attained, and one for internal purposes with stretch goals, which may or may not be completely achieved. We went on to say that they run with one set of internal numbers, the stretch goals. That point applies in the discussion that follows; the stretch plan is the Business Plan.

As this financial integration occurs, many things become possible: risk assessment (to be discussed in Chapter 21), the "top management war room" (Chapter 22), and the "running delta" (also in Chapter 22) become practical and can dramatically enhance the company's decision-making capabilities.

* * * * *

FREQUENTLY ASKED QUESTIONS

What happens if the financial people never get on board with all of this?

In short, you'll continue to operate with disconnected numbers, and hence with people marching to different drummers. The people in demand and supply will probably continue to hedge to "protect" themselves from the disconnected financial projections.

Perhaps the worst consequence is that there is no forum for controlled debate about the intrinsic conflicts that exist within a business. If the financial people exercise their concerns and questions behind closed doors, others in the organization will never have an opportunity to counter them. The end result — everyone will be working based on different assumptions and considerations. Not a good thing.

As we said before, get the financial people on board and participating early, during the Live Pilot. They're needed then, and even more so when it comes time for the full financial integration.

Chapter 19

Executive S&OP in Complex Environments

To review: Executive S&OP is, among other things, a process to balance demand and supply. This monthly process culminates in the Exec Meeting, where the leaders of the business make decisions regarding the demand/supply balance and ensure that the financial and operational numbers are in sync.

What follows is a series of examples of how Executive S&OP can be used in somewhat more complex environments than a one-business, one-location operation. Please keep in mind that these examples are suggestions, based on fairly extensive experience certainly, but not "the only way to do it."

Multi-Site, Multi-Business Executive S&OP

Let's explore the issue of where Executive S&OP decision-making should take place. Should it occur at the corporate office of a Fortune 50 conglomerate with a dozen operating businesses? How about the field sales office in Los Angeles? Or maybe the plant in North Carolina?

The answer to all of these questions is "probably not." There's a principle here: *Executive S&OP needs to occur at that level in the organization where demand and supply come together, and where responsibility for the bottom line of the business resides.* Other parts of the overall organization can play a role; they can provide input into the Executive S&OP process or they can review its results. For example:

- It would be difficult to "do Executive S&OP" at the plant in North Carolina, if in fact other key parts of the business are located elsewhere, organizationally as well as geographically. Demand and supply do not "come together" at most plants. Rather, the plants are an element of the supply side of the business, one that has an important role in the Supply Planning phase of Executive S&OP. But that role is not central; it's not the pivot point for the process.

- Similarly, the sales office in Los Angeles could not be a focal point for Executive S&OP. The people there may play a key role in Demand Planning, but they are not directly involved in the supply side of the business.

- The corporate office at the Fortune 50 corporation may review, directly or indirectly, the results of the Executive S&OP processes at the individual business units. The people there might look at aggregated sales numbers, overall inventory projections, and the like. However, Executive S&OP would not be *occurring* there. To do the process centrally for each of the 24 business units would result in a terribly inefficient use of corporate executive management's time, as they struggled through a dozen meetings of an hour and a half each.

What's even worse than being inefficient, it would be ineffective. Two reasons: most people at corporate would probably lack the *intimate* knowledge of the individual businesses necessary for effective decision making, and equally important, they're not accountable for achieving the plan; accountability for that resides with the people in the business units.

Let's now look at some other examples, starting with simpler ones and moving to the more complex.

Multiple Sales and Marketing Units

When a given producing division is providing product to other business units, it needs processes to ensure that all demands are recognized. The solution often centers on the immediate customers.

Roger was the general manager of Division P. A majority of their production went to other divisions in the corporation. Roger questioned his division's ability to use Executive S&OP effectively because they had no direct contact with the other divisions' customers. Roger said that there was no way they could do a good job of Demand Planning because they couldn't get to the customers.

His view changed when he started to look upon the other divisions as the customers. His job performance would be judged in part on how well his division was able to service these "internal customers." The better job he did, the happier his internal customers would be, and the more highly Roger's division would be regarded.

Division P's approach to Demand Planning for the sister divisions was to work closely with their people in projecting future demand, to get the best forecast numbers they possibly could. They visited these divisions once a month and were in contact between visits. Were these forecasts "highly accurate?" Of course not. Were they better than before? Absolutely. Was there more that could be done? Yes.

The sister divisions were, in effect, distributors. Since distributor inventories mask the true demand, the forecasting process needs to look through the distributors into their customers. In this way, they will see true trends and patterns of demand. Thus, the next step for Roger's division should be to work with the sister divisions' Sales and Marketing units and get access to the true demand coming from their customers. (We'll have more to say about distributors and their inventories later in this chapter.)

Multiple Plants

Many companies have more than one plant, and of course Executive S&OP has to reflect that. Naturally, companies with aligned resources have an easier time of it, and here's an example.

Company A has plants in Pennsylvania, Illinois, Texas, and California. Company A uses Lean Manufacturing very effectively, and thus has aligned resources; its plants match up closely with the product families. Therefore, it was able to set up subfamilies by plant. For example, Product Family 9 is produced both in Pennsylvania and Texas, so the company established two subfamilies: Product Subfamily 9 — Pennsylvania, and Product Subfamily 9 — Texas.

These subfamilies are forecasted and planned individually in the Demand, Supply, and Pre-Meeting steps. For the Exec Meeting, the main focus is on the total Product Family 9. However, there are times when it's necessary to look at a subfamily, for instance when there's a serious overload in one of the plants, say Pennsylvania. Scenarios could then include:

- Transferring production from Pennsylvania to Texas, with an increase in freight costs.

- Adding a third shift in Pennsylvania, with some increase in overhead at that plant.

- Offloading some other volume from Pennsylvania to Illinois, with only a minor freight cost penalty but requiring some new equipment in Illinois, resulting in a capital expenditure not in the current year's capital budget.

Obviously, cost is an important factor in this, and this is a good example of the importance of having folks from Finance & Accounting involved in the Supply Planning and Demand Planning phases in addition to the Pre-Meeting and Exec Meeting.

Having multiple plants usually means having remote plants, and that means that key people from each plant will need to take part in the overall Executive S&OP process. Normally it's not considered practical to have these folks travel into headquarters each month, nor is it necessary in this day of teleconferencing, video conferencing, Web conferencing, and whatever. What can be helpful is to bring each one of these players into headquarters once during the early phases of implementation, perhaps when their respective plants are being added to the process. Some companies then bring the appropriate people into headquarters for an Exec Meeting once a year, as a refresher, and for some face to-face contact with people whom they normally don't see in person.

Combination Families: Make-to-Stock/Make-to-Order, Make-to-Stock/Finish-to-Order, Make-to-Order/Finish-to-Order

Some families contain both Make-to-Order and Make-to-Stock products. Some are a mix of Finish-to-Order and Make-to-Stock. Or Finish-to-Order and Make-to-Order. In these cases, it can be useful to break out the product family into two subfamilies: say, one for the Make-to-Order products and the other for Make-to-Stock. These are reviewed separately during the Demand, Supply, and Pre-Meeting steps.

Then for the Executive S&OP meeting, combine them onto one spreadsheet for the total family. This spreadsheet might have to be a bit different. For a Make-to-Stock/Make-to-Order combination, it would almost certainly have to show both an inventory section and an order backlog section, so that these competitive variables can be visible. It may also be desirable to break out the demand separately into the Make-to-Stock and Make-to-Order components. A similar approach could be followed for Make-to-Stock/Finish-to-Order families.

Combination Families: Manufactured and Outsourced

Company D is in the container business. For one of its families, the product is sourced internally from one of its thirteen plants, from domestic suppliers, and from suppliers in Asia.

In this case, the product family is broken up into three subfamilies by source. The subfamilies are reviewed during the Demand, Supply, and Pre-SOP steps. The Exec Meeting looks at the family spreadsheet, which in this case shows separate supply information for each of the three different sources.

Field Inventories

Company B sells through distributors, and also through manufacturers' representatives who stock the product. The inventory at these reps is on consignment; Company B owns it until it's sold. The Executive S&OP process, to be effective, must have visibility into that inventory. Without it, a key component of the supply side of the demand/supply equation is missing, resulting in less-effective decisions.

The inventory of Company B's products at the distributors is not on consignment; the distributors own it. However, shouldn't Company B be looking at the distributors' inventories of their products, even though that inventory is not owned by Company B? We certainly think so. Actually, this piece of inventory is more important than what is at the stocking reps, even though Company B doesn't own it. Why? Because it's a much bigger number; there's a lot more inventory at the distributors than at the stocking reps.

In summary, to effectively balance supply with demand, you need to see the finished inventories in the field, regardless of who owns them.

Our colleague Bill Montgomery points out that it's often a good practice to involve distributors and reps in the forecasting process. Here also, a Pareto approach can be used: talk to the high-volume distributors and reps. Also, it may be beneficial to talk to some lower-volume, "high-value" ones — the folks who have particular insight into the market and a good feel for what's coming down the road.

S&OP for Nonphysical Products

Company M is in the aerospace business. One of its groups makes highly engineered widgets for things that fly fast: spacecraft, satellites, and missiles, among other things. Within the Systems group, there are several separate divisions that produce and sell products. However, the design of the products is done centrally within the group.

Product Design and Development performs work for the producing divisions, but it also does advanced engineering projects for NASA and others. Thus, there is a wide variety of demands placed on this department; further, Product Design and Development has a finite supply of engineering talent, which is not easy to increase in the short run.

Might this be a logical application for Sales & Operations Planning, even though there are no physical products involved?

Well, the Group Vice President had the same idea. Following successful implementations of Executive S&OP in the product divisions, he asked the design and development folks to consider the process. They did consider it, and they adopted it, and they adapted it to their particular operation. Some of the information displayed at their meetings was a bit different, but the process itself was virtually identical to that used in the divisions that make and sell the product. (See also *Report from the Field: Worldwide Support Group*, on page 138.)

We're seeing Executive S&OP applied in more and more organizations that do not produce a physical product: banks, retailers, companies that outsource 100 percent of their products, and so forth. Nowhere is it written that you must be making physical products in order to take advantage of this tool. If you have problems balancing demand for nonphysical outputs with supply, Executive S&OP might be a big help.

Global Executive S&OP

A special problem exists for large multinational corporations, operating around the world and wanting to achieve a high degree of coordination. In other words, coordinate globally; act locally. Percy Barnevik, formerly the head of ABB, a large multinational, said, "We are not a global company, but a collection of local companies with intense global coordination." We believe Executive S&OP should support this concept.

Before we get into the nitty-gritty of this, let's review some fundamentals. Executive S&OP balances demand and supply, and it integrates operational plans and financial plans. So, with a business operating globally, balancing demand and supply and integrating operational plans and financial plans may need to occur globally as well as locally.

The Goliath Widget Corporation[1] is one of these large multinationals doing a good job in using Executive S&OP to achieve that intense global coordination. They believe that the process must provide the means to globalize where necessary and appropriate, without centralizing everything and thus taking away local initiative, ownership, and energy. Here's how Goliath does it:

- The world is broken up into sections, called *entities*. An entity is defined as a geographical area where demand and supply principally align — specifically 80 percent or more of the demand is satisfied by supply sources *within the entity*. North America, Latin America, Europe, and Asia/Pacific are entities.

- The function of entities is to "localize" the Executive S&OP process to the issues and problems unique to the area. It also helps address the cultural differences of how the people handle problems and conflict, not to mention minimizing the issues of time differences and geographical separation. In other words, it gives local ownership to the process, but at the same time it provides a defined and disciplined process to deal with global issues as they arise, through coordination among entities.

---

[1] A fictitious corporation, based on a number of real ones.

- There can be no entity if there isn't both demand and supply present within the entity. For example: the South American Region has demand but no supply, and thus it is not an entity; South America's demand is supplied primarily by North America. Thus, South America has a role in the Demand Planning phase for North America and the other entities from which it draws product.

- Each of the entities does the standard monthly Executive S&OP process up through its Exec Meeting, led by a local process owner who knows the people, the culture, and the demand and supply issues.

- Please note that *inter-entity coordination* occurs in both the Demand Planning and Supply Planning phases. This is to ensure that all relevant demands are recognized and that the resources are present to meet them. In those cases where resources are insufficient due to inter-entity demand, this is addressed in the Pre-Meeting step or sooner, probably including further communication and coordination among the involved entities.

- The global processes of financial review, coordination, and decision-making occur following the Executive S&OP cycles at the entities.

Refer to Figure 19-1, which shows the monthly Executive S&OP process expanded to include the steps necessary for global coordination.

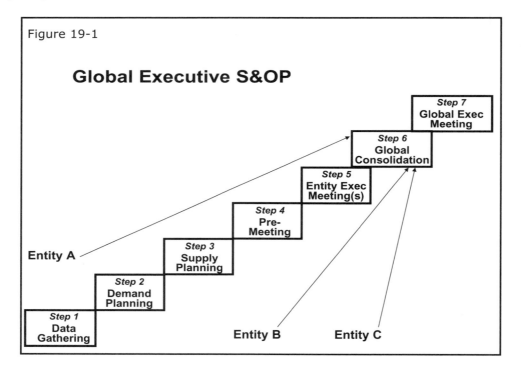

Step 1: At Goliath, data gathering activities are done centrally. They're using a large enterprise software system (ESS/ERP), so it's one central effort to close the books at month-end and distribute the resulting data electronically.

Step 2: Demand Planning is done primarily within the entities. However, sometimes portions of the markets are managed globally, meaning that some central demand people could be involved with the entities.

Step 3: Supply Planning is done primarily within the entities, and must recognize inter-entity demand. This is demand from one entity that is supplied from another entity, for example demand from South America supplied by North America.

Steps 4 and 5: The Entity Pre-Meetings and Exec Meetings are held within the entities in much the normal fashion. Again, one difference might be the need, on occasion, to recommunicate across entity boundaries in order to achieve a balance of demand and supply.

Steps 6 and 7: The Global Roll-Up & Reconciliation process and Global Executive Meeting are of course done centrally and attended (electronically) by key players from the entities. This is where reviews and adjustments of the rolled-up financials take place, as well as any rebalancing of global demand and supply. Rebalancing at this level occurs rarely, because it's almost always handled among the entities themselves during their Executive S&OP cycles.

Please note: Goliath is exclusively in the widget business, and for them this model works well. On the other hand, a conglomerate — such as Textron or General Electric with a portfolio of very different businesses — would use Executive S&OP somewhat differently. The global model shown here could work nicely for each business. However, at the corporate level, the overall global process would consist almost exclusively of financial reviews, because balancing demand and supply across different businesses with widely different products is rarely a possibility.

Executive S&OP in a Very Large Business

The Mega Corporation is a $20 billion business and virtually all of that volume is in one business unit. There is a multiplicity of products, brands, sub-businesses called SBUs (strategic business units), and so forth.

Mega struggled with how to fit Executive S&OP into the business. The challenge was how to have effective S&OP processes at a "low enough" level to make them meaningful but still to have corporate top management — the ultimate leaders of the business — in the loop. They settled on the SBU as the proper level for Executive S&OP, but with provisions for roll-up to the corporate level. This would allow primary decision-making to reside with the VP/General Managers of each of the five franchises, followed by a consolidation step and presentation to Corporate, as shown in Figure 19-2 on the next page.

If you're thinking that this looks similar to Global Executive S&OP, you're right on the mark. Each SBU leader runs his or her business with its attendant Executive S&OP process. The consolidation and corporate Exec Meeting phases keep the corporate office tied into the process; that meeting is very similar to the Exec Meeting for Goliath that we just saw in the section on Global S&OP.

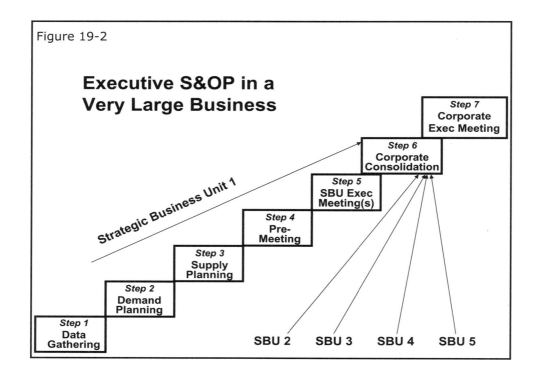

Figure 19-2

Executive S&OP in a Very Large Business

*   *   *   *   *

FREQUENTLY ASKED QUESTIONS

We have a similar situation to the one just shown for the Mega Corporation, but we're a highly matrixed organization. All of our manufacturing is centralized into one group, so the SBUs don't "own" their manufacturing. Can Executive S&OP work for us?

Absolutely. It's a bit more of a challenge in this kind of situation, but it's quite practical as long as responsibilities are clearly defined and followed. Think about the organization chart for SBU 1. There should be a line between the VP/General Manager and the executive responsible for the supply side of SBU 1's business. Does it really matter if that line is solid or dotted? Many successful users of Executive S&OP would say no, because they have exactly this situation and are making it work.

Part Four

Getting It Right and Making It Better

Prologue to Part Four: Beyond Implementation

BOB STAHL: We're nearing the end of the book. At this point, what more needs to be said?

TOM WALLACE: Well, since this part of the book is labeled "Beyond Implementation," there's a highly important topic that needs to be addressed: the issue of reimplementation.

Research has shown that a majority of companies using S&OP are not happy with the results. Many of them have attempted to implement the process, but it's simply not working well. Frequently they need to reimplement Executive S&OP because it was never really implemented the first time. Or, in some cases, the second time.

If your company is in this category, you really do need to read Chapter 20, "Fixing a Broken Executive S&OP Process," which is coming up next.

BOB: And in the chapter after that, we're going to talk about risk: how Executive S&OP can help companies deal with the risks of supply chain disruptions, both in terms of anticipation and also recovery. We feel this is particularly relevant today as supply chains stretch out and, in the process, become more vulnerable to disruptions.

Executive S&OP has the potential to be quite beneficial to companies in risk anticipation and recovery, but so far it has underperformed. We really don't see much formal S&OP activity in this risk area, and we hope Chapter 21 helps to change that.

And following the chapter on risk, we'll get out our crystal ball.

TOM: Ah yes. We'd be remiss if we failed to address the future of Executive S&OP, because the overall business environment is going to get harder not easier. Two factors bear on this: complexity and the rate of change.

The business environment will not get simpler; if anything, it'll become more complex. So also with the rate of change; it's very high today and it'll probably accelerate. This is, after all, the first part of the twenty-first century.

Executive S&OP has to support that. That's its job. So the process will have to evolve and grow and become more powerful as the future unfolds and needs increase.

Chapter 20

Fixing a Broken Executive S&OP Process

News flash: not all users of Sales & Operations Planning and Executive S&OP are happy with their results. But you knew that already, didn't you? The question is why — why are a majority of companies using the process not getting excellent results? Well, there's a host of reasons, including:

- Top management not involved

- Insufficient education

- Insufficient discipline and self-discipline

- Conflict aversion

- "It's not our job; that's for Supply Chain to worry about."

- Ongoing data problems

- Inadequate demand planning and supply planning processes

- Inadequate Pre-Meeting

- Exec Meetings that:

  – are "show-and-tell" (not decision-making sessions)

  – are unfocused

  – focus on the short term, the "crisis of the week"

  – have too much detail

  – condone finger pointing ("It's *your* fault." "No, it's not — it's *your* fault."

and on and on. We could probably list a whole bunch more but we'll rest our case here.

What if your Executive S&OP process is not working as well as you would like? For example, people begrudge the time spent in preparation, meeting attendance is poor, teamwork is not improving, the process is not productive, or all of the above. Or maybe it's not that bad, but there's a belief that it could be much better. What do to? We recommend that you do the following:

1. Gather a small group of like-minded people who believe in Executive S&OP, but agree that the current process is not working as well as it should. If possible, include someone from top management — to

provide valuable input and perhaps to serve as the Executive Champion during the reimplementation, if there is to be one.

2. Answer the question: Is top management engaged? If they are, and appear to sincerely want the process to get better, then go to work fixing the problems indicated in the Self-Audit. Given a positive situation with top management, it's likely that most of the problems are in the B-item (data) and C-item (computer) areas, and should be fixable without major problems. Perform a Self-Audit every month for the next four to six months. If your scores are reaching and remaining at a high level, then reduce the frequency of the Self-Audits.

3. If top management is not engaged, then you are facing a reimplementation. The first issue is: will top management agree to an Executive Briefing? If yes, do it; make Go/No-Go Decision #1, and proceed with the Live Pilot, which in this situation may take less than 90 days. Or, it may not. Here's why:

   • First, the steps involved in a reimplementation are largely the same is with a first-time implementation. One difference is that some of the tasks have already been done satisfactorily and won't need to be repeated. That's the good news.

   • The bad news is that the reimplementation will be more difficult, because Executive S&OP is likely viewed within the company as a failure. Hence it will have to live that down.

   • Many companies needing to reimplement are in better shape on the C and B items than the A: they've got the spreadsheets and graphs working well; the data is solid; and the data feeds are okay. The problem classically is with the people; odds are they've been undereducated (on the process), underinformed (about objectives), undermotivated, and underwhelmed. The people we're talking about here are almost always top management.[1]

As we said, the steps in reimplementation are largely the same as in a first-time implementation. This book contains a tool to help you with managing the reimplementation: the List of Tasks Involved in Implementing Executive S&OP in Appendix A. We recommend you use that document to schedule and manage the project.

4. Sometimes top management won't agree to an Executive Briefing. Why? Well, they may have received some kind of a briefing from an unqualified S&OP "expert." And/or the company didn't take the 90-Day Pilot approach and thus didn't gain the substantial learning benefits that it provides. So the problem is that top management won't agree to an Executive Briefing because they believe it has already been done. Their feeling: "Been there; done that."

If top management won't agree to an Executive Briefing, will they agree to bring a qualified Executive S&OP Expert in to conduct what we'll call an "Outsider Audit" of the process? If yes, do it. (Even though the Self-Audit has already been performed by the company's own people and is most probably quite valid, often the outsider — as we're all aware — has credibility that the insiders lack.)

---

[1] This condition is the most common cause of dissatisfaction with Executive S&OP. Frequently it comes about through what we call the "build it and they will come" approach: middle management people go to great pains to get the data, lay out the reports, develop the processes, and so on. When it's all presented to the Executive Group, if it ever is, they push back. They don't understand it; they're not familiar with the concept; they haven't bought in.

The final step in the Outside Audit should be a presentation of the audit results to top management, by both the Executive S&OP Expert and some of the group working on Executive S&OP. The Executive S&OP Expert covers the overall Executive S&OP process, objectives, benefits, and so forth; the group members present the audit results. As such, this session can also serve as an Executive Briefing, the desired outcome of which is a decision to fix what's wrong (in effect, a Go/No-Go Decision #1). Then proceed with the Live Pilot.

5. If top management won't agree to a Briefing or an Outside Audit, what should you do? Well, what you should not do is give up. Try to keep your Executive S&OP process going through all of the Pre-Meeting steps. Where practical, start to display your S&OP spreadsheets and graphs in meetings with top management. Try to present recommendations within the framework of the Executive S&OP displays. Use the same format to present alternative scenarios to support difficult decisions.

Further, keep your Executive Champion engaged and work with him or her to move the process upward in the company. He or she might be successful in getting a standing time slot, say twenty or thirty minutes, once a month at an executive staff meeting. Use this to recap the Pre-Meeting. After this has been happening for a few months, start asking the executive group to ratify the decisions made in the Pre-Meeting and to make decisions beyond their scope of authority. If this approach works well, expand it, get more of top management's time, and make it look more and more like an Executive S&OP Meeting.

Steps like these might pay off in the long run. Moreover, the downside risk appears to be almost nonexistent.

In this chapter, we've identified two documents in this book that can be of value in fixing a broken Executive S&OP process: the Executive S&OP Effectiveness Checklist (Appendix F) and the List of Tasks (Appendix A). We hope you use them and that they prove helpful.

Chapter 21

Risk Management and Executive S&OP

Risk is an important topic in business today, and supply chains are right in the middle of discussions about risk. Potential disruptions — of moderate to major consequence — are more likely today than twenty or even ten years ago due to natural disasters occurring at an increasing frequency, terrorism at the highest levels ever, and supply chains lengthening and becoming less robust.

This last point is particularly important for our purposes here. We're talking about the risks of disruptions to the supply chain. Other types of risk — stemming from currency gyrations, political instability, transformational new products from competitors, and so forth — are not on our radar screen here. Even within the supply chain, there is much more to managing the risk of disruptions than the effective use of Executive S&OP.[1] That said, our focus here is on supply chain disruptions and the role Executive S&OP can play in both anticipating them and recovering from them.

A disclaimer: in the prior sentence, we used the phrase *can play* as opposed to *is playing*. This implies that Executive S&OP is not yet doing as much in this area as it has the potential to do. That's true. On the other hand, we believe that in some cases Executive S&OP is being used to support risk management activities, but that role is not formally recognized. We'll see an example in a moment.

It's our premise that Executive S&OP is ideally suited to help companies deal with disruptions to the supply chain. It can help somewhat in the *anticipation* of disruptions and, more specifically, in the *recovery* from them once they occur. After all, its jobs include providing a window into the future, balancing demand and supply, and helping companies deal with change.

Our hope here is that this chapter will stimulate companies' thinking and lead to solid progress. Much needs to be done in this important area and we surely don't have all the answers.

Examples of supply chain disruptions include:

- Strikes: not only in one's own plants and the suppliers' plants but also dock, truck, and rail strikes

- Quality issues: product recall, inability to produce product to specification, failure of incoming material, and so forth

- Supplier failure: inability to obtain all the material one needs, perhaps as a result of being put on allocation by the supplier — plus the quality and strike issues already mentioned

- Natural disasters: fires, floods, hurricanes, earthquakes, and so forth

- Man-made disasters — fires, terrorist attacks

---

[1] For those interested in a broader view of supply chain risk, we recommend the book *The Resilient Enterprise* by Yossi Sheffi, 2005, Cambridge, MA: MIT Press.

These disruptions can be further delineated by impact (the amount of damage they will cause) and probability (the likelihood they will occur). For example, a low impact disruption might be a transient quality problem: fairly quickly corrected and causing some, but not great, difficulties in the supply chain. On the other hand, a terrorist attack — for example, 9/11 — certainly qualifies as a high-impact event, in that it triggered a virtual stoppage of the transportation system in the U.S. and led to massive upheaval in the overall supply chain.

A low probability event might be a major fire at one of the plants; this is relatively unlikely to happen. On the other hand, a demand spike — a sharp surge in demand up and back down — is a high-probability event in many companies.

In Figure 21-1, we see examples of the different types of disruptions, relating the two key factors of probability (how likely is it to happen?) and impact (how bad will it hurt?). The examples given are merely intended to help clarify the concept; they may or may not be relevant to your organization. This approach may be helpful in assessing the specific supply chain risks facing your organization and in making plans for restoring the demand/supply balance should they occur.

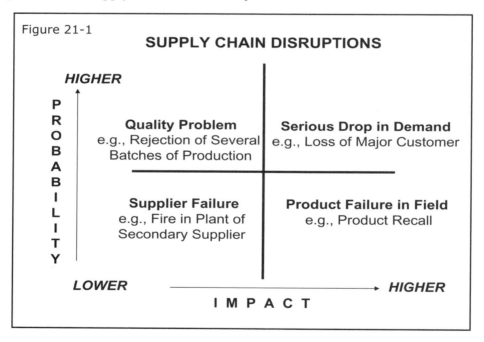

Figure 21-1

SUPPLY CHAIN DISRUPTIONS

Demand Disruptions

Supply chains, of course, include not only the view "backwards" to the suppliers but also "forward" to the customers. Thus, supply chain disruptions can include issues on both the demand and the supply side.

The most common example of a demand-triggered disruption is a "demand spike:" a sudden and unanticipated upward surge in demand. Probably the mother of all demand spikes occurred several years ago, shortly after 9/11. The Bush Administration indicated that a potential solution to chemical or biological gas attacks by terrorists was to put duct tape on all windows and doors. (Ironically, if one does this well enough, it will also keep out oxygen — not a good thing.)

We're familiar with a company that makes duct tape. As people stampeded to buy duct tape, this company's stocks were quickly depleted at the retail level, and in distribution, and then at the plant. Even after the hysteria died down, it took them quite a while to recover, refill the pipelines, and once again provide good customer service.

Most demand spikes[2] are not as severe as this one, involving as it did a new use for the product. Here's a more typical example:

Demand Spikes

Your biggest customer — whom you refer to as the "800-pound gorilla" — sends in a very large order out of the blue. This order is not in the forecast, and it's for three times more widgets in Product Family A than they've been taking in recent months. This may cause some problems, certainly, but on balance it's good news: they want to buy more of your product. How does a company deal with that? In other words, how does it recover?

Let's say that your monthly Executive S&OP cycle ended just a week before this very large order arrived. Well, you certainly can't afford to wait several weeks for the next planning cycle to address this problem. What some companies — successful users of the process — do in this situation is to immediately conduct a "mini Executive S&OP cycle." This is an accelerated version of the standard five-step Executive S&OP process, dealing only with those parts of the business affected by the demand spike: the related materials, capacity, other resources, and perhaps other customers.

The "Mini" S&OP Cycle

They conduct, quickly, a Demand Planning step, a Supply Planning step and, if necessary, hold an abbreviated Pre-Meeting and Exec Meeting. Decisions are made and the issue is resolved at the lowest level possible. If the folks in the Demand Planning step can solve the problem by shifting customer commitments around somewhat, fine. Case closed. Or perhaps the Supply Planning team can pull a rabbit out of the hat: excellent. Problem met and resolved.

But if not, the issue gets elevated to a mini Pre-Meeting for resolution and then, if the situation warrants, to a mini Exec Meeting These meetings are typically much shorter than those in the monthly cycle; they focus on the issue at hand and related factors, with probably more than a few of the participants attending via telephone.

Throughout the abbreviated process, they try to keep the steps, the report formats, and the decision-making process the same — because the people are familiar with those processes and know they're solid. And of course the information is in dollars as well as units; the Finance folks are involved in this process,

---

2   The flip side of a demand spike is a demand crash, a huge example of which is the Tylenol story of the early 1980s. After people died from ingesting Tylenol laced with cyanide, demand went to zero. Nobody wanted to buy Tylenol. Actually, supply also went to zero as Johnson & Johnson scrapped all inventories. So demand and supply were in balance, and the recovery — at least from our perspective — looks more like a new product launch, including as it did major product and package redesign.

remember? The dollar view, obviously, is necessary to make decisions that are in the best financial interests of the company.

Thus there is a coordinated and rapid response to the demand spike. At worst, and hardly ever likely, the company may conclude that it can do nothing. Or perhaps it can supply some but not all of the order when the customer wants it, with the balance later. Or just maybe it can meet all of this customer's demand and keep its commitments to other customers, who may be only "600-pound gorillas" not 800-pounders.

A few years ago, Tom co-wrote a book called *ERP: Making It Happen* with Mike Kremzar, the Procter & Gamble VP mentioned on Chapter 1. Mike stated one of S&OP's big benefits to P&G was the creation of a common, agreed-upon game plan throughout each business.

This makes mid-period corrections, of the type we're talking about here, much easier than before. Mike indicated that they no longer had to spend the first several days debating whose numbers were right; there was *only one set* of numbers. Now they could get right to work and fix the problem.

Supply Disruptions

First, let's recognize that the opposite of a demand spike is a supply crash. And, as with demand spikes, they range from relatively minor to highly serious. The very minor supply problems are typically handled by people in production, procurement, and supply chain. It's seen as part of their jobs, and they've been doing this for years.

For example, Figure 21-1 in the upper left hand quadrant shows the example of the rejection of several batches of production. Now if the product involved were a C-item — one of not much significance — then the issue would be addressed at the appropriate level in the organization and corrective action taken. On the other hand, if the product were a "Super A-item" and the company would be unable to ship that product for several weeks, the situation would be a lot more serious.

Supply crashes such as this one can be viewed as very similar to demand spikes, involving as they do a sudden, sharp dislocation of the demand/supply balance. And the recovery process is much the same.

The company can employ a variation of the process used for demand spikes: a "Mini-Executive S&OP Cycle." The variation is that the Supply Planning phase would probably begin first, followed by a Demand Planning phase, and then perhaps a revisit of the supply situation. This is not dissimilar to the issue presented in Appendix E, where we talk about highly variable supply.

Here again, if the situation can be solved in either the demand or supply phases, fine. Problem met and resolved. If not, the issue is elevated to a "mini-Pre-Meeting" and, following that if necessary, to a "Mini-Exec Meeting."

Risk Anticipation

So far we've been talking mainly about recovering from disruptions. Let's focus now on *anticipating* disruptions: certainly an important issue, as in "an ounce of prevention is worth a pound of cure."

On the demand side, Dr. Larry Lapide, of the MIT Center for Transportation & Logistics, identifies hedging, postponement, aggregation, and supply buffers as appropriate strategies for mitigating demand risk.[3] These apply also to the supply side. And, of course, they're all handled very nicely within the framework of Executive S&OP.

Larry's colleague at MIT, Yossi Sheffi, addresses the risk anticipation issue in his book, cited earlier in this chapter: *The Resilient Enterprise*. He states that the first line of defense when disaster is expected to strike is typically redundancy: extra inventory, surplus capacity, alternative suppliers, and so forth. We believe that Executive S&OP is the logical forum for the decisions to initially establish these kinds of redundancies and, over time, to modify and improve them.

These decisions *should be made* within the framework of Executive S&OP, because the amount of risk will rise and fall over time. Executive S&OP, with its forward visibility and its monthly top management participation, is the ideal process for this purpose.

Report from the Field: OTC Consumer Products[4]

Company Description: OTC Consumer Products develops, produces, and markets non-prescription medicines; primary customers include mass merchandisers (WalMart, Target), drug chains (Walgreens, CVS), and supermarkets (Kroger, Safeway).

Their Experience: OTC is an experienced and highly successful user of Executive S&OP. They feel that this process enables, among other things:

1. Timely identification of issues

2. More effective, consistent decision-making

3. Improved flexibility to deal with change and conflict

The company makes effective use of the Mini-Executive S&OP process for dealing with the risk of disruptions to the supply chain. Interestingly, they use it both for actual disruptions (recovery) and also for potential disruptions (anticipation). Here are two examples:

---

[3] *Journal of Business Forecasting*, Summer 2007.

[4] The identity of the actual company has been disguised, at the company's request

Recovery. Several years ago, one of OTC's key manufacturing facilities got hit hard by a rash of hurricanes, shutting down the company's ability to supply certain forms of their most popular product. OTC's Mini-S&OP process includes meeting weekly as an integrated and cross-functional team, deciding on product and customer priorities, as well as what to communicate to customers. The Executive Group was kept in the loop with periodic updates and formal presentations at the Exec Meeting. They did this until they reached targeted inventory levels, and the situation normalized, at which time the Executive Group authorized the disbanding of the Mini-S&OP team. OTC uses this same process for significant changes in demand.

Anticipation. In the latter half of 2007, OTC convened a cross-functional Mini-S&OP team based on news about potential changes in children's dosing of cough/cold medicines, for safety reasons. This had the potential to sharply impact customer service and inventory. The Mini-S&OP team did scenario planning for the Executive Group, and thus positioned the company to respond quickly and effectively in the event of a product recall.

The Moral of the Story: We believe that the experiences of OTC Consumer Products and others prove that Executive S&OP can play an important role in risk avoidance and recovery.

Here's an example of Executive S&OP supporting risk anticipation, once again from our friends at the Acme Widget Company. Since we last saw them, they've implemented Executive S&OP and have done a first rate job of it. The scene is an Exec Meeting.

Good Day at Acme Widget

Executive S&OP Process Owner: *Since we've introduced the new products into Family 5, sales are increasing a lot. Starting this summer, Marketing is forecasting 100,000 per month for that family.*

Based on that, we're going to need additional equipment in Plant A by November. The lead time to procure, install, and make the equipment operational is six months, which means that we'll need to place an order three months from now — in May.

President: *How solid are you Marketing folks with that forecast? What's the range?*

VP Marketing: *We're comfortable with it. The high-side forecast is 120,000 and the low is 80,000.*[5]

President: *Let's test those for the new equipment buy.*

Process Owner (calling up the S&OP graph containing the low-side forecast): *Okay, as you can see here, at 80,000 we won't need the new equipment until February. And . . .* (calling up a different graph,

---

[5] "Range forecasts," containing both a high number and a low number, are generally considered superior for new product introduction, as opposed to "point forecasts," i.e., one number only.

containing the high-side forecast) . . . *here's the picture on 120,000. It says that we'll need the equipment on-line in August. That means we need to order now.*

VP Operations: *We're dealing with two different capacity strategies here: lead and lag. If we lead and buy now, we run the risk of having excess capacity for many months. If we lag and don't buy, but the high numbers materialize, we'll be incurring the costs of high overtime, expediting, poor customer service, and lost business.*

President: *Right now I'm leaning towards the high plan. I think it makes the most sense strategically but I'm concerned about the financial risk. Marty, could you have your folks in Finance dollarize these plans against the different levels of sales? I'd like to reconvene tomorrow afternoon and put this to bed.*

CFO: *Sure, John, we'll be ready.*

Conclusion

There's a bit of a paradox here. We've felt for some time that Executive S&OP is not contributing to the challenges raised by the risks of supply chain disruptions. But perhaps we were wrong. As we dug into this, we learned several things.

First, Executive S&OP has been helping in this area for some time. However, its contributions have not been recognized as supporting risk management. Thus there's been more happening than meets the eye, so to speak. But even allowing for that, much remains to be done.

We hope to see, over the next few years, more and more companies utilizing Executive S&OP *formally* as a primary management tool to deal with risk, for both anticipation and recovery. Ways in which this could be done might include:

- Making risk issues a permanent agenda item for each Exec Meeting

- Also at the Exec Meeting, reviewing actual and planned redundancies — hedges, excess capacity, and the like — and modifying them as conditions change

- Identifying, to the extent possible, the degree of anticipated risk facing individual product families and displaying this information on the product family graphs and spreadsheets

- Formally reviewing risk recovery experiences to learn how future recoveries might be done better and also how to better anticipate risk

As we said earlier, we don't have all the answers. We don't even know what all the questions are. But we are convinced that the Executive S&OP process has a key role to play in this area. We challenge the successful users of the process — both current and yet to come — to integrate risk management into it.

Chapter 22

The Future of Executive S&OP[1]

A coworker described the planning process at the company where one of us then worked: "With our eyes fixed firmly on the past, we back confidently into the future." Hmmm. That's obviously not the way to do it and, by the way, that company is no longer around.

Executive S&OP is largely about the future, forward visibility, anticipation. It stands to reason, then, that a book about this process should also be forward looking. So here it is: where we see Executive S&OP heading over the next five to ten years.

First, it will continue to grow in popularity because of these reasons:

- As more and more companies are successful with Executive S&OP, the word gets around. Further, as executives from those companies sometimes move to other organizations, they take their enthusiasm for the process with them and implement it there.

- As we saw earlier, the Lean Manufacturing community is discovering Executive S&OP. This trend will accelerate because Lean and the Executive S&OP process work together extremely well. This synergy will become increasingly obvious to many Lean users, even though the process was not invented as a part of Lean Manufacturing.

- As more and more supply chains extend around the world, Executive S&OP increasingly will be viewed as essential to harmonize the entire supply chain. It sits at the pivot point, the center of the supply chain, which is where the demand/supply balance needs to occur.

- Next, software will play a greater role in Executive S&OP. As complexity and the rate of change increase across the industrial landscape, the need is emerging for S&OP software to become more powerful, effective, and useful to executives and managers — particularly its simulation capabilities.

- We're seeing more and more uses of Executive S&OP outside of traditional manufacturing:

  - Retailers today are faced with a much higher volume of their products coming from half a world away. Executive S&OP, with its forward visibility, is proving to be helpful in dealing with the extended lead times that result. Radio Shack is a good example of this; they get most of their products far from the United States and they are using an excellent set of S&OP processes to help with that.

  - Companies that we call "designer/distributors" are using Executive S&OP widely. These are companies that design the product, distribute the product, and market the product — but do not make the product. They use contract manufacturers exclusively. Microsoft comes to mind; they don't produce packaged software, X-Boxes, keyboards, and the like — but they surely design, distribute, and sell a bunch. Does it matter who owns the factory? Executive S&OP doesn't care.

---

[1] Much of this chapter is based on material in Chapter 8 of *Sales & Operations Planning: The Executive's Guide.*

– Engineering and design organizations don't produce a physical product but they're beginning to use Executive S&OP, as we saw in Chapter 15. Both of us have experience with companies utilizing Executive S&OP in their centralized engineering groups. Those folks have demand and supply issues also.

– We're starting to see service businesses use the process. One of the largest banks in Australia is reporting great success using Executive S&OP in its consumer loan division. First, demand for consumer loans can be quite variable. Second, the supply of trained people to process them cannot be increased overnight; the new people must be hired and then trained. Executive S&OP's forward visibility and its focus on balancing demand and supply make it a natural for this kind of environment.

Report from the Field: The Kangaroo National Bank[2]

Company Description: The Kangaroo National Bank (KNB) is based in Australia, with operations there as well as in New Zealand and the United Kingdom. It employs over 20,000 people; as with most banking operations, many of its operations are relatively people-intensive.

Their Experience: During 2002–2003, KNB was faced with a good news/bad news kind of situation. The good news was that interest rates were declining substantially and that created greater demand for consumer loans. The bad news was an unprecedented level of backlog: loan applications in house but not processed. Demand (for loans) had sharply outstripped the ability of the bank's workforce to process them. As the backlog grew, lead times stretched out and unhappy applicants went elsewhere for their loans.

This is another classic demand/supply balance problem. Demand is variable: rising and falling due to interest rates, economic conditions, consumer confidence levels, the seasons of the year, and so on. The supply resources consist largely of people. Much of the loan application process can be automated but, prior to loan approval, a human being needs to be in the loop. Too few people means increased backlogs and hence increased lead time for customers to get their money and hence lost business. On the other hand, too many people can mean substantial unnecessary costs with their attendant drain on profitability.

KNB turned to Sales & Operations Planning to fix the problem of demand/supply imbalances, even though they could find no other banking company using it. They implemented the process and their results have been excellent:

• 24% productivity improvement over two years

• 8% increase in output during the same period

---

[2] The identity of the actual company has been disguised, at the company's request.

- 6% reduction in unit cost

- Reduced rework levels resulting from higher staff skill levels and increased morale

- Shorter lead times and superior customer service

Plus the S&OP project paid for itself in a little over six months.

The Moral of the Story: Our colleague from Down Under, Phil Heenan, sums it up well: "We've had a number of people from this organization come to our courses, which are aimed at manufacturing companies. No matter, they took what they learned and put it to work at the bank. I think this shows that balancing supply and demand is critical in almost all businesses, not just manufacturing companies who have been the traditional users of S&OP and associated techniques."

The Top Management War Room

Please use your imagination for just a bit as we peer confidently into the future. We predict that, within a few years, the following kinds of capabilities will be widespread.

Imagine that Executive S&OP is operating successfully in the company of which you're the President. You and your staff are meeting once a month to authorize Sales and Operations Plans that will harmonize demand and supply and to integrate those plans with the financials. In an Exec Meeting, while discussing a product family that contains a highly significant new product launch, you raise an issue:

"I'm getting some input from the field that our competition may be working on a similar product. If they beat us to the market, we'll have just dumped millions of dollars into a "me-too" product, and that's just not an option. If we can move our new product launch up by six weeks, I'm certain we can get to the market first. Can we do that? And, if so, what else might be impacted?"

Your Supply Chain director, Susan Carter, is projecting the S&OP display for this product family onto a large screen from her PC, which contains all of the relevant demand, supply, and financial data. Susan asks for a brief time-out while she runs "what-if" scenarios using your S&OP simulation software. Within a few minutes, she has answers:

- Plan A is feasible and has the lowest cost but it will require getting certain material from a supplier who has had quality and delivery problems in the past — not a good thing for a new product launch.

- Plan B is also feasible and has moderate costs, but will cause shortages on products 234 and 345.

- Plan C can work and has the lowest total cost, but will cause serious stockouts across much of the product line, because of capacity constraints in Fabrication.

Armed with these facts, you and your staff are well equipped to make the right decision. You may select Plan B: it's feasible; it has only slight negative impact; and it accelerates the new product launch. But there may be more; let's say Carol the CFO raises a question:

> *"Now that we've picked Plan B, I have a question. We're moving the new product from next quarter into this quarter. To do that, we're pushing out production of established products into next quarter. I've got to give an earnings projection to Wall Street before long, so what do I tell 'em?"*

Susan replies: *"Carol, here are the deltas on Revenue and Gross Margin between the current plan and Plan B. They don't appear to be major, but you'll probably want to take it into account in developing your earnings call."*

The phrase "top management war room" comes to mind. We're looking forward to the day when this type of capability is widespread: Executive S&OP using simulation software running at virtually the speed of light, allowing rapid development of alternative scenarios; supporting major demand/supply decisions with facts, not guesses; in a top management setting.

The Running Delta and the Red Zone

There's more. Today, future plans for demand and supply are authorized at the Exec Meeting and, shortly thereafter, they begin to change. Why? For any number of reasons:

- Customers change their minds and we have to shift schedules. Thus, demand and supply have changed.

- A critical process in the plant goes down, due to an unanticipated machine failure, and we have to shift schedules. Thus, supply and its related demand have changed.

- A key supplier has a flood, perhaps caused by a hurricane. Everything's up in the air, no pun intended. The demand and supply picture has changed dramatically.

- You decide to accelerate a new product launch. Here also, demand and supply have changed from how it looked at the last Exec Meeting.

Wouldn't it be nice to know how far your current plans have drifted from what you authorized? What's needed is the capability to calculate very rapidly the difference between a) the dollars in the volume plans authorized in Executive S&OP and b) the dollarized sum of the detailed schedules currently in place.

We call this the "running delta." This means you could walk into your office in the morning, hit a few keys on your keyboard, and see the running delta: how closely are the current plans meeting what you and your colleagues authorized?

Now pretend you're the head financial executive in this business. Every 90 days, you face one of the most difficult parts of your job: making the earnings call to Wall Street, or to corporate so that the CFO can make the call. Within days of the end of the quarter (called the "red zone") that doesn't sound so difficult. But it can be and often is, because of the factors cited above. The running delta will certainly make red zone calls, for the current quarter, more valid and more certain – as well as guidance calls made for future quarters.

Audit Trail of Decisions Made

In some companies, seven-figure decisions are made routinely by people with five-figure incomes. We saw an example of this earlier from the executive who complained about "turning knobs not connected to anything." Seven-figure and sometimes eight-figure decisions were made routinely at the level of detailed scheduling, and not in the President's office. Executive S&OP helps to minimize this kind of problem.

But even so, wouldn't it be nice to have a "system of record" — the capability to archive, for each decision of any substance, who made the decision and why? This would have been a good thing ten and twenty years ago, but now it's even more important in this era of enhanced governance requirements,[3] which have been placed on businesses by their governments.

Further, for internal purposes, it's often helpful to look back and see *why* we decided to do something; and what the conditions and assumptions were that underlay the decision. This is not to point fingers and to affix blame, but rather *to learn* from what we did so that we can do it better next time. As we said earlier, better decision-making processes lead to better decisions. The system of record is part and parcel of better decision-making processes.

*　　*　　*　　*　　*

To sum up, industry needs these kinds of capabilities: the top management war room, the running delta, and the system of record. It's ready for them; and they're now available. Thanks to some superb new simulation software, these kinds of capabilities will become widespread before long. It's no longer a question of if but merely when.

Given this, more attention will be given to the financial integration side of Executive S&OP. The use of S&OP-generated financial planning numbers in leading edge users today is quite good, and this practice will become stronger and more widely used in the future. It will play an increasing role in the making of red zone and guidance calls by the CFO. But that's not all.

Adam Szczepanski, a CFO we know, has experienced the benefits of Executive S&OP in two different companies. Adam had this to say: "This process can do a lot more for the CFO than assist in making earnings calls. All CFOs should have a strategic Financial Plan that increases the value of the enterprise. The contribution of Executive S&OP is that it provides formal input on a monthly basis into the strategic direction. It brings life to a strategic process that usually occurs only once or twice per year."

---

[3] In the United States, we call this Sarbanes-Oxley.

Due to these factors, Executive S&OP will move more visibly into the executive suite. It will become widely recognized as an essential element in the top management tool kit, enabling executives and managers to run their companies better — in many cases far better — than before.

It directly involves relatively few people within a company. Done well, however, it can have a highly postitive affect on many people inside and outside the company, throughout its supply chain, and beyond.

*   *   *   *   *

We hope this book proves helpful to you whether you're investigating Executive S&OP, implementing it, or trying to improve it. We definitely welcome your feedback, so please don't hesitate to get in touch.

Thanks for listening.

Tom and *Bob*

info@tfwallace.com

Appendix A

List of Tasks Involved
in Implementing Executive S&OP

Our intent here is to provide a list of what generally needs to be done for a successful implementation.

Please note: this is a generalized list and must be tailored to become the individual company's plan. As such, some tasks may not be necessary and can be dropped, while others may need to be added. Overall, this list follows the Implementation Path diagram, which was introduced on page 72. It assumes that Excel™ or other spreadsheet software will be used and thus no software selection step is shown.

The list is intended to be entered into your project management software; to eliminate the tedious task of manually entering all this data, simply download it from our Web site — www.tfwallace.com and go to Free Downloads section.

PHASE I-A — LEARNING AND DECISION #1

010   Conduct Exec Briefing

020   Make Go/No-Go Decision #1

030   Assign Preliminary Responsibilities and Team Memberships

040   Conduct Kickoff Session

PHASE I-B — PREPARATION FOR THE LIVE PILOT

050   Confirm Responsibilities and Team Memberships

060   Identify Product Families and Subfamilies

070   Determine Product Family Units of Measure

080   Identify Supply Resources to Be Tracked

090   Determine Capacity Units of Measure

100   Determine Planning Horizon

110   Select Pilot Family

120   Set Demand/Supply Strategies for Pilot Family

130   Determine Sources and Automate Feeds for Actual Sales and Forecasts

140   Determine Sources and Automate Feeds for Actual and Planned Production

150   Determine Sources and Automate Feeds for Actual Finished Inventories and Backlogs

160   Develop Formats for Spreadsheets and Graphical Displays

170   Develop Formats for Capacity Displays

180   Design How the Five-Step Process Will Be Used

190   Develop Explanation of the Executive S&OP Process Steps and First-Draft of Executive S&OP Policy

PHASE I-C — CONDUCTING THE LIVE PILOT

200   Conduct the Data Gathering Step for the Pilot Family

210   Conduct the Demand Planning Step for the Pilot Family

220   Conduct the Supply Planning Step for the Pilot Family (and Resources if possible)

230   Conduct the Pre-Meeting for the Pilot Family

240   Conduct the Exec Meeting for the Pilot Family Including a) Full Explanation of Processes b) Review of Draft of Executive S&OP Policy c) Decision-Making

250   Make Go/No-Go Decision #2

PHASE II — EXPANSION

260   Determine Product Families to be Added in Next Cycle

270   Set Demand/Supply Strategies for Next Group of Families

280   Conduct Second Five-Step Cycle, Adding Product Families

290   Begin Resource Requirements Planning, if Not Already Done in the Pilot

300   Begin Addressing New Products, if Not Already Done in the Pilot

310   Begin Comparison of Operations Plan to Master Schedule

320   Determine Product Families to Be Added in Next Cycle, if Necessary

330   Set Demand/Supply Strategies for Next Group of Families, if Necessary

340   Approve Executive S&OP Policy

350   Test the Executive S&OP Process Against the Executive S&OP Checklist

360   Conduct Third Five-Step Cycle, Adding Product Families, if Necessary

370   Determine Product Families to Be Added in Next Cycle, if Necessary

380   Set Demand/Supply Strategies for Next Group of Families, if Necessary

390   Test the Executive S&OP Process Against the Executive S&OP Checklist

400   Conduct Fourth Five-Step Cycle, Adding Product Families, if Necessary

PHASE III — FULL IMPLEMENTATION

410   Ensure That All Product Families and Resources are Covered within Executive S&OP, Either Individually or in Groupings

420   Add Full Financial Tie-In

430   Formalize Business Plan Review within Exec Meeting

440   Add Full Resource Requirements Planning

450   Add Full Simulation

460   Evaluate Other Routinely Held Meetings for Discontinuance or Integration into Executive S&OP Sessions

470   Test the Executive S&OP Process Against the Executive S&OP Checklist

480   Imbed the Executive S&OP Process in the Business

Appendix B

Using Control Charts for Executive S&OP

This appendix describes how to develop and use Control Charts to support Executive S&OP. Control charts are a necessary part of verfying this data, thus making it credible. The actual tool is from the Six-Sigma toolbox.[1]

Control Charts are graphs used to track the performance of an ongoing process. With regard to Executive S&OP, Control Charts track data performance when it has intrinsic variability. The most obvious example of data with intrinsic variability is actual sales. Control Charts are also used to support:

- conversion of unit sales volume projections to gross revenue projections

- allocation of unit production volume plans to specific resource(s)

- conversion of unit volume production plans to a specific resource run rate (hours)

- conversion of unit inventory projections to a storage unit of measure (cubic feet)

- conversion of unit shipping volumes to a transportation unit of measure (rail cars, trucks, etc.)

- conversion of unit volumes to a "soft resource" unit of measure such as engineering, site installation, and so on

- and many others.

Constructing a Control Chart

A Control Chart is a graph showing the mean (average), along with the upper and lower control limits. The upper and lower control limits represent a statistical boundary. If these limits are set at three times the mean absolute deviation (MAD), they will represent greater than a 99 percent probability that all future data points will fall within that range. This is part of the logic of the bell-shaped-curve.

Let's take a simple example and construct a Control Chart. Here's a table showing actual sales of a family of products for the last ten months. Shown are the sales, along with the actual calculated deviation from the mean. The mean is determined by taking the total sales for all ten periods divided by the number of periods or 9320 / 10 = 932.

1	600	-332
2	800	-132
3	1400	468
4	1200	268
5	600	-332
6	1020	88
7	950	18
8	1150	218
9	750	-182
10	850	-82
Total	**9320**	2120 *

*Absolute value (ignoring sign)

---

[1] For a complete discussion of this topic see "The Memory Jogger" series, published by GOAL/QPC, Methuen, MA: www.eoq.org/Goalqpc.htm.

The next step is to calculate the mean absolute deviation. This is accomplished by dividing the total absolute deviation (shown at the bottom of the Mean Deviation column) by the number of data points or 2120 / 10 = 212.

The following abbreviated table displays the statistical probability from the bell-shaped-curve analysis. In this case, it would indicate the probability of the next actual sales data falling within the upper and lower control limits, if set as indicated.

Reliability	Limit Factor
57.6%	1.05 times MAD
89.4%	2.00 times MAD
98.4%	3.00 times MAD

In the chart below, the upper and lower control limits are the mean (932) + or – 3 x MAD (3 x 212 = 636) or 1568 and 296, respectively.

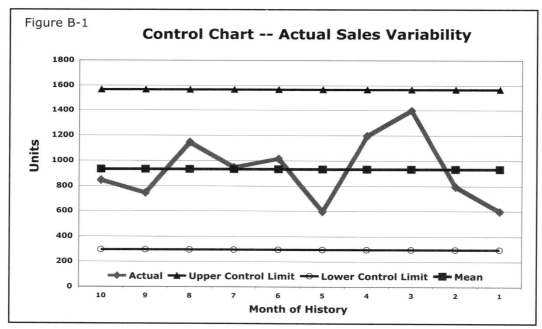

Figure B-1

The use of Control Charts is a vital part of proper data management. Here it would be used to:[2]

• determine the range of expected sales volume variability,

• determine if the next plot of actual sales is the result of common cause or special cause.[3]

---

[2]   If you're thinking that this same logic is used in the calculation of safety stock, you're correct, but that's not our focus here.

[3]   Both common cause and special cause are TQM terminology. Common cause refers to normal, somewhat anticipated events; special cause refers to a more random, largely unexpected occurence.

If a future actual demand for the period were to fall within the upper and lower control limits, that would be normal and would be the result of common cause. If it were outside these limits, it would not be normal but would be the result of special cause. In the second instance, cause and corrective action would be appropriate to properly understand and act upon the cause of the abnormal variation. Depending on the answer, it may affect the future management forecast.

Using Control Charts

Executive S&OP is a process that is fairly data intensive. Beyond the example above, using Control Charts to manage the simplifying assumptions about mix is essential.

For purposes of demonstration here, we'll convert the unit sales volume plan (forecast) of Family A to gross sales revenue projections. For each of the last ten months, Figure B-2 shows the history of the average unit sales price for a unit of Family A. You can see the average sales price went up (from $5.30 per unit to $5.58 per unit) between period 5 and 6, and the variability narrowed. This was probably the result of a price increase/change.

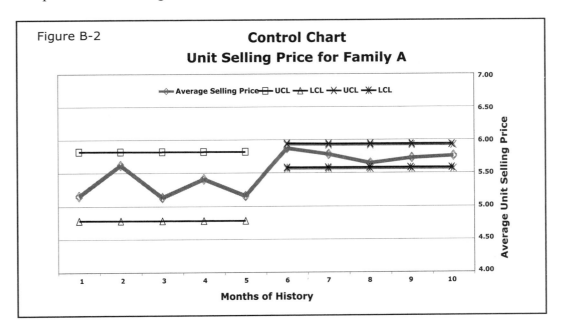

Figure B-2

Control Chart
Unit Selling Price for Family A

The primary use of this simplifying assumption is to eliminate the need to forecast the mix to get accurate revenue projections for Family A volume forecasts. Using the table below, you can draw some very reliable conclusions:

- The probable projection (mean) for 932K units per month for Family A of product will be $5.37 million per month.

- It will be no lower than $5.20 million, and no higher than $5.54 million, given a 99.2 percent probability.

Validating the Assumptions

As we have seen, one of the things that allows Executive S&OP to work is the extensive use of simplifying assumptions, thus avoiding the need for full SKU-level granularity. Proper use of Control Charts must support all of the simplifying assumptions mentioned at the beginning of this appendix. This is to insure that the dynamics of current events are tracked and monitored.

If you don't track the effect of current events on the assumptions, when it comes time to make hard decisions, top management will probably lack the confidence to be firm in their decisions. With solid validating data about assumptions, however, this should not be the case.

Family A Revenue Projection Range

Control Chart Recordings		Volume	Total
Maximum	Upper Control Limit $5.94	932,000	$5.54 Million
Probable	Mean $5.76	932,000	$5.37 Million
Minimum	Lower Control Limit $5.58	932,000	$5.20 Million

Here's Rick Hall, VP of Operations at the Homac Companies: "Doing this eliminates the anecdotal events from casting doubt on the validity of the Executive S&OP outputs. This is true for demand, supply, and financial elements. In our experience, many good questions that have surfaced have been answered, validated, and acted upon through the use of statistical data tracking used to form the simplifying assumptions."

The tracking and monitoring of these assumptions is done each month in the appropriate step of the Executive S&OP process. In this case, the revenue conversion assumption would be tracked during the Demand Planning (Step 2) or Supply Planning (Step 3). It would be brought into other steps only if there were a point that needed to be made.

Appendix C

Software for Executive S&OP

A question we're often asked is: what software do most companies use for their Executive S&OP process?

And the answer is, simply, Excel™ or other spreadsheet software.[1] Companies extract data from their ERP software system, their CRM system, their legacy systems, and so forth, and then load it into Excel™ for processing and display. Virtually all successful users do it this way or they do something close to it. It's the way that Sales & Operations Planning has "grown up" over the last quarter century.

There's both good news and bad news with this, and until recently, the good news has far outweighed the bad.

- Good news — "everybody" already knows Excel™. So the software issue has not been a distraction to the primary work of achieving organizational behavior change. Successfully implementing Executive S&OP is primarily a people-centric task, not software-centric.

- Bad news — without more powerful software, there is lost potential for even greater benefits from Executive S&OP. New capabilities — full simulation, financial linkage, compliance with government regulations, and others — are increasingly important as businesses and their operating environments become more complex and more subject to rapid change.

There is more good news, however. We're seeing the emergence of powerful S&OP-specific software to further enhance the Executive S&OP practices. This more powerful software will support, among other things:

- Complete and very rapid simulation, at both the volume and mix levels, in units and dollars, both inside and outside the Planning Time Fence

- Full integration of Financial Plans and Operational Plans, enabling the business to be run internally with "one set of numbers"

- Volume/mix alignment inside the Planning Time Fence

- Archiving of decisions made, along with the relevant data, to support governmental requirements

Some of these new software tools use Excel™ as the mechanism for graphical display of data. They will, however, be able to retrieve, store, and quickly manipulate much larger amounts of data than Excel™ can.

---

[1] Throughout this appendix, we'll refer to spreadsheet software as Excel™, recognizing that there are other spreadsheet products on the market. Excel™ is used by an overwhelming majority of companies and, in our experience, is superior to the others.

Lately we've been getting more than a few questions from potential users and software suppliers about what a good S&OP software package should contain. Some software suppliers claim to have S&OP software but fall quite short of fulfilling the criteria that follow.

In response to this situation, we've developed a list of criteria for truly effective software for Executive S&OP. Our intent here is to assist companies in evaluating software for Executive S&OP, and to help software suppliers produce more complete and powerful software.

Software Selection Criteria

The criteria come in two sets: a) capabilities already existing in Excel™, and b) new functionality not in Excel™.

Obviously, if a software vendor is using Excel™ for its display tool, then the first set of criteria are met. If not, we submit the following "Excel™ kinds of capabilities as essential:

1. **Pivot Tables** — The ability to easily slice and dice detailed historical data in any number of different ways; on both the demand and supply sides of the business. This capability is used to mine data for developing and managing simplifying assumptions for the future, as well as to investigate significant variability when it is experienced.

2. **Graphs** — The ability to easily and quickly tie data tables to graphs and charts.

3. **User Friendly** — The ability to easily navigate through the various features and functionality, including a "dashboard" type of mechanism.

4. **Full and Rapid Unit Simulation: Volume** — The ability to simulate alternative plans involving both demand (each, cases, gallons, etc.) and supply (hours, head count, tons, warehouse space, etc.) at the volume level, utilizing mix assumptions. This unit simulation answers the question: "Can we do it outside the Planning Time Fence?" These simulations should be done easily and virtually in real time, for example, in an Exec Meeting, without having to break up the meeting and reconvene.

In addition, a first-rate set of software for Executive S&OP should have the following:

5. **Full and Rapid Unit Simulation: Mix** — The ability to simulate alternative plans involving both demand (each, cases, gallons, etc.) and supply (hours, head count, tons, etc.) at the mix level, utilizing granular (SKU) detail. This unit simulation answers the question: "Can we do it both inside and outside the Planning Time Fence?"

6. **Full and Rapid Financial Simulation: Volume and Mix** — The ability to tie dollars to both of the above simulations. Once the unit simulation(s) show that we can do it, the financial simulation answers the question: "Do we want to do it — does this make financial sense?"

7. **Continuous Alignment of Volume and Mix** — The sum of the mix plans, for both demand and supply, is continuously compared to the volume plans. The deltas, where they exist, are displayed to involved users.

8. **Continuous Alignment of Units and Dollars** — A dollarized view of the unit plan is continuously available, and reflects the most recent changes to the unit plan at both the mix and/or volume levels.

9. **Mix Assumption Variability Testing** — The ability to test the variability of the simplifying mix assumptions: any one, or in combinations if more than one.

10. **Financial Conversion Variability Testing** — The ability to test the variability of the simplifying financial assumptions (average selling price, average margins, average costs): any one, or in combinations if more than one.

11. **Demand Variability Testing** — The ability to test the variability of forecasted demand, based on past demand data.

12. **Control Charts** — Needed to track the continuing validity of all assumptions — both mix and financial. When updated plots from the current month fall outside the upper or lower control limits, the assumption would be reviewed and possibly changed.

13. **Conversion to Financials** — Conversion of both detail and aggregate volumes to dollars and financial reports of all types from units, based on simplifying assumptions about revenue rates, and again testing for variability.

14. **Uploading/Downloading** — Easy uploading of data from ERP/CRM/legacy files.

15. **Archiving** — Archived audit trail of decisions made by whom and based on indicated data.

16. **Successful Users** — One or more companies that are operating a highly successful Executive S&OP process, supported by the software in question and exercising the functions identified here.

A Bit of Advice

With regard to getting started, there are two paths you can follow:

1. Use Excel™ to get started, and then shift to more powerful software after you've come up the learning curve with Executive S&OP practices, and after you find better software. In this way, you'll not only be smarter about the Executive S&OP practices themselves, but have a better knowledge of what software features you truly need.

2. Get S&OP-specific software that meets the above criteria and use it right from the start.

If you select choice #2, recognize that you'll be on two learning curves simultaneously: one with the new Executive S&OP processes and their attendant organizational behavior change, and the other learning curve being the new software. The risk is that the software may become a distraction from the management and behavioral issues that make Executive S&OP successful.

Our advice: if you're convinced you need S&OP-specific software, then go for it. If you're not certain of that, get started with Excel™ and get Executive S&OP working well. Then, if you see a need, investigate S&OP-specific software.

Appendix D

The Difference between Production Planning and Executive S&OP

Perhaps the best way to contrast Sales & Operations Planning with its predecessor, Production Planning, is to view them graphically. On the next page, please see Figure D-1, showing the Production Planning method.

Notice that the Sales Planning and Production Planning boxes are separate and sequential. What's implied by this is that Sales and Marketing people put together a forecast and hand it off to Operations, who puts together a Production Plan, which is sent directly into Master Production Scheduling.

Figure D-2, depicting Sales & Operations Planning, looks quite different. It shows both the Sales Planning function and the Operations Planning function occurring jointly, not sequentially. It indicates that there is interaction between the Sales Plan and Operations Plan, which of course is what we've been presenting throughout this book.

The result of the cross-functional Sales & Operations Planning process is the companywide game plan for Sales & Marketing, Operations, Finance, and Product Development — far more than a Production Plan.

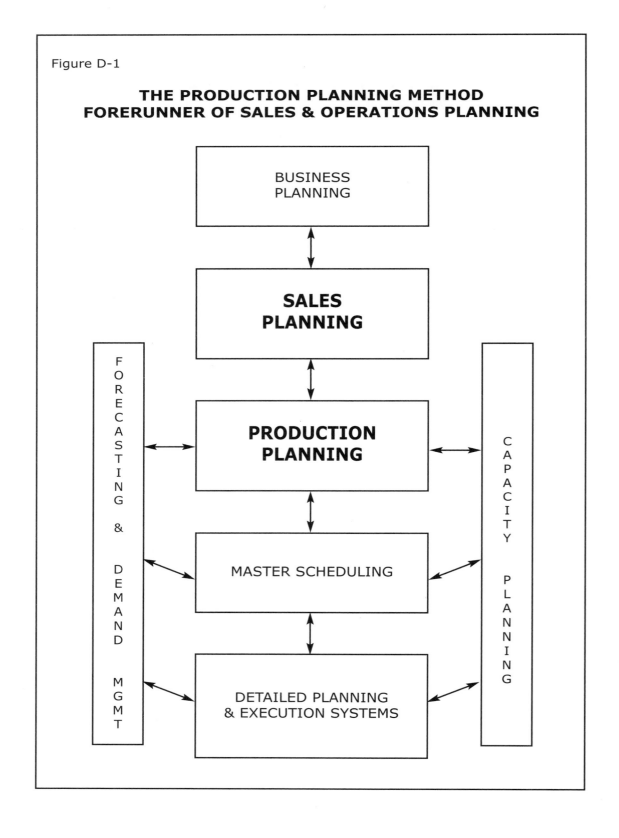

Figure D-1

**THE PRODUCTION PLANNING METHOD
FORERUNNER OF SALES & OPERATIONS PLANNING**

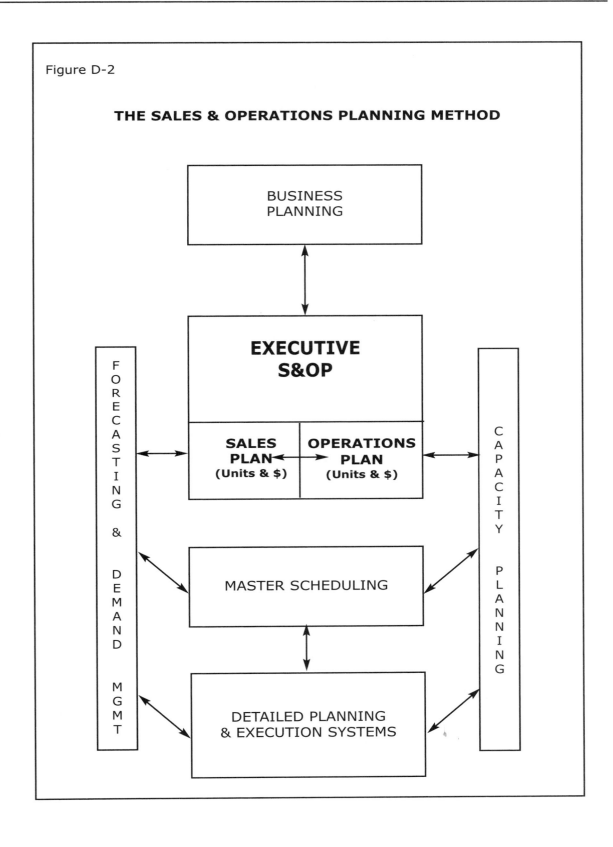

Figure D-2

THE SALES & OPERATIONS PLANNING METHOD

Appendix E

Highly Variable Supply

To use terms from statistics, the standard approach to Executive S&OP treats demand as the independent variable and supply as being dependent. That's why we talk about demand and supply, rather than supply and demand, as the economists do. Demand is the driver.

This is most often the case, but not always. Earlier we saw the example of constrained versus unconstrained demand, the latter being what the company could sell were it not for constraints on the supply side. In this case, supply is the driver — at least until supply is increased until it no longer becomes a constraint.

Highly variable supply is another case of supply being the driver, primarily determining what's going to be sold. Many examples of this occur in the food processing business, where the size of the crop to be harvested determines how many cases of corn, beans, cherries, or whatever are going to be sold.

In this case, the standard Five-Step model for Executive S&OP doesn't do the job. It needs to be modified, to *begin* with an initial Supply Planning phase, then go to Demand Planning, and to a second Supply Planning phase, as shown in Figure E-1.

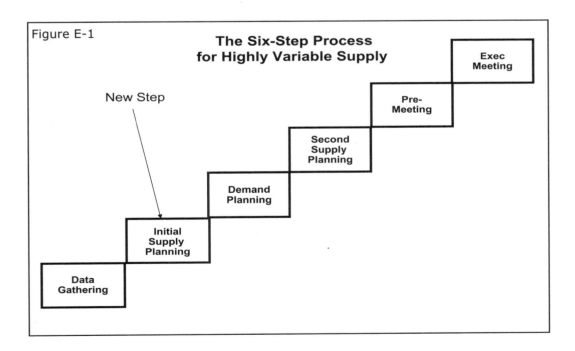

Figure E-1

The Six-Step Process for Highly Variable Supply

This preliminary Supply Planning step, often headed up by Purchasing, attempts to identify the size of the crop that will be available, which of course is a sort of forecast in its own right. This information is passed to the Sales and Marketing people for the Demand Planning phase, where they take into account the predicted supply in formulating their forecasts.

Following this, the new forecasts are passed to the second Supply Planning step. This is necessary to ensure that the specifics of the new Demand Plan are producible. Let's look at the following example from a packer of frozen and canned vegetables:

1. In the preliminary Supply Planning phase, the availability of string beans is projected at one million bushels.

2. Demand Planning people use that number to set their forecasts for string beans. They forecast the equivalent of 300,000 bushels for the canned string bean family and 700,000 for frozen, which is a sizeable increase from last year.

3. The Supply people must then verify that they can freeze and package 700,000 bushels worth of string beans — along with all the other demands for freezing capacity. Plus they need to verify that they have freezer space for that volume, and so forth.

The rest of the Executive S&OP cycle — the Pre-Meeting and the Exec Meeting — happens in the standard manner.

Appendix F

The Executive S&OP Effectiveness Checklist

This checklist is intended to serve as an aid in evaluating the Executive S&OP process within a company. The responses to a given item in the checklist can be 4 (excellent), 3 (good), 2 (fair) and 1 (poor or non-existent). If a given item is not applicable to the company, mark it as NA.

	Ex	Gd	Fr	Pr
1. Executive S&OP is a monthly process involving both middle management and top management, including the President (General Manager, COO, Managing Director).	4	3	2	1
2. The monthly Executive S&OP cycle consists of a Demand Planning phase, a Supply Planning phase, a Pre-Meeting, and an Exec Meeting that includes the President.	4	3	2	1
3. A written Sales & Operations Planning policy details the participants, responsibilities, timing, and objectives of each step in the process.	4	3	2	1
4. Meeting dates for the Pre-Meetings and Exec Meetings are scheduled well into the future, to maximize attendance.	4	3	2	1
5. The Exec Meeting is rescheduled if the President is unable to attend. Other participants who cannot attend a given meeting are represented by their designated alternates, who are empowered to participate in the decision-making process.	4	3	2	1
6. A written agenda is issued at least two work days before each Exec Meeting, highlighting major decisions that need to be made at that meeting.	4	3	2	1
7. The Exec Meeting operates at an aggregate, family level and rarely focuses on individual items.	4	3	2	1
8. The number of product families is in the range of 5 to 15. Subfamilies are used in the Pre-Meeting steps where appropriate.	4	3	2	1
9. Sales & Marketing "own" the Sales Forecast. They understand and accept their responsibility: to provide forecasts that are reasoned, reasonable, reviewed at least monthly, and reflect the total demand.	4	3	2	1

	Ex	Gd	Fr	Pr
10. Operations "owns" the Operations Plan. They understand and accept their responsibility: to develop plans that support the Sales Forecast, meet the demand/supply strategies, and are cost-effective for production.	4	3	2	1
11. The planning for products sourced offshore is done with full recognition of the longer, and potentially more variable, lead times often involved.	4	3	2	1
12. Customer service performance measures (on-time and complete shipments) are reviewed at each Pre-Meeting and Exec Meeting.	4	3	2	1
13. In order to reach target customer service levels, finished goods inventory levels for products sourced offshore are set higher than for domestically sourced products, to compensate for greater supply variability.	4	3	2	1
14. Demand/supply strategies for each product family are formally reviewed quarterly in the Pre-Meeting and Exec Meeting with a view towards increasing customer service targets, reducing finished goods inventory targets, and reducing customer order backlog targets.	4	3	2	1
15. Sales, operations, inventory, and backlog performances are measured against plan at each Pre-Meeting and Exec Meeting. When performance is outside the agreed upon tolerances, then investigation and corrective action is initiated.	4	3	2	1
16. The S&OP spreadsheet contains all key information about a product family on one page: performance to plan, customer service statistics, Sales Forecasts, and Operations Plans; it extends at least fifteen months into the future.	4	3	2	1
17. In addition to quantitative information, the S&OP spreadsheet also shows qualitative, verbal information in the form of assumptions and issues that need to be recognized.	4	3	2	1
18. To identify plant overload/underload problems, separate capacity displays are used where there is not a one-for-one match between product families and production resources.	4	3	2	1
19. Capacity issues at contract manufacturers are reviewed in the Supply Planning and Pre-Meeting phases, and are treated in much the same way as for company-owned plants.	4	3	2	1
20. Effective communications processes regarding demand and supply are in place between the company and its offshore suppliers.				

	Ex	Gd	Fr	Pr
21. New product development issues that may impact the demand/supply relationship are a permanent agenda item for the Demand Planning Phase, Supply Planning Phase, Pre-Meeting and Exec Meeting.	4	3	2	1
22. Potential risks of inventory obsolescence at contract manufacturers are routinely reviewed in the Supply Planning and Pre-Meeting phases, and are elevated to the Exec Meeting where appropriate.	4	3	2	1
23. The Master Schedule is routinely compared with the Operations Plan in Executive S&OP to ensure that the Master Schedule is set at the levels authorized in the Exec Meeting.	4	3	2	1
24. Executive S&OP is a decision-making process. The Pre-Meeting Team decides what recommendations to make to the Exec Meeting, and the Executive Team decides to accept those recommendations or adopt an alternative.	4	3	2	1
25. Simulation is routinely used to evaluate alternative solutions to problems and opportunities.	4	3	2	1
26. Members of the Finance & Accounting function play important roles in the Demand Planning, Supply Planning, Pre-Meeting, and Exec Meeting phases to ensure that the plans have financial validity.	4	3	2	1
27. In the Exec Meeting, dollarized versions of the Sales & Operations Plan are compared with the Business Plan (annual budget, annual operating plan). As appropriate, the Business Plan is updated to reflect the new realities identified in Executive S&OP.	4	3	2	1
28. Executive S&OP is used to help with risk anticipation and recovery regarding large changes in demand.	4	3	2	1
29. Executive S&OP is used to help with risk anticipation and recovery regarding large drops in supply.	4	3	2	1
30. In the spirit of continuous improvement, a brief critique of the Exec Meeting is held before the end of the meeting. Feedback is solicited from all participants.	4	3	2	1
31. Minutes of the Executive S&OP meeting detailing all decisions made are distributed within two work days after the meeting.	4	3	2	1

	Ex	Gd	Fr	Pr
32. The Executive S&OP process has become the framework for decision making regarding all major demand/supply issues.	4	3	2	1
33. Improvement has been achieved in at least four of the following six performance areas: higher customer service, lower customer order backlogs, shorter customer lead times, higher inventory turnover, reduced unplanned overtime, lower hiring and layoff costs.	4	3	2	1

SCORING FOR SALES & OPERATIONS PLANNING CHECKLIST

of 4s: _____ * 4 = _____

# of 3s: _____ * 3 = _____

# of 2s: _____ * 2 = _____

# of 1s: _____ * 1 = _____

TOTAL = _____

TOTAL _____ divided by: _____ (33 minus # of NAs) = SCORE: _____

Score Evaluation: 3.5 – 4.0 = Excellent

3.0 – 3.4 = Good

2.0 – 2.9 = Fair

< 2.0   = Poor

Appendix G

Waterfall Chart

A waterfall chart is a tool to help identify and diagnose bias in the forecast. A biased forecast is one who's forecast error is always in the same direction. Examples might include the following:

- To overcome chronic shortfalls in production, the forecast is made artificially high, to "fool" manufacturing into producing more product.

- A sales compensation system that pays the salesforce more if they exceed the forecast, encouraging them to forecast low.

A waterfall chart simply tracks the forecast data over time so that actual sales can be easily compared to the forecast at various intervals of time: one month before, two months before, and so on.

Following are, first, a table for capturing the data and next a simple graph showing one of the intervals — three months away. In this example, actual sales are always lower than the forecast when it was three months away. It can also be seen that as the forecast horizon gets shorter, the forecast gets closer to actual, but remains wrong in the same direction.

Figure G-1

Waterfall Chart - Medium Widget Family

2007	Jan	Feb	Mar	Apr	May	Jun	Jul	Aug	Sep	Oct	Nov	Dec
Dec-02	**70**	80	90	100	100	100	100	100	100	100	100	100
Jan-03		**70**	80	90	100	100	100	100	100	100	100	100
Feb-03			**70**	80	90	100	100	100	100	100	100	100
Mar-03				**70**	80	90	100	100	100	100	100	100
Apr-03					**70**	80	90	100	100	100	100	100
May-03						**70**	80	90	100	100	100	100
Jun-03							**70**	80	90	100	100	100
Jul-03												
Aug-03												
Sep-03												
Oct-03												
Nov-03												
Dec-03												
Jan-04												
Feb-04												

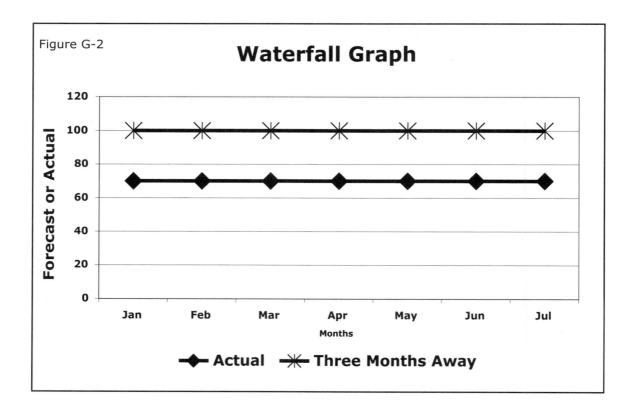

Figure G-2

Appendix H

Glossary

ABC Classification — The grouping of items based on their importance. "A" items are the most important; "B's" are less so; and "C" items are the least important of all. This stratification can be applied to items in inventory, products, product families, customers, and more. ABC classification is based on Pareto's Law, the 20/80 rule, which states that 20 percent of the items in a group will have 80 percent of the impact.

Abnormal Demand — Demand not in the forecast, frequently from a customer with whom the company has not been doing business.

Aggregate Forecast — See: Volume Forecast.

Aligned Resources — Resources that match up very closely with the product families. For example, all of the production for Family A is done in Department 1 and Department 1 makes no product for any other family; similarly for Family B and Department 2, and so on. Determining future capacity requirements for aligned resources is simpler than for matrix resources. See: **Matrix Resources**.

Assemble-to-Order — See: **Finish-to-Order**.

Available-to-Promise (ATP) — The uncommitted portion of a company's current inventory (On-Hand Balance) and future inventory, as expressed by the Master Production Schedule. ATP is a tool for promising customer orders.

Bias — The amount of forecast error build-up over time, plus or minus. This is a measure of overforecasting or underforecasting. See: **Sum of Deviations**.

Bill of Resources — A listing of the important resources required to produce and deliver a given product or product family. Used in **Resource Requirements Planning** and **Rough-Cut Capacity Planning**.

Build-to-Order — Term popularized by Dell Computer; it has a similar meaning to **Finish-to-Order** and **Assemble-to-Order.** See: **Finish-to-Order**.

Business Plan — The financial plan for the business, extending out three to five fiscal years into the future. The first year of the plan is typically the annual budget and is expressed in substantial detail, the future years are less so.

Capable-to-Promise — An advanced form of **Available-to-Promise (ATP)**. ATP looks at future production as specified by the master production schedule. Capable-to-Promise goes further; it also looks at what could be produced, out of available material and capacity, even though not formally scheduled. This capability is sometimes found in advanced planning systems (APS). The latter include the traditional **Capacity Requirements Planning** process and the newer Finite Capacity Planning/Scheduling, which not only recognize specific overloads but make recommendations for overcoming them.

Capacity Planning — The process of determining how much capacity will be required to produce in the future. Capacity Planning can occur at an aggregate level (see **Resource Requirements Planning**) or at a detailed level. Tools employed for the latter include the traditional **Capacity Requirements Planning** process and the newer Finite Capacity Planning/Scheduling, which not only recognizes specific overloads but makes recommendations for overcoming them.

Capacity Requirements Planning (CRP) — The process of determining the amount of labor and/or machine resources required to accomplish the tasks of production, and making plans to provide these resources. Open production orders as well as planned orders in the MRP system are input to CRP, which translates these orders into hours of work by work center by time period. In earlier years, the computer portion of CRP was called infinite loading, a misnomer. This technique is used primarily in complex job shops.

Collaborative Planning, Forecasting, and Replenishment (CPFR) — A process involving participants in the supply chain centering on jointly managed planning and forecasting, with the goal of achieving very high efficiencies in replenishment. CPFR has been referred to as "second generation **Efficient Consumer Response.**"

Control Chart — A graphic comparison of process performance data with predetermined computed control limits. The primary use of control charts is to detect assignable causes of variation in the process as opposed to random variations.

Control Limit — A statistically determined line on a control chart (upper control limit or lower control limit). If a value occurs outside of this limit, the process is deemed to be out of control.

Demand Management — The functions of sales forecasting, customer order entry, customer order promising, determining distribution center requirements, interplant orders, and service and supply item requirements. **Available-to-Promise** and **Abnormal Demand** control play a large role in effective Demand Management.

Demand Manager — A job function charged with coordinating the **Demand Management** process. Frequently the Demand Manager will operate the statistical forecasting system and work closely with other marketing and salespeople in the Demand Planning phase of **Executive S&OP.** Other activities for the Demand Manager might include making decisions regarding **abnormal demand,** working closely with the Master Scheduler on product availability issues, and being a key player in other aspects of the monthly **Executive S&OP** process. This may or may not be a full-time position.

Demand Plan — The forecast, customer orders, and other anticipated demands such as interplant, export, and samples. See: **Sales Plan.**

Demand/Supply Strategies — A statement for each product family that defines how the company "meets the customer" with that product, its objectives in terms of customer service levels, and targets for finished inventory or order backlog levels. For example, Family A is **Make-to-Stock** (i.e., it is shipped to customers from finished goods inventory), its target line fill is 99.5 percent, and its target finished inventory level is ten days' supply.

Demand Time Fence — That period of time in the near future inside of which the unsold forecast is ignored in the **Master Schedule.** In many companies, the Demand Time Fence is set at or near the finishing lead time for the product. The logic is that the unsold forecast can't be produced due to insufficient time and thus should be ignored. See: **Planning Time Fence.**

Design-to-Order — An order fulfillment strategy that calls for detailed design of the product to begin after receipt of the customer order. This is frequently used in companies that make complex, highly-engineered, "one-of-a-kind" products. See: **Finish-to-Order, Make-to-Order, Make-to-Stock.**

Detailed Forecast — See: **Mix Forecast.**

Distribution Requirements Planning (DRP) — A technique that employs the logic of MRP to replenish inventories at remote locations such as distribution centers, consignment inventories, customer warehouses, and so forth. The planned orders created by DRP become input to the **Master Schedule.**

Efficient Consumer Response (ECR) — An approach in which the retailer, distributor, and supplier trading partners work closely together to eliminate excess costs from the supply chain, with the goal of enhancing the efficiency of product introductions, merchandising, promotions, and replenishment.

End Item — An individual finished product.

Engineered Cycle Time — In **Lean Manufacturing,** the capacity of the resource expressed in the time required to produce one item. An engineered cycle time of 20 means that the resource is capable of producing one item every 20 seconds. See: **Takt Time.**

Enterprise Resource Planning (ERP) — An enterprise-wide set of management tools with the ability to link customers and suppliers into a complete supply chain, employing proven business processes for decision-making, and providing for high degrees of cross-functional coordination among Sales, Marketing, Manufacturing, Operations, Logistics, Purchasing, Finance, New Product Development, and Human Resources. Enterprise Resource Planning is a direct outgrowth and extension of Manufacturing Resource Planning and, as such, includes all of those capabilities. ERP is more powerful than MRP II in that it: a) applies a single set of resource planning tools across the entire enterprise, b) provides real time (or near real time) integration of sales, operating, and financial data, and c) extends resource planning approaches to the extended supply chain of customers and suppliers.

EPE Interval — In **Lean Manufacturing,** this is the minimum time between production runs of each part produced in a process. (EPEI = Every Part Every Interval.) The EPEI calculation determines the maximum frequency at which each item can be run without creating problems because of the amount of set-up time required.

Exec Meeting — The culminating step in the monthly **Executive S&OP** cycle. It is a decision-making meeting, attended by the President/General Manager, his or her staff, and other key individuals.

Executive S&OP — The executive portion of the overall Sales & Operations Planning set of processes. Its mission is to balance demand and supply at the aggregate level and to align operational planning with financial planning. It is a cross-functional decision-making process involving the General Manager of the business and his or her staff, along with managers and other support people. Executive S&OP includes the functions of **Demand Planning, Supply Planning,** the **Pre-Meeting,** and the **Exec Meeting,** occurring on a monthly cycle and displaying information in both units and dollars. Used properly, Executive S&OP enables the company's managers to view the business holistically, provides them with a window into the future, and serves as the forum for discussing relevant policy and strategy. See: **Sales & Operations Planning.**

Family — See: **Product Family.**

Final Assembly Schedule (FAS) — See: **Finishing Schedule.**

Financial Interface — A process of tying financial information and operating information together. It is the process by which businesses are able to operate with one and only one set of numbers, rather than using data in operational functions that differ from that used in the financial side of the business.

Financial Planning — The process of developing dollarized projections for revenues, costs, cash flow, other asset changes, and so forth.

Finish-to-Order — An order fulfillment strategy where the customer order is completed shortly after receipt. The key components used in the finishing or final assembly process are planned, and possibly stocked, based on sales forecasts. Receipt of a customer order initiates the finishing of the customized product. This strategy is useful where a large number of end products, most often due to a high degree of optionality within the product, can be finished quickly from available components. Syn: **Assemble-to-Order, Build-to-Order.**

Finishing Schedule — The schedule that defines the operations required to complete the product, from the level where its components are stocked (or Master Scheduled) to the end item level. The schedule also assigns the resources (equipment, manpower) to be utilized, and specifies timing.

Forecast — See: **Sales Forecast.**

Forecast Consumption — The process of replacing uncertain future demand (the forecast) with known future demand (primarily customer orders).

Forecast Error — The amount that the forecast deviates from actual sales. Measures of forecast error include **Mean Absolute Deviation (MAD)** and **Sum of Deviations (SOD).** See: **Variability.**

Forecast Frequency — How often the forecast is fully reviewed and updated. A monthly frequency is common.

Forecast Horizon — The amount of time into the future that the forecast covers.

Forecast Interval — The size or "width" of the time period being forecasted. The most commonly used intervals are weekly or monthly.

Independent Demand — Demand for an item is considered independent when unrelated to the demand for other items. Demand for finished goods and service parts are examples of independent demand.

Just-in-Time — The forerunner of **Lean Manufacturing.**

Kanban — A method used in **Lean Manufacturing** in which consuming (downstream) operations pull from feeding (upstream) operations. Feeding operations are authorized to produce only after receiving a Kanban card (or other trigger) from the consuming operation. In Japanese, loosely translated it means card or signal. Syn: demand pull.

Lean Manufacturing — A powerful approach to production that emphasizes the minimization of the amount of all the resources (including time) used in the various activities of the enterprise. It involves identifying and eliminating nonvalue-adding activities in design, production, **Supply Chain Management,** and customer relations.

Load Profile — See: **Bill of Resources.**

Line Fill Rate — The percentage of order lines shipped on time and complete. See: **Order Fill Rate.**

Lower Control Limit — Control limit for points below the central line in a control chart. See: **Control Limit.**

Make-to-Order — An order fulfillment strategy where the product is made after receipt of a customer's order. The final product is usually a combination of standard items and items custom designed to meet the requirements called out in the customer order. See: **Design-to-Order, Finish-to-Order, Make-to-Stock.**

Make-to-Stock — An order fulfillment strategy where products are finished before receipt of customer orders. Customer orders are typically filled from existing finished goods inventory. See: **Design-to-Order, Finish-to-Order, Make-to-Order.**

Manufacturing Resource Planning (MRP II) — See: **Enterprise Resource Planning.**

Master Schedule — The tool that balances demand and supply at the product level, as opposed to **Executive S&OP**, which balances demand and supply at the aggregated **Product Family** level. It is the source of customer order promising, via its **Available-to-Promise** capability, and contains the anticipated build schedule for the plant(s) in the form of the Master Production Schedule.

Material Requirements Planning (MRP) — The first step in the evolution of ERP. This set of techniques uses bills of material, inventory data, and the **Master Production Schedule** to calculate requirements for materials. It makes recommendations to release replenishment orders. Further, since it is time phased, it makes recommendations to reschedule open orders when due dates and need dates are not in phase. Originally seen as merely a better way to order inventory, today it is thought of primarily as a priority planning technique (i.e., a method for establishing and maintaining valid due dates on orders). See: **Manufacturing Resource Planning, Enterprise Resource Planning.**

Matrix Resources — Resources that do not match up with the product families. For example, Department 1 makes products in Families A, C, D, and G. Determining future capacity requirements for matrix resources is somewhat more complex than for aligned resources. See: Aligned Resources.

Mean — The arithmetic average of a group of values.

Mean Absolute Deviation (MAD) — The average of the absolute values of the deviations of observed values from some expected value. MAD can be calculated based on observations and the arithmetic mean of those observations.

Mix — The details. Individual products, customer orders, pieces of equipment, as opposed to aggregate groupings. See: **Volume.**

Mix Forecast — A forecast by individual products. Sometimes called the detailed forecast. It is used for short-term scheduling for plants and suppliers (and may be required for certain long lead time, unique purchased items).

On-Hand Balance — The amount physically in stock, irrespective of booked customer orders.

Operational Takt Time — See: **Takt Time.**

Operations Plan — The agreed-upon rates and volumes of production or procurement to support the **Sales Plan (Demand Plan, Sales Forecast)** and to reach the inventory or order backlog targets. The Operations Plan, upon authorization at the **Exec Meeting,** becomes the "marching orders" for the Master Scheduler, who must set the Master Production Schedule in congruence with the Operations Plan. Syn: **Production Plan.**

Order Fill Rate — The percentage of customer orders shipped on time and complete as opposed to the total number of orders. Order fill is a more stringent measure of customer delivery performance than line fill. For example, if only one item out of twenty on a customer order is unavailable, then that order counts for zero in the order fill calculation. The line fill percentage in this example would be 95 percent. See: **Line Fill Rate.**

Pacemaker — The point at which work is scheduled in a **Lean Manufacturing** environment. Components produced upstream of the pacemaker are pulled to the pacemaker finishing schedule. Work flows to processes downstream of the pacemaker on a first-in first-out basis.

Planning Bill of Material — An artificial grouping of items in a bill-of-material format used to facilitate forecasting and Master Scheduling.

Planning Time Fence (PTF) — The period of time inside of which detailed planning must be present in the **Master Schedule.** Normally, the Planning Time Fence approximates the cumulative lead time of the product plus 25 to 50 percent. Sometimes called the Critical Time Fence. Most Master Scheduling software will not alter the Master Production Schedule within the PTF, only outside of it.

Plant Scheduling — The process of creating the detailed schedules needed by the plant(s). Plant schedules can include the **Finishing Schedules,** fabrication schedules, and so forth.

Postponement — An approach that calls for waiting to add options into the product until after the customer order is received and then finishing the product very quickly. See: **Finish-to-Order.**

Pre-Meeting — The preliminary session prior to the **Exec Meeting.** In it, key people from Sales & Marketing, Operations, Finance, and New Product Development come together to develop the recommendations to be made at the Executive S&OP session.

Product Family — The basic planning element for **Executive S&OP,** where the focus is on families and subfamilies (volume), not individual items (mix).

Product Subfamily — A planning element sometimes used in **Executive S&OP** that provides a more detailed view than product families, but not at the extreme detail of individual products. Product Family A, for example, might contain three subfamilies — A1, A2, A3 — and each of those might contain a dozen or so individual products. See: **Product Family.**

Production Plan — See: **Operations Plan.**

Projected Available Balance — The inventory balance projected out into the future. It is the running sum of on-hand inventory, minus requirements, plus scheduled receipts and (usually) planned orders.

Pull — The process of flowing production from upstream (feeder) processes to downstream (finishing) processes in which nothing is produced by the feeder until the downstream "customer" signals a need.

Resource — Those things that add value to products in their production and/or delivery.

Resource Planning — A generalized term applied to **Manufacturing Resource Planning, Business Resource Planning,** and **Enterprise Resource Planning.**

Resource Requirements Planning — The process by which the **Operations Plan in Executive S&OP** can be converted into future capacity requirements. Frequently the Operations Plan, expressed in units of product, is "translated" into standard hours of workload (which is a common unit of measure for production operations). Resource Requirements Planning can be used at the departmental level, or for subsets of departments, down to individual pieces of equipment or specific skill levels for production associates. This process can also be carried out for material requirements from suppliers, for warehouse space, and for non-production operations such as product design and drafting. A similar process, called **Rough-Cut Capacity Planning,** operates at the mix level in conjunction with the **Master Schedule.**

Rough-Cut Capacity Planning. See: **Resource Requirements Planning.**

Running Sum of Forecast Error (RSFE) — The cumulative sum of forecast error, plus or minus, over time. As such, it is a measure of bias. Also called Sum of Deviations (SOD).

Safety Stock — An amount of inventory held to protect against fluctuations in demand and/or supply.

Safety Time — A technique in MRP whereby material is planned to arrive ahead of the requirement date. This difference between the requirement date and the planned in-stock date is safety time.

Sales & Operations Planning (S&OP) — A set of business processes — **Executive S&OP, Master Scheduling, Distribution Planning, Plant** and **Supplier Scheduling,** and so forth — that helps companies keep demand and supply in balance, align units and dollars, and link volume planning with detailed mix schedules and plans. It does that by first focusing on aggregate volumes — product families and groups — so that mix issues — individual products and customer orders — can be handled more readily. The **Executive S&OP** component of Sales & Operations Planning links the company's Strategic Plans and **Business Plan** to its detailed processes — the order entry, **Master Scheduling, Plant Scheduling,** and purchasing tools it uses to run the business on a week-to-week, day-to-day, and hour-to-hour basis. See: **Executive S&OP.**

Sales Forecast — A projection of estimated future demand.

Sales Plan — The details backing up the **Sales Forecast.** It represents Sales & Marketing management's commitment to take all reasonable steps necessary to achieve the forecasted level of actual customer orders.

Stockkeeping Unit (SKU) — An individual finished product. In the more rigorous use of the term, it refers to a specific, individual product in a given location. Thus, product #1234 at the Los Angeles warehouse is a different SKU from the same product at the Chicago warehouse.

Subfamily — See: **Product Subfamily.**

Sum of Deviations (SOD) — See: **Running Sum of Forecast Error.**

Supermarket — Within **Lean Manufacturing,** this is a set amount of inventory (finished goods or work-in-process) that allows **Pull** processes to function when demand is not totally linear.

Supplier Scheduling — A purchasing approach that provides suppliers with schedules rather than individual hard copy purchase orders. Normally a supplier scheduling system will include a contract and a daily or weekly schedule for each participating supplier extending for some time into the future. Syn: vendor scheduling.

Supply Chain — The organizations and processes involved from the initial raw materials through manufacturing and distribution to the ultimate acquisition of the finished product by the end consumer.

Supply Chain Management — The planning, organizing, and controlling of supply chain activities.

Supply Planning — The function of setting planned rates of production (both in-house and outsourced) to satisfy the **Demand Plan** and to meet inventory and order backlog targets. Frequently, **Resource Requirements Planning** is used to support this.

Takt Time — In **Lean Manufacturing,** Takt Time sets the basic rate of production. It communicates the frequency of demand and thus the frequency at which products must be produced at the **Pacemaker.** Takt Time is derived from the **Sales Plan,** while Operational Takt Time is derived from the **Operations Plan,** reflecting inventory draw down or build up, plant shutdowns, and other factors. Thus, these values can be thought of as the demand for capacity, i.e., what the resource will be required to produce. **Engineered Cycle Time** refers to the supply of capacity, i.e., what the resource is capable of producing.

Time Fence — A point in the future that delineates one time zone from another. See: **Time Zones.**

Time Phasing — The process of expressing future demand and supply by time period.

Time Zones — Periods within which changes are managed in certain ways, reflecting the realities of the operating environment. For example, in many plants, achieving a 30 percent increase in output might be impossible within three days; difficult and costly, but attainable, within three months; and very practical within three years.

Two-Level Master Scheduling — A Master Scheduling approach where an end product type or category (not a specific product) is Master Scheduled along with selected key options, features, attachments, and common parts.

Upper Control Limit — Control limit for points above the central line in a control chart. See: **Control Limit.**

Variability — In the larger sense, this is the amount that individual elements in a time series deviate from the average. In some cases, variability is random and inherent in the process being observed. See: **Forecast Error.**

Vendor Managed Inventories — A process that places the replenishment decision-making in the hands of the supplier. It's the supplier's job to ensure that the customer does not run out of stock and to keep the inventories at the agreed-upon levels.

Volume — The big picture. Sales and production rates for aggregate groupings — product families, production departments, etc. — as opposed to individual products, customer orders, and work centers. See: **Mix.**

Volume Forecast — A forecast by product groupings such as families, classes, and so forth. Also called the aggregate forecast or the product group forecast, it is used for sales planning, for **Capacity Planning** at the plants and suppliers, and for financial analyses and projections.

Waterfall Chart — A graphical chart that displays time-phased demand variations of forecast-to-actual for the purpose of identifying bias in the forecast.

Index